About the Authors

Matthias Stiefel was educated at the Graduate Institute of International Studies, Geneva. From 1980 to 1986 he directed the United Nations Research Institute for Social Development's (UNRISD) Participation Programme which engaged in a large number of highly innovative research investigations in a cross-section of countries in Latin America and Asia. In 1986 he embarked on a personal experiment for five years, becoming a farmer on a smallholding in southern Portugal. At the same time, he continued to do international consultancy for various agencies, including UNICEF and IFAD. He is currently Deputy Director of the Programme for Strategic and International Security Studies at the Geneva Graduate School of International Studies and acts as senior adviser to the Director of UNRISD. He is the author of various books, reports and papers on the political and social aspects of development, humanitarian aid and development co-operation.

Marshall Wolfe was educated at Williams College, USA, and Oxford University where he was a Rhodes Scholar. He joined the United Nations Secretariat in 1946 shortly after it was founded. From 1963 to 1978 he served as Director, Social Development Division, at the UN Economic Commission for Latin America (ECLA), in Santiago, Chile. For two years, he also co-directed UNRISD/ECLA's Research Programme on a Unified Approach to Development Analysis and Planning. He is the author of *Elusive Development*, as well as various papers on development, mainly published in the *CEPAL Review*.

The United Nations Research Institute for Social Development (UNRISD) was established as an autonomous agency to promote multi-disciplinary research on the social dimensions of contemporary problems affecting development. Its work is guided by the conviction that, for effective development policies to be formulated, an understanding of the social and political context is crucial. The Institute attempts to provide governments, development agencies, grassroots organizations and scholars with a better understanding of how development policies and processes of economic, social and environmental change affect different social groups. Working through an extensive network of national research centres, UNRISD aims to promote original research and strengthen research capacity in developing countries.

Current research themes focus on the social dimensions of economic restructuring, environmental deterioration and conservation, ethnic conflict, the illicit narcotic drugs trade and drug control policies, political violence, the mass voluntary return of refugees, and the reconstruction of war-torn societies, as well as ways of integrating gender issues into development planning.

A Voice for the Excluded

Popular Participation in Development:
Utopia or Necessity?

Matthias Stiefel

&

Marshall Wolfe

Zed Books Ltd
London & New Jersey

in association with

The United Nations Research Institute
for Social Development (UNRISD)
Geneva

A Voice for the Excluded: Popular Participation in Development: Utopia or Necessity? was first published in association with the United Nations Research Institute for Social Development, Palais des Nations, 1211 Geneva 10, Switzerland, by Zed Books, 7 Cynthia Street, London N1 9JF and 165 First Avenue, Atlantic Highlands, New Jersey 07716, USA, in 1994.

Cover design by Andrew Corbett
Typeset by Ray Davies
Printed and bound in the United Kingdom
by Biddles Ltd., Guildford and King's Lynn.

A catalogue record for this book is
available from the British Library

US CIP is available from the Library of Congress

ISBN 1 85649 247 8 Hb
ISBN 1 85649 248 6 Pb

Contents

To the memory of Andrew Pearse

Preface

As the United Nations Research Institute for Social Development celebrates its thirtieth anniversary and we cast a glance at its work over this period, the Popular Participation Programme undoubtedly stands out as one of its major success stories. In many ways, it represents the most ambitious and systematic effort made within the United Nations system to grapple with the complex and controversial theme of participation. It has played a pioneering role at both the substantive and methodological levels.

At the substantive level, the programme is remarkable for situating the study of participation within a broad spectrum of ideological and institutional settings and organizational initiatives. Thus the programme has sponsored investigations into the meaning and content of participation in widely divergent contexts ranging from communist regimes to military dictatorships and from mobilizing states to liberal systems. The coverage of the social groups excluded from participation is equally impressive, ranging as it does from the organized working class to workers in the informal sector, from the peasantry to the rural landless and from the ethnic minorities to poor women. The organizational initiatives also display a remarkable diversity, comprising local spontaneous groups, local and national NGOs, social movements, political parties, peasant associations, co-operatives, trade unions, neighbourhood committees and a variety of state-sponsored institutions.

At the methodological level, the programme worked through a global network of researchers and activists. It attempted to promote sustained interaction between researchers and organizations of the excluded. Through its newsletter, *Dialogue about Participation*, it initiated a creative discourse among hundreds of thinkers and activists engaged in promoting participatory processes in different parts of the world. The project administration was decentralized to the point where national and regional groups assumed responsibility for its direction and development.

This volume by Matthias Stiefel and Marshall Wolfe constitutes a synthesis of dozens of studies sponsored by the programme, many of which have already been published by UNRISD or elsewhere. Although most of these studies were carried out in the early 1980s, the authors have attempted in this book to relate the theory and practice of participation to the greatly changed global and national contexts of the 1990s. In view of the continuing vitality of the idea of participation, the book will be of interest to a diverse world-wide audience of researchers, activists, policy makers and officials of international and donor agencies.

Dharam Ghai
Director, UNRISD

Foreword

A Voice for the Excluded is an important book. The central dilemma it confronts is indicated by the book's subtitle, *Popular Participation in Development: Utopia or Necessity?* Andrew Pearse, who inspired the Popular Participation Programme and decisively shaped its goals and methodology, should have been given the last word on its results. Unfortunately he died in 1980, only one year after the research really got under way. It is only fitting that the programme's co-director, together with a member of the core group guiding the work who was also a long-time colleague of Andrew's, should reflect on the programme's significance. They have the last word on the project, but not on the issues it attempted to address. These will continue to haunt us for as long as human societies exist.

Andrew Pearse was one of the most insightful social scientists observing, analysing and writing about what happened to ordinary rural people when their customary local institutions and ways of making a living were disrupted by the processes of historical change that are commonly labelled development. Most of his own field work was in the Caribbean and Latin America, but he was a careful scholar who made comparative studies of similar processes in Africa, Asia and elsewhere. For him, the dominant continuing social process of our times was the accelerating incorporation of hitherto largely self-provisioning communities into urban-based national and international networks of production, exchange and domination. Most of the world's people were being uprooted from their traditional livelihoods before new ones had been generated in the industrializing and urbanizing world system.

Andrew's primary concern was how these processes of incorporation might be modified in specific situations to enable ordinary working people to improve their livelihoods and pursue their aspirations in liberty. In his view, the essence of any quest for popular participation was the politics of freedom.

When I became the Director of UNRISD in 1977, Andrew was revising his overview report of the Institute's Green Revolution Project that he had directed in the early 1970s. This was published in 1980 under the title *Seeds of Plenty, Seeds of Want*.[1] This book contained the central hypotheses of the Popular Participation Programme that Andrew was urging UNRISD to develop. Similar ideas of 'struggles over the terms of incorporation' had already been formulated in Andrew's earlier book, *The Latin*

American Peasant,[2] which was based on many years of field research throughout the region. He had written part of this influential monograph while he was working with the Chilean Agrarian Reform Research and Training Institute (ICIRA) in the late 1960s and had finished it at UNRISD. Neither of these important books ever received the widespread acclaim that they richly deserved. Perhaps this was because they were ahead of their time when published, while later their messages had already become superficially accepted as part of the conventional wisdom about development.

Andrew played a key role in designing the UNRISD research strategy for the late 1970s and early 1980s. Research priorities of the Institute included three central themes. The first was the struggle for livelihood, which has always been the primordial preoccupation of working people. The second was development policy. Andrew believed that if policy was 'any sustained course of action adopted and pursued by a group for its advantage', then development policy embraced the attempts of governments, poised upon the dominant interest groups and class interests in each country, of corporate entities, NGOs and other groups to stimulate economic growth and to influence social change according to their particular goals and values. All policy arenas from high councils of governments and transnational executive board rooms to junior officers' clubs, union-meetings, NGO offices and student groups merited attention.

The third theme was participation. This was seen in the UNRISD approach to be the encounter between the pursuit of livelihood by popularly-based groups and the policies being pursued by the state and other 'developers'. The terms of participation were determined in specific situations by the outcomes of organized efforts to increase control over resources and regulative institutions on the part of groups and movements of those hitherto excluded from such control. In other words, participation always implied a struggle for greater self-empowerment. It was inevitably conflictive.

Andrew's model of incorporation, as I understood it, was by no means evolutionary or teleological. Incorporation into a single world system was a historically observable process that commenced several centuries ago. It was practically impossible to posit credible alternatives to incorporation other than catastrophic ones. The terms of incorporation, however, were anything but inevitable. They depended primarily on social relations – on individual, group and class interests, values, institutions, technologies, demographic change and politics, among many other factors.

Incorporation could be a step in a 'long march' from peasant cultivator to unionized urban worker. But it could also be a step towards growing social chaos, to nihilist, nationalist and fundamentalist fanaticisms, or to a repressive custodial state. The role of 'free will' was very much a part of Andrew's cosmology. He had been a conscientious objector in the war and was awarded the French Legion of Honour for his contribution towards 'de-nazifying' the German school curriculum during the allied occupation. He believed that social researchers shared an obligation to try to use their position and insights to influence social outcomes. He was too realistic about human nature, however, to expect that convincing the powerful of the need for greater popular participation would be enough to bring it about. He wrote, 'Future conjunctures in which a peasant-based strategy would become future policy are unlikely to occur without the activities of (peasant) organizations and movements becoming a recognized political force in the polity, whether attached to supporters of the government or exercising power in opposition ... .'[3] Popular organization was, in his view, a necessary, but not a sufficient, condition to bring about greater participation. Effective peasant organization in some circumstances could bring on harsh repression. Also, he warned that defending a popularly based strategy from internal abuse and from state or private exploitation was as important and difficult as adopting such policies in the first place.

The UNRISD research into popular participation reviewed in Part II of this book took place well over a decade ago. Meanwhile, national and international contexts have changed, as have the concerns and priorities of governments and of international organizations. These changes and their implications, accompanying greater globalization, world economic recession and the disintegration of 'real socialism', are reviewed in Part III. The issues and dilemmas dealt with in the UNRISD research, however, remain as pertinent as ever. Only the language and emphasis have changed. Two of the few generalizations the authors permitted themselves to draw from the research remain particularly relevant today. One is the unpredictability of outcomes of efforts by the hitherto excluded to increase their control over resources and regulative institutions in specific contexts. We must always expect the unexpected. A second is that, 'In the last analysis, there may be no alternative to the efforts of a reformist state and a reinvigorated and organized civil society in which the excluded can make their voices heard.'

Before writing off these results as trivial, or dismissing efforts at achieving greater popular participation as marginal, one should ask a counter-factual question. What would have happened in each of the specific cases studied by UNRISD if there had been no organized effort by the excluded to increase their resources and control? In other words, imagine a society without the social conflicts associated with unions, strikes, peasant land seizures, national liberation movements and the like. One conjecture might be that such a brave new world would resemble paradise as it could not be inhabited by ordinary mortals. Another might be that, for the same reason, such a conflict-free society would resemble a well-run battery chicken farm, a giant cattle feed-lot, or a well-kept zoo.

The UNRISD inquiry into popular participation benefited from the enthusiastic intellectual and material co-operation of many scores of participants at all levels who received no material support from the programme for their contributions. This was perhaps best illustrated by the four published issues of *Dialogue about Participation* and the many more that could have been published if the programme had been able to continue.

The support for the programme by the Inter-American Foundation deserves special mention. The Foundation's staff, and especially Charles Reilly, spent many days with Andrew and myself discussing premises of the project and its objectives and making innumerable valuable suggestions. The IAF provided the major financial support that made the research programme possible. This, incidentally, also explains why the major research efforts under the programme took place in Latin America. Research in Thailand, India and China was facilitated by enthusiastic co-operation of a few national institutions and researchers, as well as, in the case of Thailand, by financial support from the Norwegian government through the FAO. Unfortunately, UNRISD never had the staff or financial resources to commence a similar research effort in Africa, where it was perhaps most badly needed.

In UNRISD's research strategy, the Popular Participation Programme was designed to bridge the gap between research concerned with struggles of uprooted peasants for livelihood, on the one hand, and issues of development policy, on the other. Struggles for livelihood had been the central concern of the Institute's earlier Green Revolution project led by Andrew, and it was the focus of the research on food security and food systems that began simultaneously with the inquiry into popular participation. Development policies had been the primary concern of the Institute's work on 'A Unified Approach to Development Analysis and Planning', led by Marshall Wolfe. The Participation Programme was meant to deal explicitly with the political dimensions of the elusive United Nations quests for greater food security and for more integrated development planning. To the extent that the popular participation research was successful in better illuminating these fundamental development issues, it owed a great debt to Andrew Pearse and to Marshall Wolfe for their pioneering efforts in these fields. It also was greatly indebted to Orlando Fals Borda and his collaborators for prior research on popular participation in rural co-operatives, and to the previous Director of UNRISD, Donald McGranahan, for initiating these earlier innovative research programmes into social development.

In my opinion, the Popular Participation Programme was successful. It attracted numerous highly qualified participants and generated a wide range of debates and informative provocative publications. I hope it advanced a little the levels of international and national discussions and understanding of some fundamental issues in social development. This is more than can be said about much development research that was a great deal more costly and pretentious.

Solon Barraclough
Former Director, UNRISD

Notes

1. Pearse, Andrew, *Seeds of Plenty, Seeds of Want: Social and Economic Implications of the Green Revolution*, UNRISD and Oxford University Press, Geneva and Oxford, 1980.
2. Pearse, Andrew, *The Latin American Peasant*, Frank Cass, London, 1975.
3. Pearse, Andrew, op. cit. in n. 1, p. 247.

Acknowledgements

UNRISD's Participation Programme represented in many ways a unique effort to combine the collective energies and commitment of social scientists from many countries under the umbrella of a United Nations research body in order to enhance collectively both our understanding of participatory processes and struggles of the excluded and the struggles themselves. This book reflects part of the findings generated by the programme. Our gratitude goes first to all those who participated in it, who gave it form and reality and made it to some extent their own. We think of the many researchers, social scientists and at times activists that participated in some of the field projects, the debates, the seminars or in a more regular and continuous way as members of the programme's regional or central core groups. They are too numerous to be listed here, but some are mentioned in the Annexes to this book.

Our gratitude also goes to the late Andrew Pearse, who was instrumental in the initiation and original conception of the programme. With his death we lost a friend, a colleague, and a constant source of support, inspiration and vision, and the programme lost its intellectual father. Many of his ideas and thoughts remain present in the conceptual approach that characterized the programme and to a large extent this volume.

While this book is based upon the findings of the Participation Programme and constitutes to some extent its final overview, it also attempts to go further and to reflect upon the relevance of these struggles and their lessons to the world of the 1990s. Naturally we alone are responsible for the use that we have made of the many findings and ideas generated within the programme, and particularly for the extrapolations made from the past to, we hope, enlighten the future.

Our thanks also go to UNRISD, its Directors – Solon Barraclough at the time of the active programme and Dharam Ghai at present – its staff and its Board who not only gave practical, administrative, financial and moral support to the programme and to this book but who had the courage to support it politically in spite of the sensitive nature of many issues raised.

The Inter-American Foundation, and particularly Charles Reilly, deserve special recognition, both for the important intellectual contribution that they made in the initial stages of the programme and for providing most of the funding. The research in Thailand was funded by a generous grant from the Norwegian government. Without such external financial support the Participation Programme could not have been carried out.

Finally, we would like to express our deep gratitude to our families, in particular Rebecca Irvin and the late Virginia Abellera Wolfe, to our children, and to all those who have been close to us, supported us and encouraged us with unending patience throughout the years that it took for this book to be completed.

Matthias Stiefel   Marshall Wolfe
Geneva   Vermont
April 1993   April 1993

Part I

Concepts of Participation

An Inquiry into Participation

Why participation?

A Voice for the Excluded examines the interacting political, economic and other transformations in the world that bear upon the prospects for popular participation today. It then considers the ways in which grassroots movements, governments, the 'family' of intergovernmental organizations and their non-governmental counterparts are confronting or evading questions of the relevance of popular participation to these transformations. First, however, it draws upon a broad inquiry into popular participation in development, launched by the United Nations Research Institute for Social Development (UNRISD) in the late 1970s and continued into the 1980s, in the confidence that the debates and field researches of those years remain relevant. A major shortcoming of the present renewed discourse on participation is its disregard of even recent history, the conceptions and prescriptions that flourished a few years ago. As the Spanish saying has it, this disregard exposes the 'new' proposals to the risk of 'inventing gunpowder in the twentieth century'.

The initiative to launch the UNRISD inquiry followed a critical assessment of past and present development strategies and trends and, more specifically, of the findings of previous UNRISD research on 'rural co-operatives', on the 'green revolution' and on a 'unified approach to development analysis and planning'.[1] The processes of economic growth and socio-political change then under way in the so-called Third World had scarcely improved the levels of consumption or the productive capacity of the strata starting with the least assets, status and power except, probably, through widening access to education and health services. Furthermore, these processes subjected the disadvantaged strata to continual disruption of their previous sources of livelihood, security and social cohesion.

From the standpoint of the values and conceptions of 'social development' that inspired the work of UNRISD, it seemed obvious that the disadvantaged, in many countries the majority, would have to 'participate' actively rather than passively – that is, achieve a greater capacity to advance their own interests and control their own livelihood, becoming a voice in the shaping of 'development' – if the trends toward greater inequality, exploitation and marginalization were to be reversed.

In fact, by the late 1970s, 'popular participation' had entered the vocabulary of many development experts and had been endorsed in various United Nations declarations and resolutions. An imposing array of official and private programmes identified 'participation' as a more or less central component of their functioning, and a certain number of research projects were focusing on the topic. At the same time, confusion and vagueness seemed to predominate concerning the operational meaning of 'popular participation'. Evidence was scarce and ambiguous as to the consequences of purportedly participatory initiatives that had been pursued over some length of time. The governmental and other sponsors of such initiatives seemed reluctant to seek a precise definition of the term and even to be in tacit agreement to refrain from considering participation in terms of social class and power. Existing field studies dealt mainly with the history and internal strengths and weaknesses of particular projects or organizations, giving priority to technical and management issues in ways that obscured the social and political factors underlying such issues. At the other extreme, some advocates of 'another development' or 'alternative styles of development' insisted on participation in terms that implied the necessity of a worldwide transformation of societal organization and values, without linking this vision convincingly to the real struggles and aspirations of the disadvantaged in specific settings.

The earlier UNRISD researches had confirmed the views of a long line of political and social theorists that the central issue of people's participation is the distribution of power – exercised by some people over other people and by some classes over other classes – and that any serious advocacy of increased participation implies a redistribution of power in favour of those hitherto powerless. Andrew Pearse, who originally proposed the inquiry and became its co-director, was a strong advocate of this position on the basis of his many years of research among rural people in Latin America and his later experience as director of UNRISD's global examination of the socio-economic repercussions of the Green Revolution. Adoption of the term 'participation' for an inquiry starting from such a premise had the advantage of linkage to an internationally accepted desideratum or banner-word; but carried a potential danger of enmeshing the inquiry in the multiple connotations of the term (described in some detail in Chapter 2).

The first stage following UNRISD's decision to confront 'participation' was thus to formulate a definition and research approach guarding against this danger; linking participation to a wider context of political, social and economic change; aimed at findings accessible and useful to the people called on to participate as well as their would-be guides and allies in the social sciences and in the multifarious organizations concerned with 'development'. After two seminars on the issue held in Geneva in 1978 and 1979, UNRISD tackled these questions in a conceptual paper circulated for discussion.[2]

Definition and dimensions of participation

The working definition of participation proposed for the purposes of the inquiry was the following: 'the organized efforts to increase control over resources and regulative institutions in given social situations, on the part of groups and movements of those hitherto excluded from such control.'

By specifying 'the organized efforts ... of groups and movements', the definition deliberately excluded certain broader interpretations of participation that might be legitimate for other purposes. After all, everyone 'participates' in society, whether as an effective actor or a passive victim. By specifying 'control', the definition aimed to rule out evasion of the central issue of power. It excluded certain technocratic or paternalistic approaches that aim to provide access to resources and institutions while withholding control. The reference to 'resources and regulative institutions', however, left open the question whether the aims and consequences of participation should be 'system-maintaining' or 'system-transforming'. In fact, as the inquiry later confronted Third World economic crises, discrediting of the welfare state and policy movements toward 'privatization' of public enterprises and services, the relevance of popular control over existing resources and institutions became increasingly problematic. The reference to 'given social situations' was intended to ward off overgeneralizations and the quest for universalized prescriptions characteristic of some criticisms of development during the 1970s. The reference to 'those hitherto excluded' aligned the inquiry with the interests of the disadvantaged, but naturally could not foresee the many forms and degrees of exclusion that the inquiry was to encounter, or the importance of the 'newly excluded' who were being deprived by economic and political mutations of the measure of control they had previously achieved. It also left out of account the likelihood that the most disadvantaged and impoverished groups had so little capacity for organized efforts that they would fall outside the purview of any investigation focusing on such efforts.

The research approach fitted into a view of 'development' as, *inter alia*, a process of incorporation, with 'traditional' social groups, relationships and institutions gradually but inevitably being incorporated into new, 'modern' and larger social, economic, cultural and political settings. In the course of this process pre-existing livelihood arrangements, values and channels of representation (usually vertical) would break down. Some social groups would dissolve and new ones emerge. All would have to struggle over the terms in which they would find a place in the new and larger social system. Participatory efforts could thus be viewed as 'struggles over the terms of incorporation', a conception Andrew Pearse had elaborated in his work on Latin American peasants.[3]

It followed that the inquiry's conception did not imply a dualistic view, as in certain marginalization theories, of development processes in which part of the population was 'included' and other parts definitively 'excluded'. The problem was rather that the poorer strata were being incorporated – included – in current national and international development processes, but on highly unfavourable terms; they were being excluded from control over the decisions and regulative institutions that governed these processes.

UNRISD identified six 'dimensions' of participation. These really constituted different perspectives or points of entry into the study of the question, perspectives from which to define a research agenda to deal with participation in the real world:

1. As 'encounter' between the hitherto excluded and those elements in the society that maintain or enforce exclusion. From this perspective, the excluded groups confront the controllers and supporters of sets of social arrangements that determine patterns of access to resources, services, status and power, seeking a new deal. 'Sets of arrangements' may be systems of tenancy, laws introduced to enforce or override custom, the fixing of food prices, existing school or health services, taxation, institutionalized clientelism or corruption, institutionalized ethnic or religious discrimination, etc. Encounter sequences embrace many continually changing forms of interaction, from tradition-sanctioned mutual accommodation between the power holders and the disadvantaged, through forms of bargaining and compacting, persistent friction and institutionalized or informal political skirmishing, through to armed confrontation and violent repression of the weaker groups by the local or national power holders. Viewing participation as encounter draws attention to the weaponry and tactics of effective struggle. It points to the relevance of popular resistance to real processes of 'modernization' or 'development' and of defensive revolts as forms of participation of last resort. It proceeds logically to an assessment of the gains and losses of the encounter from whatever point of view the observer wishes to take.

2. As 'movements' and 'organizations' of would-be participants. Enhanced understanding of the structure, *modus operandi* and social context of the organized efforts emerging among the poor and powerless in the course of their encounters was central to the purposes of the proposed research. This perspective pointed to a broad range of questions: factors influencing capacity to maintain permanent organizational structures; leadership and member ability to choose and control leaders; class homogeneity or heterogeneity of the organized group; alliances between organized groupings of the excluded and religious organizations, nongovernmental organizations, political parties, trade unions and other established 'macro-organizations of the poor'; concrete goals and demands making for group solidarity or the reverse; forms and tools of struggle, within or outside the limits of established legality; bureaucratization of 'organized efforts' following upon increases in their scope and permanence and resistances to such bureaucratization.

3. As 'biography'; i.e. the individual participatory experience. From this perspective, decisions to participate in the organized efforts on which the research would focus are individual ones that can be fully understood only by examining the life experience of the individual. Individual consciousness is the crucible in which social forces are translated into human action, and the crucible itself is moulded during a lifetime by those experiences accessible to the location that the individual occupies in a particular society. Biographical testimony from members of participatory movements about their personal experience and the evolution of their perception of the social world around them should therefore be of great importance in complementing the perspectives of 'encounter' and 'organizations'. Testimony of this kind calls for dialogue on terms of equality and within a shared cultural perspective between researcher and activist or rank-and-file participant.

4. As 'programme' or 'project' proposed and executed by a government agency, voluntary organization or international body. The distinctive feature of this perspective is that the programme or project has been initiated from above or outside; that the impetus for participatory activity does not come from the disadvantaged group but from some relatively privileged or powerful entity that has its own idea of what ought to be done, can command certain human and financial resources and believes the participation of a 'target group' can be enlisted provided it applies the correct methods.

As was indicated above, the initial explorations of 'participation' within UNRISD found this perspective inadequate and in some ways misleading. Nevertheless, it referred to a significant component of what was really happening. Such programmes and projects had become part of the setting of encounters and organized efforts for many of the disadvantaged. Whether or not they could be expected to generate major changes for the better in the livelihood of the poor, or to be replicated and expanded on a scale making this possible, some of them evidently functioned more effectively and corresponded better to their proclaimed purposes than others. Serious and critical evaluations of their origins, their sources of support and their functioning in the field should have a place in the proposed inquiry. In this area, questions such as the following had to be asked:

How does the programme under scrutiny relate to wider national policy and its social and ideological context? If the programme is initiated in a society characterized by gross inequalities of power and wealth, how is this reflected in the participatory programme, its staffing and its aims? Does the initiative stem from 'system-maintaining' objectives of social control, or from 'system-transforming' objectives of groups inside or outside the state apparatus aiming to change the distribution of power and livelihood opportunities, from social amelioration concerns of external sources of funds and advice, or from an unresolved mixture of all these? At the local level, what systems of incentives and motivations shape the recruitment and actions of the officials and field workers in promotion campaigns? How does the 'change agent' relate to the 'target group' of the programme? What level of participation seems actually to have been achieved; to what extent does it seem potentially self-sustaining once the focus of the programme has shifted elsewhere; which sectors of the target group participate most effectively and which benefit most? How do state-supported programmes relate to pre-existing grassroots initiatives; through co-operation, competition, or supplantation? Lastly, how do the intended beneficiaries, the 'participants' themselves, assess the gains and costs of their participatory action? To what extent and under what circumstances can localized and externally promoted 'participation' lead to democratic political organization and a real voice in the control of resources and regulative institutions?

5. As 'component of national policy'. Under this heading, three quite different perspectives were relevant to the inquiry.

The first had to do with participation considered literally as a 'component' of the current development policies and plans undertaken by the state, with their typical emphasis on industrialization, targets for increases in the national product and expansion of public social services and infrastructural investment. At what stage in policy-making does 'participation' enter in and for what reasons; is it viewed simply as a technique for implementing technocratically designed plans? This raised the broad question of the capacity of the national state to plan development, which would receive increasingly negative answers during the 1980s, and also the question of the compatibility between national planning, with its propensity to quantitative targets and bureaucratic implementation, and the inherently disorderly and conflictive nature of participation as the inquiry conceived it.

The second perspective concerned the long-debated questions of representative democracy and direct democracy. Could the formally democratic systems of national elections, parliaments and political parties become really effective channels through which the hitherto excluded could achieve some control over resources and regulative institutions? The recent experience of the countries with the best-established systems of democratic representation and the best informed public opinion gave quite ambiguous answers. In the countries with which the inquiry was primarily concerned, with a highly concentrated distribution of wealth, power and access to information, current events suggested that formally democratic institutions could function only as long as the hitherto excluded did not participate, or did so only as clientèles manipulated by governing élites. If their organized efforts seriously threatened the distribution of power, these efforts were repressed, generally by military force at the disposal of the élites. Thus, in 'rich' countries as well as 'poor', confidence in the potential of representative democracy for the achievement of social justice was far from vigorous.

Or could participatory movements practising direct democracy eventually undermine the power structures and determine national policy from below, as advocates of 'another development' seemed to envisage? Some authentically participatory movements were internalizing hopes of this kind, and while it seemed unlikely that such hopes would become widely predominant among the hitherto excluded, the inquiry would have to give them sympathetic attention.

Thirdly, the question of participation as a component of national policy took a radically different form in the case of governments seeking to mobilize the whole population in the name of development, or to organize the hitherto excluded for the purpose of carrying through and consolidating revolutionary shifts in the distribution of power. These governments generally rejected the traditional instruments of representative democracy, but made popular participation an explicit and central feature of policy, expressed in new institutions, laws, mass parties and public ideology. The inquiry was not prepared to take the claims of these policies at face value and recognized that 'reasons of state' defined by a single 'people's party' or a new ideological élite were likely to justify the concentration of decision-making and the conversion of mass mobilization into manipulation. Nevertheless, it was evident that revolutionary and state-directed mass mobilizations were transforming the lives of the hitherto excluded in a good many countries. The inquiry was particularly concerned to explore the real interactions of national mobilization ideologies and policies with popular strivings for a voice in control of resources and institutions at local level.

The research outline formulated two general cautions relating to the study of participation as a component of national policy:

First, officially declared national policy normally represents the temporary resolution of conflicts and contradictions between different forces within the state or able to influence the state. Since these forces have diverse interests, aims and ideological preconceptions, the policies they support cannot be expected to merge into a fully consistent ensemble, or to lead to fully coherent implementation. The extent to which a declared policy is reflected in what is actually being done can be expected to shift over time as different forces or individuals exercising a share of power come to the fore or fall into eclipse. It is important to analyse what forces support which parts or interpretations of a given policy and why if we are to understand the possibilities and limits of state backing for popular participation.

Secondly, the nature of complex social organizations such as the nation state sets limits to participation. Whatever the shortcomings of the state as an arbiter of policy and however self-serving the rationalizations of the forces dominating policy-making, some kind of central authority must strive to reconcile local and class interests, cope with the problems of technological modernization and environmental degradation, deal with a continually changing world economic and political order, and, in short, try to achieve a certain degree of coherence and effectiveness in the elusive domain of 'development policy'. Human nature sets other limits. If national policy strains too hard or too dogmatically to universalize participation the outcome is likely to be apathy and conformism.

6. 'Anti-participatory structures and ideologies'. A study of popular participation taking the side of the hitherto excluded requires, finally, an examination of the structures that resist their strivings for a voice in decision-making and of ideologies that dominant classes create (or rather 'secrete') to maintain existing power monopolies and forms of exploitation. Societies develop complex batteries of defences against popular participation, and even those institutions supposed to realize the participation of the many are vulnerable to the 'iron law of oligarchy' and thus liable to turn into instruments of manipulation operated by the few.

The characteristic contemporary patterns of economic growth, of 'modernization' and of 'nation-building' all have strongly anti-participatory traits. The incorporation of rural neighbourhoods and local institutions into larger, more complex urban-centred systems removes whatever capacity for decision-making the local community might have possessed and renders its traditional institutions obsolete. (The same process, of course, erodes the anti-participatory power of local élites.) Most modern technologies leave little autonomy of action and little margin for adaptation to the local user, although some technologies now beginning to emerge may have quite different implications. Bureaucracies and large economic enterprises tend to be anti-participatory in their functioning. As was indicated above, these evolving structures require functions from the state that set practical limits to participation, although continual participatory strivings can test the limits and, it is to be hoped, modify the functioning of the central authority.

While directly repressive measures against popular participation have recurred throughout history and up to the present, the anti-participatory character of dominant ideologies has provided the most pervasive form of control, as they have moulded the attitudes of different classes and groups to one another. Hardy mental stereotypes about the innate character and propensities of social classes, castes, 'races' distinguished by physical traits, and groups having cultural or religious affiliations different from those of the dominant group, have served this purpose. So have the cultural stereotypes through which most societies have maintained the subordination of women. In more subtle ways, dominant classes have glorified the heredity and processes of socialization entitling them to rule, and have consigned others to the more modest roles for which their heredity and socialization qualify them. The ways in which the family, schooling and mass communications reproduce and reinforce the stereotypes are particularly important. (One might even ask whether the socially most revolutionary trend of recent decades, and the most important to the future of participation, has not been the melting of parental authority and the deconstraining of the new generations.) Altogether, the critique of anti-participatory structures and ideologies opens up a field for inquiry that is an indispensable complement to direct study of participatory encounters, groups and movements, programmes and policies.

Debate, research and basework

The inquiry proposed to start tackling this formidable agenda of questions and perspectives by opening a debate among theorists, researchers and practitioners, a kind of collective exercise to clarify and render more useful and socially relevant the idea of participation in advancing livelihood and human development. Work was then to proceed to field research – the systematic collection, verification and analysis of information on organized groups and movements of the hitherto excluded and on participatory initiatives and organizations. Such field research was originally envisaged in four specific settings: peasants and rural workers; workers participating in management; ethnically defined participatory movements and situations; and urban marginal settlements. The evolving organizational roles and initiatives of women were obviously important in their own right as well as in their links to the settings mentioned above, but since a separate UNRISD programme was expected to deal with these questions, the participation inquiry provisionally set them aside.

The inquiry proposed to experiment with innovative inter-disciplinary approaches and to attract committed researcher-activists who would be free to explore complementary topics and approaches; for example, popular cultural manifestations as channels for popular self-identification and self-assertion. The projects were, as far as practicable, to use participatory methods as a complement to traditional methods of social science research and to link such research with what was called 'basework'. Basework was conceived as the practical extension of research to the field and the application of its results at the grassroots level, through which it was 'to receive the political and existential impulses which come directly from flesh and blood experiences of participatory movements and institutions and the situations in which they are generated and have their being'.[4] Practically, basework implied close interaction with the groups and movements of the excluded, ensuring that the conduct of research and its findings would respond to their perceived needs for tactically useful information, including information on the struggles of their counterparts elsewhere. This implied circulation of findings in forms and in languages really accessible to the different groups and movements. The inquiry viewed this as important not only for the effectiveness of the leadership, but also for a process of internal education through which the membership would acquire capacity to participate in decision-making, control its leaders and find a rationale for long-term solidarity. An essential element of the inquiry, therefore, would be investigation, in dialogue with the groups and movements themselves, of the potential role of 'participatory' or 'action research' in generating member consciousness and empowerment. Research and basework should feed back into a continuing debate, 'a prolonged act of reflection', to be carried out through circulation of ideas and preliminary research findings, open to all interested in 'participating', and through discussion meetings.

The first step towards debate was the circulation of the proposed research approach itself to some 150 potential collaborators concerned with the issue of participation at different levels of theory and practice. The response was overwhelming, the suggestions and criticisms so diverse that the programme decided to publish all the comments interspersed in the text of the proposal, a demonstration of the multiple meanings attached to participation within different frames of reference deriving from ideology, political-bureaucratic imperatives and practical experience.[5] The programme carried on this global debate between 1979 and 1983 through a periodic publication: *Dialogue about Participation / Diálogo sobre la Participación*, with the number of 'participants' rising from 150 to over 1,000. Participants covered a very broad spectrum of countries, academic disciplines, ideologies and activist experiences, linked only by their common interest in the questions posed by the inquiry. Regional thematic sub-debates were organized, usually by the co-ordinators of national research projects, which were to proceed as autonomous explorations of the main themes of the inquiry. Moreover, three global sub-debates focusing on main conceptual issues were organized, dealing with 'The Urgency Factor and Democracy' (i.e. the case for revolutionary mobilization and central planning vs. representative democracy); with 'Participation: The View from Above' (i.e. the view of the state and the shapers of its policies); and with 'Clientelism, Patronage and Popular Participation'.[6]

Meanwhile, a series of meetings involving researchers and activists from Asia and Latin America (Oxford 1980, Bogota, Managua, Bangkok and Bombay 1981) discussed methods and questions for field studies. In view of the very limited staffing and funding of the programme itself, the availability and interests of national research institutions and social scientists, and also of external sources of funds, were decisive in the geographical distribution of field studies and in the character of the groups and movements studied. Latin America received the widest and most varied coverage, largely because special funding became available for participation research in this region and because the programme coincided with and encouraged a re-thinking among Latin American social scientists and theorists of political democracy, social movements and self-defensive participation among the excluded that stemmed from the region's traumatic experience of popular defeats and military authoritarianism during the 1970s. Studies of peasant movements, trade unions and urban neighbourhood associations, and of participation as a component of national policy were carried out in Bolivia, Brazil, Chile, Colombia, Guyana, Mexico, Nicaragua and Peru, generally by teams of researchers dealing with different aspects of these topics.

In Asia, studies of non-party political formations and of social activists in India responded to preoccupations of national researchers that were somewhat different from the questions that came to the fore in Latin America. Peasant movements and incipient forms of peasant resistance in an extremely anti-participatory setting were studied in Thailand. Plans for research in China, which might have opened up some particularly controversial questions, could not be carried beyond a preliminary exploration owing to lack of funds.

Several other projects envisaged had to be abandoned, mainly for lack of funding. The programme was unable to initiate research in Africa or other major regions. Several of the 'dimensions' of participation discussed in the research proposal, in particular the questions of biographies, programmes and projects, and anti-participatory structures and ideologies, could be dealt with only in the context of studies focused on other questions. One of the settings of particular interest to the programme, that of ethnic or tribal minorities striving to cope with aggressions and exclusions from 'national' social and economic orders had to be set aside to a hoped-for later stage, except in cases in which ethnicity played an important role in peasant mobilization, such as in the Bolivian studies, and to some extent the studies in Colombia and India. It became increasingly evident that omission of research and debate on the participation or exclusion of women was unjustifiable but examinations of this question in Asia and Latin America could be initiated only late in the course of the programme, and only in the context of regional sub-debates.[7]

An attempt was made to reflect the participatory approach in the very organization of the programme which gradually evolved and took shape as a result of impulses and suggestions received through the central debate. The programme thus increasingly moved away from the traditional UN research model, with power concentrated in a central office, towards a style in which the motors of the programme operated more strongly from the periphery than from the centre – i.e. from some of the research centres and groups in charge of actual field research and sub-debates which were attuned to local and national development needs in a critical spirit, already involved in basework with participatory movements and at the same time committed to rigorous standards of social analysis and synthesis. In early 1981 the programme was thus radically reorganized on a highly decentralized and participatory basis, with collective decision-making bodies being established at the regional and global levels (central core group and regional core groups).[8]

Like the groups and movements it was trying to understand and help, the programme suffered many vicissitudes and could, as we have noted, realize its aspirations only in part. It suffered a particularly grievous blow in its early stages from the untimely death of Andrew Pearse, the programme's principal source of ideas and initiatives, a sociologist committed to the empowerment of the disadvantaged. The programme also suffered from a continuous paucity of resources in relation to its ambitious objectives and the many temptations to broaden its thematic and geographical scope. It faced latent opposition from various quarters due to the controversial and sensitive nature of its central focus and its unconventional *modus operandi*.

One persistent shortcoming of the debate was that the programme was better able to call forth and circulate differing points of view and experiences than to conduct a real dialogue or extract a synthesis. Feedback between the global debate and the research in progress was thus limited or erratic. Also, the findings from field studies were suggestive rather than conclusive in regard to the prospects for participation. This was inevitable given the constraints of resources and institutional contacts that dictated the study of peasant movements in a few countries, trade unions in others, national mobilization policies and other 'dimensions' in still others, and given the unexpectedly contradictory and traumatic transformations of the national settings themselves. The programme inevitably fell short of its aim of advancing much beyond the current fragmented, unstructured approaches to the study of participation to reach a holistic approach relating the many forces and processes that reproduce or challenge existing relations of domination and exclusion. The aim of supporting and promoting through 'action research' or 'basework' the organized efforts of the hitherto excluded to participate in the running of their societies also led only to relatively modest and inconclusive results, although in several countries the research did respond to preoccupations voiced by popular organizations that translated the findings into local languages, circulated and discussed them, and presumably were later able to make use of them in their struggles. Also, in some countries, the programme could play at crucial moments a catalytic role in bringing together intellectuals, activists and grassroots movements and organizations.[9]

Research was generally welcomed by participatory movements if it helped them better to understand their social identity and to analyse their own problems of organization and strategy. The close involvement of social movements studied in the research itself influenced in some cases the very contents and orientation of the research. A number of projects were actually initiated at the request of such movements, and in other cases their involvement in the research process led to a change of focus of the research, for example away from the study of participatory organizations and movements to a study of the concrete obstacles and constraints that the movements were facing, i.e. the study of anti-participatory structures and ideologies, and of political and legal spaces open for action.

Altogether, the programme generated a substantial body of findings that, in combination with research carried out under other auspices with which the programme tried to keep in touch, should help toward a better understanding of the problems of participation in the terms in which the research proposal defined it. Part II of this volume attempts to sum up and make use of the findings for this purpose.[10]

Rethinking of preconceptions on participation

This attempt to sum up the findings of UNRISD's inquiry into participation and relate them to the world of the early 1990s would do well to resist temptations to over-generalization, superficial comparisons, and the kind of pseudo-practical recommendations that decorate many international surveys dealing with social questions. National settings and historical trajectories are unique; spaces for the participation of the excluded open and close unpredictably. Forecasts of outcomes are generally far off the mark. One might plausibly urge on the organized efforts of the excluded tactics of cautious realism in the face of political, cultural and economic constraints, but in at least a few cases utopian voluntarism has probably inspired movements to change the distribution of power in their favour. Would-be guides and allies need sufficient humility to leave the choice of tactics to those who will experience the dangers and consequences of defeats, but not to the point of complete renunciation of confidence in capacity to interpret and help.

On at least three important points the findings did suggest a need for re-thinking of certain explicit or implicit assumptions entering into early stages of the debate and formulation of hypotheses:

First, the studies bring out the indeterminacy of the path of participatory experiences and movements. They imply that there is no clear linear sequence from non-participation to participation, from exclusion to incorporation, from local movements to national ones, from the micro-social to the macro-social. More specifically, it is misleading to think in terms of a model of 'genuine' participation present as a potentiality in the encounter of previously unorganized and tradition-bound people with 'development', to be filled with content by successive approximations in the historical process. In this respect, the studies support neither the 'modernization' theories of the 1950s and 1960s, for which both mobilization and modernization were cumulative and irreversible processes – albeit with temporary retrogressions and diversions; nor variants of Marxist social analysis that also postulate the cumulative character of class struggle and class consciousness; nor the expectations of 'social movements' evolving into 'national popular movements' entertained by some Latin American contributors to the inquiry. At its beginning, the inquiry into participation, while not committing itself to any of these positions, did incorporate a somewhat evolutionary and teleological element in some formulations of its view of 'incorporation'. It even offered as a dominant theme 'the idea of a long march from traditional cultivatorship to organized urban worker. The long march in this case becomes a many-sided symbol of change, and as long as we do not force the image, its use reminds us that the many scenes of participation which it passes through are related to each other and that they depict stages in an evolutionary sequence, which in the under-industrialized camp is the dominant trend of our times'.[11]

The studies suggest that the struggles of the groups and movements of the excluded are too diverse in their origins and outcomes to be summed up by the image of a 'long march' in any definable direction. No social science paradigm has been able to embrace and explain, let alone predict, the contradictory course of social change. Moreover, as became clearer during the 1980s, the prospect of their continuing incorporation into industrial employment as a basis for organization was largely an illusion. As Chapter 9 demonstrates, the 'dominant' trend in much of the world has rather been toward more radical exclusion from economic and social orders in crisis and from the opportunities offered by new technologies. The organized efforts of the hitherto excluded as well as the newly excluded have had to focus on survival strategies and forms of protest to which most of their previous organizational experiences are barely relevant. Even in the high-income industrial or post-industrial countries, the declining active membership and tactical confusion of social democratic parties, trade unions and other long-established popular organizations in the face of the erosion of welfare state institutions and wage and job security, conquests that previously seemed unchallengeable, demonstrate that the 'terms of incorporation' are never settled definitively.

Secondly, and in partial contradiction to the above generalization, the studies throw into relief the structural limits to participation that were discussed above. National processes and policies set the framework within which organized efforts, even at the local level, take place, acquire meaning, and can 'succeed' or 'fail'. The image of people organizing locally and spontaneously to confront dominant forces and structures appears doubly incomplete because (1) it is often only through the mediation of those structures – including the state, national political parties, trade unions and voluntary organizations – that participatory movements become effective social actors; and (2) it is often within such structures that meaningful participation can take place. In this manner, the very notion of encounter becomes considerably more complex than it seemed at first, with its connotation of David against Goliath. Political participation at the national level, in terms of party politics, pressure groups and formal structures for intermediation emerges as an ineluctable dimension of 'organized efforts'. This does not imply, of course, that the state or other large bureaucratized organizations can be dependable allies of the excluded. The studies indicate, however, that the groups and movements of the latter have to make use of them without taking their pretensions at face value, have to seek realistic tactics and alliances in the continuing struggle for control over them.

Thirdly, the studies demonstrate the wide differences in rationalities between the social actors engaged in encounters: politicians, technocrats and bureaucrats, military and police officers, national and local élites, employers, ideologists, religious leaders, academic figures in different disciplines, students, national and local leaders of popular organizations, the rank and file of these organizations, and the unorganized masses of the excluded. These 'actors' often seem to be following scripts in separate, incompatible dramas, indifferent to or contemptuous of one another.

Fourthly, in its early focus on Latin America, the participation programme dealt with a region in which organized social movements and strivings from the disadvantaged classes were vigorous, relatively autonomous *vis-à-vis* the state, and ambitious in their aims of transformation, although they confronted anti-participatory structures and ideologies that were particularly powerful and ruthless at the time the research took place. In discussions within the programme at a later stage to focus on Asia, there was consensus that this would have to give relatively more attention to state participatory schemes and to those of national and international organizations trying to work with groups having little or no initial capacity for organized efforts.

An end and a beginning

In practice, the Participation Programme suffered a fate ironically similar to that of many participatory initiatives dependent on state or other institutional support. Its activities came to an inconclusive end through shortage of funds, institutional uneasiness over its future course in so controversial a policy area, and subsequent departure or diversion to other research tasks of its central core group. Various national and regional social research institutions continued independently to pursue the question, to exchange information, and to seek alliance with groups and movements of the excluded.[12]

The programme left behind a considerable body of published research findings, summed up in Part II of this volume, but the preparation of a final global survey of this material and the ideas thrown up in the debates remained in suspense. Meanwhile, during the 1980s, the appeal of the term 'participation' waned, in part because of its uses to legitimize policies that were predominantly manipulative and paternalistic, in part because the increasing dominance of neo-liberal prescriptions for 'development' and internationally dictated 'adjustment policies' to cope with crises left no room for 'organized efforts', whether inspired from above or from below.

The delay in producing an overview of studies and debates carried out in the early 1980s might seem to deprive the present text of timeliness. The groups and movements then studied and the national contexts of their struggles have changed enormously in a decade. However, the delay has at least two positive consequences.

First, it has forced the authors to place the ideas of participation current at the end of the 1970s, which are summarized in Chapter 2, as well as the studies themselves, in a more adequate historical context, to consider their relevance to a world in which past expectations have been devastatingly disappointed, in which new potentialities and challenges have emerged, and in which the indeterminacy of the future is more evident than ever before. Chapter 9 grapples with this new context of the early 1990s.

The problem of specifying the settings to which the inquiry's findings are now relevant suggests the magnitude of changes in the world order and in ways of thinking about social development since the late 1970s. The originators of the inquiry took it for granted that it would focus primarily on 'developing countries' or the 'Third World'. The latter term recurs throughout the present text. Even during the months of preparation of this text, however, the disintegration of the 'Second World' of 'real socialism' rendered the term practically obsolete. Divisions of the world into 'developed' and 'developing' countries, 'rich' and 'poor' countries, or 'North' and 'South' have their own drawbacks. Thus we have retained 'Third World' as a convenient label, no more susceptible to misleading connotations than others.

It is more important for present purposes that, in spite of widening gaps of various kinds between the 'First World' and the remainder of the world's peoples, the differences in forms of 'exclusion' and in challenges to 'organized efforts' are not as clear cut as they seemed a few years ago.

The First World also is experiencing declining state capacity to provide services and reduce income inequalities, and declining public confidence in the legitimacy of its efforts. Established popular organizations, in particular trade unions and class-based parties, are decreasingly able to defend their members' interests or mobilize mass support. 'Informalization' of livelihood is on the rise. Migrations are bringing millions of 'hitherto excluded' from the poor countries to cope with new patterns of exclusion as well as new opportunities. Social movements are becoming just as diverse and challenging to the pre-existing order in the First World as elsewhere.

Secondly, the problems of 'participation' have returned to the forefront of attention for several reasons and at several levels. On the one side, the processes of political democratization that have swept most of the world since the later 1980s and their contradiction with dwindling confidence in the capacity of the state or the economic system to respond effectively to popular demands for social equity and security have placed the organizations purporting to represent the people in a paradoxical combination of enhanced legitimacy and impotence.

On the other side, many governments and international institutions such as the World Bank are looking to 'participation' as a means of making their development projects function better, helping people cope with the impoverishment and unemployment associated with the adjustment policies that economists argue are necessary, and, possibly, counter the rising ungovernability and anomy that threaten to make any coherent policy unviable. They are also looking to 'participation' as an indispensable dimension of the environmental policies and population control policies that can no longer be evaded or postponed. In this effort, they are turning increasingly to voluntary organizations as executors of participatory initiatives, in the expectation that they will prove more flexible and better attuned to 'working with people' than state technocrats and bureaucrats. Chapter 10 pursues some facets of the new status of 'participation'.[13]

A new wave of theoretical, polemical and prescriptive writings responds to these preoccupations. This book can do no more than call attention to this discourse, which combines efforts to label and justify the 'new social movements' arising and mutating in Europe and North America with attention to the organized efforts of the excluded in the rest of the world.[14] Most of the ideas now entering into international discourse have a long history. The transformed economic, social and political context in which their application is envisaged does not justify treating them as new discoveries. The saying that those who ignore history are condemned to repeat it is pertinent to a great deal of 'development' policy, including the question of participation. We do not presume to teach 'lessons', but hope to make a modest contribution to the dispelling of historical ignorance.

Notes

1. See *Rural Co-operatives as Agents of Change: A Research Project and a Debate*, UNRISD, Geneva, 1975; Pearse, Andrew, *Seeds of Plenty, Seeds of Want: Social and Economic Implications of the Green Revolution*, UNRISD and Oxford University Press, Geneva and Oxford, 1980; and *The Quest for a Unified Approach to Development*, UNRISD, Geneva, 1980. As a result of this critical assessment of previous UNRISD research, 'participation', together with 'livelihood' and 'policy' were identified as the three main themes on which the Institute's research should focus. Participation was seen as the crucial factor in any interaction between the popular pursuit of livelihood and the realization of government policy. See *An Approach to Development Research*, UNRISD, Geneva, 1979. See also the Foreword to this book by Solon Barraclough who, as Director of UNRISD, played a crucial role in defining and initiating the new approach.

2. Pearse, Andrew and Stiefel, Matthias, *Inquiry into Participation: A Research Approach*, UNRISD, Geneva, May 1979.

3. See Pearse, Andrew, *The Latin American Peasant*, Frank Cass, London, 1975.

4. UNRISD, *A Glance at the Past and Directions for the Future*, mimeo, Geneva, July 1980b, p. 1.

5. Cohen, Selina, ed., *Debaters' Comments on 'Inquiry into Participation: A Research Approach'*, UNRISD Participation Programme, Geneva, October 1980.

6. The three papers were published in *Dialogue about Participation* (see issues 1, 3 and 4 respectively). The debate stemming from the paper on the 'urgency factor' was also published, but termination of the Participation Programme itself has prevented publication of the other two debates.

7. Two publications reflect the findings of this work: one focuses on the changing role of women in participatory movements in India and Thailand (Omvedt, Gail, *Women in Popular Movements: India and Thailand during the Decade of Women*, UNRISD, Geneva, 1986); the second one on the role of women's organizations in social mobilization in Latin America (Jelin, Elizabeth, ed., *Women and Social Change in Latin America*, UNRISD and Zed Books, Geneva and London, 1990).

8. An Annexe to this volume contains a list of research projects and sub-debates carried out under the UNRISD Participation Programme, of researchers and research institutes that were involved, as well as of central and regional core group members.

9. A few research reports dealt more particularly with the issue of participatory or dialogical research; also at the end of the programme some think-pieces were written on the question reflecting some of the experiences of the research. See for example: Das, Arvind N., *Research, Participation and Action: Some Methodological and Practical Issues*, unpublished manuscript, UNRISD, 1985; PIDT, *Understanding Social Reality*, unpublished manuscript, PIDT/UNRISD, New Delhi, 1984.

10. An Annexe to this volume contains a list of the published reports as well as other unpublished material generated by the programme and available from various commercial publishers or at UNRISD. A preliminary summary of results from the regional sub-debates in Latin America was presented at a joint UNRISD-

CLACSO seminar held in Buenos Aires in August 1984. See CLACSO, 'Movimientos Sociales y Participacion Popular', *David y Goliath – Boletin CLACSO*, vol. XIV, no. 46, 1984, pp. 5-20.

11. Pearse, Andrew and Stiefel, Matthias, 'Launching the Debate' in *Dialogue about Participation 1*, UNRISD, Geneva, June 1981.

12. While no separate research programme on participation exists today at UNRISD, key questions of participation raised by the earlier programme are present in most of the recent and current UNRISD work. Such is the case, for example, in the research presently carried out on ethnic conflicts, political violence, sustainable development and changes in Eastern Europe as well as in the preparatory work for the 1995 World Summit for Social Development carried out by UNRISD. Relevant publications are listed in a separate annexe at the end of this volume.

13. A wide-ranging discussion of this new status and its problems can be found in Bhatnagar, Bhuvan and Williams, Aubrey C., eds., *Participatory Development and the World Bank: Potential Directions for Change*, World Bank Discussion Papers, The World Bank, Washington, DC, 1992.

14. For recent theoretically-oriented treatments with ample bibliographies, see Scott, Alan, *Ideology and the New Social Movements*, Unwin Hyman, London, 1990; and Pieterse, Jan Nederveen, *Emancipations, Modern and Postmodern*, special issue of *Development and Change*, vol. 23, no. 3, July 1992, Sage Publications on behalf of the Institute of Social Studies, The Hague. See also Escobar, Arturo and Alvarez, Sonia E., eds., *The Making of Social Movements in Latin America: Identity, Strategy and Democracy*, Westview Press, Boulder, Colorado, 1992. This last compilation, in particular, contains important new contributions to the discussion of questions of institutionalization and interlocutors.

The Many Faces of Participation

The term 'popular participation' entered into international discourse on development during the 1960s and achieved wider currency during the 1970s, at a time when the myth of development itself was experiencing contradictory impacts of utopian redefinition ('another development') and disillusionment with state capacity to control or plan. The term itself and the actions it suggested were adaptable to quite different ideological frames of reference and immediately came under suspicion for the same reason. Different actors in the development drama conceived of participation in very different ways and promoted or opposed participatory initiatives with different time perspectives and expectations. The hopes for participation derived from and renewed a long historical evolution of theories and practice of democracy, co-operation and communitarian and socialist utopias, but the 1970s discourse paid only sporadic attention to this history.

During the 1980s participation lost ground in international discourse, sharing in the eclipse of development conceptions oriented to social justice and human welfare. A United Nations International Seminar on Popular Participation, held in Ljubljana in 1982, focused on government policies and expectations from participation, rather than on the 'popular' dimension. At the beginning of the 1990s hopes for participation as a way out of otherwise insoluble crises of human relationships and livelihood are reviving. In February 1990, the African governments, together with various United Nations agencies, non-governmental organizations and African people's organizations, held an International Conference on Popular Participation in the Recovery and Development Process in Africa, at Arusha, Tanzania. In May 1990, the United Nations Children's Fund (UNICEF), which has been particularly concerned at the paucity of beneficiary initiative in its own local projects, organized a Global Seminar on Participatory Development in Florence, Italy. The documents of these meetings show that long-standing ambiguities remain concerning tutelage by the state or by NGOs and other external allies vs. popular spontaneity and autonomy; and in regard to the requirements of a market-ruled kingdom of necessity vs. popular aspirations to social justice and security.

The following pages will discuss the main conceptions of or approaches to popular participation as they emerged in the 1970s and earlier, and as they manifested themselves in the UNRISD debates and research. Chapter 9 will return to them as they relate to the crisis-ridden world of today. The summary does not pretend to be exhaustive, and most of the conceptions are not mutually exclusive, either logically or in their practical consequences. Real policies and initiatives have generally based themselves, simultaneously or over time, on an eclectic mixture of several conceptions, or at least have contained elements borrowed from several. All approaches have been susceptible to distortions and mystifications.

Pluralist democracy

The conception with the longest history and widest acceptance has focused on participation as the ideal functioning of pluralist representative democracy. Political parties competing within codified rules of the game then become the main channels through which the whole adult population can have a voice in the selection of leaders and policies. This conception has supposed free competition in ideas and criticisms; protection of the rights of minorities; two-way communication between the citizens and their elected leadership through a wide range of organizations representing different constituencies, in addition to the competing parties; and many kinds of formal and informal consultations among citizens. It has also supposed a broad underlying consensus that allows all major social groups to feel themselves represented within the system in spite of obvious differences in ability to make themselves heard. It has been compatible with widely differing degrees and kinds of government intervention in society, but thus far has been associated with capitalist or 'mixed' welfare state systems. It has implied a distrust of concrete utopias and blueprints for their achievement, including centralized planning, that might endanger the majority's right to change course.

Pluralist democracy has been formally endorsed and at least intermittently practised by the majority of states since World War II. Governments and social scientists in the First World prescribed it almost as a matter of course for new countries emerging through decolonization. Its application has met with well-known reverses and criticisms, of which the following are particularly relevant for present purposes.

First, it has been argued, particularly in regard to countries with rural majorities and high illiteracy, that only educated and well-off minorities are able to enter the political competition. If the rural majority and the urban poor vote at all they do so at the dictate of landowners, caciques or government officials. The 'participating' minorities are then able to serve their own interests at the expense of the voiceless majority. (With economic and demographic changes generating large underclasses practically excluded from employment and even from stable shelter, similar arguments are now being applied to significant minorities in certain 'rich' countries.) It has been argued that the excluded are more likely to gain from mobilizing régimes, motivated to seek their support to counterbalance the power of the previous élites. This argument has applied particularly to agrarian reforms, since one can find at least a few instances of decisive action by dictatorships and many instances of delay and emasculation of programmes by parliamentary allies of landowning élites. In general, however, the weight of evidence does not suggest that the dispossessed have fared better under mobilizing dictatorships than under élite-controlled democracies, in which clientelistic networks may offer them appreciable rewards and some sense of participating.

A related argument against pluralist representative democracy, linked to the reasoning discussed under 'legitimization of power' below, is that the divisiveness of competition by rival parties clashes with the cultural background of 'non-Western' peoples accustomed to decisions by consensus or by reliance on traditional authorities. It has also been argued, from the experience of multi-ethnic African and Asian countries, that the formation of competing political parties almost unavoidably becomes linked with ethnic divisions rather than policy choices or class interests, so that pluralist democracy cannot function as it does in more homogeneous societies.

As electoral participation widens with the advance of urbanization, literacy and exposure to mass media, without significant narrowing of the gap between the élites and the majority or the incorporation of the latter into autonomous class-based organizations, different arguments against pluralist democracy come to the fore. Charismatic populist leaders gain the confidence of the majority through extravagant promises and some real benefits, once they come to power. Mobilized voting then displaces more structured efforts to gain control over resources and institutions. The populist leadership tolerates minority opinion only grudgingly, identifying it with 'enemies of the people'. The anti-populists interpret their own exclusion as an evil consequence of excessive participation. In practice, the populist régimes have commonly brought about some changes in the composition of élites but no sustainable redistribution of power to the majority. Their propensity to incoherent economic policies, arbitrariness and corruption have generally brought about their breakdown and replacement by overtly anti-participatory régimes, although mass loyalty to populist leadership has persisted or recurred. A few régimes, such as that of Mexico, have managed to institutionalize original combinations of populist appeals, co-option or repression of opposition, and technobureaucratic management to achieve over relatively long periods political stability and economic growth, but at a price of growing popular alienation and apathy.

The different kinds of international discourse represented by the UNRISD programme and the Ljubljana seminar did not give more than intermittent attention to formal pluralist democracy as a means for the dispossessed majority to participate in control over resources and institutions. The breakdowns, impasses and manipulations visible in electoral systems in most of the Third World argued for their ineffectiveness for the advancement of majority interests. The continuing, although waning, credibility of the centrally planned 'real socialist' systems and of certain military or one-party mobilizing régimes made their participatory claims seem promising. Moreover, the participation of representatives of these régimes in United Nations gatherings such as the Ljubljana seminar ensured that their claims would be heard with respect. In the 1970s the advocates of 'another development' looked to China and Tanzania as models, and the Velasco military government in Peru had embarked on participatory schemes with apparent innovativeness and conviction. In a good many other countries authoritarian régimes were so well entrenched and so adverse to pluralism that only participatory initiatives too localized and unobtrusive to attract their suspicion seemed practicable, and this limitation influenced many organizations that aspired to bring practical help to the dispossessed.

Since then, as will be discussed in Chapters 9 and 10, the resurgence of pluralist democracy has been extraordinary, in national societies with quite different past trajectories. It has become more widely agreed that other forms of participation, however legitimate and promising, cannot do without political means of making themselves heard at the national level, if only to fend off bureaucratic arrogance and corruption. Ability to give or withhold votes, for all its shortcomings, is indispensable to the efforts of the 'hitherto excluded'.

Modernization

A conception widely influential among policy-making élites and social scientists has viewed participation as a dimension of modernization. If capital formation and transfer of technology were to generate self-sustaining 'development', they would have to go hand in hand with cultural, political and social 'modernization': including the transfer of democratic political institutions from the West, and the transfer of values emphasizing efficiency and consumerism. Popular participation then became a therapy, to transform 'backward', 'traditional', 'unresponsive' populations into citizens ready to assume their duties and seize their opportunities in a predetermined development process. In this process, the majority would receive diverse incentives as well as compulsions to participate in activities outside the family and the neighbourhood, gradually gaining in ability to organize and defend perceived interests. This conception has implied that some groups, at least for a few generations, would remain unable or unwilling to be incorporated into a 'modern' and 'efficient' social order; that is, they would be excluded or bypassed by history. Advocates of this conception have generally devalued or distrusted traditional community and extended family ties as forms of participation. Such ties would or should disintegrate in the course of modernization. They have also shared a preoccupation that participation in politics and in consumption might run ahead of participation in production and in technological innovation. Participation might then stifle development by stimulating premature struggles over distribution and preventing accumulation of a surplus for investment.

By the 1970s this conception had lost a good deal of credit through the rise of dependency theory and related attacks on the 'Western' bias of modernization. The long-term viability of continually expanding and modernizing production and consumption was coming into question. The proportion of the world's population able to participate to some degree was obviously growing, but ecological and demographic trends made it seem unlikely that the laggards would ever be able to catch up by following available route-maps of modernization. The dilemmas presented by modernized consumption patterns accessible to minorities prepared to guard their privileges by force versus expanding political participation and demands for redistribution seemed likely to be permanent rather than transitory, both within countries and between countries in the world system. Democratically legitimized régimes that see increasing inequality through the unleashing of market forces as the only way forward are now confronting new versions of these dilemmas.

The missing ingredient

Policy-making élites have also viewed participation as a means or set of techniques available to government agencies for the purpose of making development programmes function better and the development process itself more efficient and more equitable. That is, popular participation has been seen as a 'missing ingredient' to be achieved through fool-proof or bureaucrat-proof ways of adding 'participation components' to projects and activities. In fact, this approach is associated with a conception of development itself as an aggregation of 'development projects' rather than as a complex process of societal change. It introduces participation only at the stage of implementation of projects handed down from above, and defines the people affected as 'target groups' or 'beneficiary groups'.

Advocates of this approach have generally looked to traditional communities and systems of reciprocity as more adaptable to their purpose than modern party and interest-group organizations. Applications go back to the community development and 'animation rurale' programmes embarked on in many countries in the 1950s, some of them backed by considerable public resources and high-level government support. Their generally disappointing results generated diagnoses pointing to their subjection to centrally imposed targets and techniques, their failure to allow for cultural traits and conflicts of interest within the communities they served, and their propensity to manipulate rather than liberate. Since then, programmes using different labels and purporting to meet the criticisms of their predecessors have waxed and waned. Repeated experience of the inefficiency and costliness of the bureaucratic apparatuses available for implementing 'planned' development programmes, particularly in rural settings, and of the lack of communication between these apparatuses and the intended beneficiaries have kept alive the hope of accomplishing objectives more cheaply, defusing popular discontent and tapping the potential of human initiative.

In spite of its negative evaluation of bureaucratic agents, this conception could not dispense with a supposition of basic state rationality, benevolence and representativeness in society, and of societal consensus on development goals. Programmes whose experience cast doubt on these suppositions risked disavowal by their government sponsors. Practically none of the initiatives could solve the problem of duplicability of localized successes, or shield them against political and economic instability in the wider society. The supposition of a 'missing ingredient' became less plausible with rising scepticism concerning the capacity of the state to manage development.

More recently the forced abandonment of state responsibilities for social services and subsidies to the levels of living of the poor has thrown attention back to the potential of localized self-help with modest support from the state or non-governmental organizations. This trend, accompanying a shrinkage in the planning capacity and aspirations of the state, becomes rather a substitute for a development policy than a missing ingredient. It has at least meant greater appreciation of the survival strategies of the poor, and has involved a wide range of small-scale initiatives close to the approaches discussed under 'conscientization' below.

The self-reliant poor

Even before the crises of the 1980s, a good many governments looked to a more restricted version of the conception summarized above, viewing participation as a means of relieving pressures for social services and subsidies under conditions in which the style of development could not offer satisfactory livelihood or 'modern' employment to a large part of the population. Self-help, self-reliance and reciprocity were then encouraged for the production and exchange of goods among the poor and for the provision of housing and community services: areas in which participation did not perturb the existing distribution of power and wealth. The poor were to maintain themselves in a kind of parallel economy, functioning under laws quite different from the modern economy, until the latter might become ready to absorb them. Policies of this kind encountered a persistent misunderstanding between the parties: governments supported them to some extent so as to relieve themselves of responsibilities; the poor participated to some extent in the hope of being rewarded by resources from the government. Under present conditions, however, governmental hopes of this kind can reach an uneasy coexistence with strivings from below, when groups of the dispossessed and their allies find no alternative to organized survival strategies and can expect from the authorities not much more than toleration of these strategies.

Legitimization of power

Authoritarian governments have viewed popular participation (although not overtly) as a set of techniques (plebiscites, mass demonstrations of support for the régime, mobilization of 'voluntary' labour for public purposes, revival or invention of 'traditional' consensual community institutions, etc.) legitimizing their rule and allowing for controlled expression of popular sentiments while eliminating autonomous channels for organization and representation. The rhetoric of participation and also of national cultural uniqueness is thus used to promote manipulated alternatives to 'divisive' pluralist democracy. A good deal of self-deception may enter in, and the degree of authenticity in the participation and the cultural traditions may be unclear even to the sponsoring authorities as well as the groups called on to participate. This approach has been used to some degree by all populist régimes and one-party states and quite systematically in régimes such as the 'New Society' of the Marcos period in the Philippines. It was present in 'African Socialism' and similar ideologies adopted by the ruling élites of various newly independent African countries.[1] Authoritarian participatory rhetoric has motivated rejection of the term by some adherents to other conceptions, as indicated below under 'mystification'. This approach differs from the conception next to be discussed in its lack of a coherent rationale for societal transformation in the interest of the majority.

Revolutionary and post-revolutionary mobilization

A conception widely influential in the Third World during the 1960s and 1970s held that 'participation', if it were to bring about real gains for the dispossessed majority, would have to consist of revolutionary mobilization under the guidance of a vanguard party or enlightened élite. The currents of opinion adhering to this proposition generally relied on variants of Marxist-Leninist theory, but it was also advocated independently of such theory. It was argued that the intolerable poverty of the Third World majority, the urgency of transformation, the complexity of the policy choices involved, the threat of imperialist aggression and counter-revolutionary subversion from defeated classes, and the necessity of comprehensive planning did not leave room for more pluralistic, localized, autonomous or open-ended approaches. This argument entered into the UNRISD programme through a sub-debate on the 'urgency factor', but none of the field researches confronted its applications to reality, with the partial exception of an exploratory mission to China.

While the conception called for empowerment of the hitherto excluded majority, it left this majority no scope for choice of what to do with its empowerment. It offered no safeguards against arbitrary and unrealistic decisions by an infallible leadership and conformist ritualism substituted for autonomous and critical participation. Its pretensions have collapsed with astonishing rapidity, through the self-admitted impasses of the régimes supposed to exemplify it. An examination of the erratic trajectories of policy in such régimes and their human costs indicates that the alleged advantages of planning and ability to act decisively were illusory, and even the real achievements in social equality and security have come under attack as causes of productive stagnation and psychological antipathy to innovation. Moreover, in a good many Third World countries, 'urgency' has justified military and bureaucratic élites with little or no revolutionary authenticity or claim to majority support. Authentic participation for the defence of perceived popular interests could survive only in the interstices left by the inability of the formal mobilizing and planning mechanisms to regulate all aspects of social intercourse.

Conscientization and self-liberation

A family of conceptions very different from those summarized above has viewed participation mainly in terms of local groups defending and/or transforming their own lifestyles and sources of livelihood, evolving their own ideas and tactics in the course of struggle against exploitative power structures, ideologies and economic systems. These conceptions have supposed a very high potential for popular creativity and also for traditional knowledge and indigenous technology. They have denied the capacity of bureaucratized state power, whether under capitalist or socialist forms of economic and political organization, to achieve just social orders. In general, they have limited the legitimate role of external allies to that of catalysts helping in the early stages of organization. They have generally been reluctant to speculate on the future management of complex societies. They have either disregarded the constraints imposed by national states within the world system, or hoped that these would wither away as local groups become more autonomous and form 'networks' among them. Differences have emerged mainly concerning the degree of spontaneity to be expected and the legitimacy of guidance from outside the group, i.e. 'conscientization'. One activist and participant in the UNRISD programme has affirmed: '... it is concluded, without further ado, that communities must be guided towards social responsibility, or "conscientized". I utterly disagree with this conclusion and with the neologism coined by Paulo Freire (conscientization), because I consider that the appearance of a conscience, whether individual or collective, is not an induced event, but a spontaneous occurrence.'[2]

The real initiatives corresponding to these conceptions have proved vulnerable but also resilient and remarkably varied during the past two decades. They have been easy to repress, and have touched upon the lives only of shifting minorities within most national societies. The contradictions between the ideal of autonomy and the real dependence of local groups on external allies have been recurrent, as have the contradictions between the concrete aspirations of the local groups and the egalitarian anti-consumerist ideologies of their allies. The conceptions themselves have come under criticism for their anti-political bias, isolating the local groups from national class-based organizations and making them paradoxically dependent on the state as the only institution capable of responding to their needs for services and subsidies.

At the same time, the ties between local self-defensive movements of the dispossessed and national or international movements with religious, gender, ethnic and environmental agendas have become remarkably complex. The potential of conscientization or self-liberation to transform for the better the lives of the majority remains an open question, but the efforts are bound to persist, both as one dimension in popular survival strategies and as one dimension in the international effort to rethink or replace the myth of development.

Social movements

Conceptions having considerable affinity to the above go back to social upheavals in the First World during the 1960s, when a wide range of new movements focusing on 'quality of life' issues or anti-militarism seemed to displace traditional class antagonisms and struggles over distribution as the main focus of challenge to the existing systems of domination. Some of the studies sponsored in Latin America by the UNRISD programme viewed participation mainly as an evolving process of the emergence of 'social movements' and their coming together into broader 'popular movements' capable of challenging the national power structures and eventually controlling the state in the interest of the majority. Their authors argued for the necessity of combining many different bases and motivations for 'organized efforts' (class, local, regional, ethnic, gender, student status, etc.). Their hopes emerged from a period of disillusioning experiences with political parties, electoral mechanisms, revolutionary strategies and development planning. In a good many countries in Latin America military governments had eliminated previous channels for political and interest-group participation and forced a search for viable alternatives. The resulting distrust of centralized 'vanguard parties', state planning and theoretical blueprints for the future led to a high valuation on spontaneous popular action and on civil society as opposed to the state, but gave more importance to power and transformation at the national level than did the advocates of conscientization and self-liberation. Political parties were looked to as components but not manipulators of the eventual 'popular movements'. Class struggle was viewed as an important but not unique dimension of social transformation. These conceptions were inherently pluralist but viewed pluralism rather differently from the advocates of representative democracy, since popular choice between competing political parties would be less important than interactions between social and popular movements seeking common ground. The majority of the UNRISD studies combined a scrutiny of organizations of national or regional scope devoted to collective action for limited ends with an examination of the actual or potential roles of these organizations as components of social and popular movements.

Trade unions and other collective action for limited ends

Collective action focused on the advancement of class or group rights and interests through collective bargaining, organized pressures on the authorities, and co-operatively managed production, buying and selling, has a long history and corresponds closely to the UNRISD definition. Participation here takes the form of a continuing struggle over the distribution of incomes and access to livelihood and services, in which solidarity gives strength to a numerous social group engaged in production whose members individually have neither assets nor power. The participants may also act in accordance with one or more of the other conceptions of participation, but their immediate struggle leaves open the question of their acceptance or rejection of the existing economic and political order, and also the question of a liberating transformation of their values. Collective action for limited ends also leaves open the question whether the organized participants should go out of their way to incorporate weaker and less easily organized categories of the disadvantaged, or take a stand on questions outside the area of production, such as ecological menaces or the rights of women and minorities. The contradiction between motivations to broaden solidarity and motivations to maintain group advantages seems inherent in this form of participation.

Since the nineteenth century, the future of trade unionism, the most dynamic component of class-based participation, seemed assured by the expectation that the industrial working class would continue to grow in size and concentration in large enterprises. The future of peasant unions and other organizations for defence of traditional means of livelihood seemed much less promising, since the latter were expected to disintegrate in the course of modernization. By the 1970s, the former expectation was already losing plausibility. Since then, as will be discussed in Chapter 9, the unexpected rapidity of technological change and the international mobility of capital seeking lower labour costs have shrunk employment in the previous strongholds of union organization and generated new occupations and concentrations of labour presenting different organizational challenges. More recently, of course, economic crises have eroded union capacity to defend employment security and income levels.

Worker management

A relatively well-defined movement with its own body of experiences and techniques, more influential in Europe than elsewhere and central to national policy in Yugoslavia until recently, has concentrated on participation in the sense of worker management in industry and other economic enterprises, in the expectation that this could eventually become the main form of organization of production and distribution, and the basis of a new society. Various successful enterprises have been presented as models, but their number and influence do not seem to have increased significantly since the 1970s. Roles for trade unions as administrators of social services for their members, financed by dues and sometimes state contributions, and participation by union representatives in the directorates of industries have been more widespread but do not seem to have brought about significant empowerment of members. Hopes that worker management would replace bureaucratized 'real socialism' during the recent disintegration of the latter seem to have been ephemeral. The approach has been briefly incorporated in national policies in a few Third World countries, as in Peru during the 1970s. In these countries, however, worker management has more often appeared as a dimension of survival strategies: workers, particularly in public transport, have taken over bankrupt enterprises abandoned by their owners or by the state and kept them going as best they could. Small enterprises in the informal sector are also sometimes managed co-operatively by their workers, although even in this part of the economy capitalist entrepreneurial management seems to be more common.

Defence of the natural order

According to one line of argument among social scientists, authentic participatory movements usually derive from a shared set of beliefs justifying group defence or recovery of an imagined traditional social order, based on natural rights and forms of hierarchy and reciprocity, that is threatened by outsiders or by unintelligible forces disrupting lifestyles and sources of livelihood. The resulting 'organized efforts' do not necessarily aim at control of the state or transformation of the economic system, but the consequences can be either revolutionary or reactionary according to interactions with other forces and ideologies and with the state's efforts to maintain order. Periods of questioning of the legitimacy and viability of the existing political and economic order naturally bring forth a resurgence of national myths and quests for bases of collective identity, which may be partly spontaneous, partly manipulated by the state itself or by movements seeking power. Movements of this kind can take on extremely 'excluding' and xenophobic forms, clashing violently with participatory currents that hold to more universalistic and forward-looking conceptions of human rights and social justice, in particular those calling for gender equality and religious freedom. The revolutionary-religious transformation of Iran is the most obvious case in point. At the same time, advocates of conscientization and of the spontaneous development of social movements have insisted on the need to draw on the historical memories and cultural resources of the oppressed. The movements combining demands for cultural autonomy and defence of traditional means of livelihood have found allies particularly among environmentalist movements. A struggle for popular consciousness may then ensue between rival articulators of historical myths and ethical-religious doctrines. The various outcomes are likely to be as inspiring, baffling and horrifying to proponents of other conceptions of participation in the future as in the past.

Mystification

Ever since the cry of the French students in 1968 – 'Je participe ... ils profitent' – 'participation' has undergone criticism as a deliberately misleading slogan masking an evasion of the realities of power or the laws of economics. Criticisms have come from economic and political orthodoxy, insisting on the incompatibility of premature or spontaneous participation with governability and development, and from the Marxist left, insisting on the futility of participation divorced from a strategy for the taking of power and transformation of relations of production. At the same time, advocates of self-liberation, direct democracy and autonomous social movements have objected mainly to the contamination of the term itself in international and national political usage. They have argued that the purposes of the organizations and governments endorsing it deprive it of legitimacy as a focus for research and action. More narrowly, 'participation' might amount to a source of livelihood and status for activists and researchers whose previous schemes for development were reaching an impasse. The *Debaters' Comments*[3] on the original UNRISD research proposal ranged from enthusiastic approval to expressions of all the above reasons for scepticism.

*

The various conceptions of or approaches to popular participation summarized above reflect the views of intellectual-ideological activists, social scientists, politicians and administrators who have codified them and tried to act on them. They have manifested themselves in projects and expressions of solidarity with minorities among the dispossessed classes and groups whose 'participation' is hoped for. Here they interact with organizational initiatives from below whose extent and continuity can only be guessed at. The results of this interaction for the dispossessed, depending on real experiences and the capacity of the wider environment to reward participation, are unavoidably contradictory. They include a generalized distrust of outsiders based on past manipulation and unfulfilled promises; a more sophisticated evaluation of outsiders as needed but undependable allies; and an internalization of the vocabularies and views of these allies, whether from conviction or as a means of manipulating them and forging links with more influential components of the societies. The clash of conceptions of participation and the competition of governmental, nongovernmental, and anti-governmental allies/manipulators has become a part of the environment within which the 'excluded' struggle to survive and adapt to or escape from their exclusion.

Notes

1. Bangura, Yusuf, *Authoritarian Rule and Democracy in Africa: A Theoretical Discourse*, UNRISD Discussion Paper No. 18, Geneva, March 1991.

2. Angulo, Alejandro, *An Experiment in Participatory Development*, UNICEF Innocenti Global Seminar on Participatory Development, Florence, May 1990.

3. Cohen, Selina, ed., *Debaters' Comments on 'Inquiry into Participation: A Research Approach'*, UNRISD, Geneva, 1980.

Part II

Experiences of Participation, Pseudo-Participation and Anti-Participation

What use can the findings of studies of struggles receding into the past be to the present organized efforts of the hitherto excluded and their allies? Not primarily to provide models of successful tactics to be imitated, or even cautionary tales of tactics to be avoided, although the latter may be closer to relevance. Probably the most useful lesson will be to expect the unexpected, to keep in mind that the character of exclusion and of the groups excluded along with the environments with which they must cope are continually changing. Tactics derived from time-honoured theories about the nature and role of classes or from the projection of trends that happen to be dominant at a given moment risk leading organized efforts into traps.

At the same time, reflections of past realities have an enormous influence on present realities. The ways groups among the dispossessed identify themselves along with legitimate allies and adversaries, the utopias they look to, their historical memories and myths build potentialities and constraints on action that correspond only erratically to changes in material circumstances. Action-oriented interpretations generally lag behind current realities, but they may also jump ahead in visions of the shape of the future. The would-be guide to the choices open to these perplexed groups has to balance objective factors of power and livelihood alternatives with dominant or sub-conscious self-images.

In the world today, people originating in tradition-bound peasant communities, or their children, may enter the ranks of the marginal urban poor, become unionized industrial wage workers, enter the lower middle class, through formal education, as public employees or teachers, enlist as soldiers or guerrillas, migrate abroad to work and send home remittances, prosper through smuggling or drug traffic, be converted by drought or civil war into starving refugees. Many individuals make more than one transition to relatively advantageous inclusion in the social order, then back to extreme exclusion.

Women are as complexly involved in these transitions as men, partly through similar precarious migrations and occupational shifts, partly through tensions stemming from changing relations between sexes and between generations. Their life-chances depend less than before on family ties. With the nearly universal rise in educational levels of women, many move into political, professional and commercial activities previously barred to them. International movements aiming at gender equality affect their capacity for organized efforts directly and indirectly. Much larger numbers, particularly from poor peasant households, find themselves, temporarily or otherwise, in urban factories, domestic service or sex work, and these labour markets, like those for women professionals, are becoming increasingly internationalized. Women rise to leadership positions as well as responsibility for family subsistence in villages and urban neighbourhoods deprived of men through migration, political persecution or war. At the same time, reactionary and fundamentalist movements strive with intermittent success and considerable support from insecure males to expel women from their new occupational roles and from a voice in public life.[1]

Analysis in terms of distinct social classes becomes shakier as more and more individuals and families experience what has been called 'multi-insertion' in economy and society. The different categories of people discussed below may be easily distinguishable at one particular point in time, but their present struggles cannot be understood without reference to their journey over time, their links to the struggles of other groups, and the fact that 'exit' – shifting from one setting to another – is one of the commonest ways out of defeats and impasses.

The following sections rely on the researches sponsored by the UNRISD Participation Programme, plus a few similar studies under other auspices. They make no attempt to cover systematically the wealth of research and polemics on the dispossessed and policies relevant to them. They do not focus so much on the analysis of participatory organizations and experiences as such, and the manifold organizational and other reasons that condition failure and success, but rather on the broader societal and historical context within which these experiences take place, which throws light on the deeper forces and trends that crucially influence these experiences. They aim to stimulate certain actors in the drama of 'participation' to think about what they are doing or pretending to do, and to help them become more sensitive to the ambiguities in their relationships to other actors, through discussion of certain episodes in the history of participation, then through a confrontation with what seem to be the main trends of change in the world today.

The first three chapters in Part II deal with the organized efforts of three major categories of the hitherto excluded: the peasants and rural workers; the urban wage workers; and the urban poor distinguished by settlement patterns rather than relation to production. The last three chapters deal with different dimensions of the environment within which the organized efforts take place: with the efforts of certain states to 'institutionalize' participation behind their own objectives of reform or revolution; with the hopes for emergence of new forms of collective empowerment of the 'hitherto excluded' through the evolution of 'social movements' into 'national popular movements'; and, finally, with the relationships between the hitherto excluded and the interlocutors other than the state who try to help, enlighten or manipulate them.

The selection of topics depends partly on the kinds of evidence furnished by the field research, heavily weighted toward Latin America and two countries of Asia. The treatment of the topics is uneven and makes no pretence to comprehensiveness. It focuses on certain questions central to the purposes of the UNRISD Programme. We had originally hoped that other categories and dimensions could be discussed in this Part: in particular, the movements of ethnic minorities and groups culturally distinct from a dominant 'national' pattern; the role of popular culture and historical memories as conscientizing and legitimizing factors in participatory movements; and the role of clientelism and patronage as specific aspects of the relations between the hitherto excluded, the politically and economically dominant forces, and the state. However, material on these questions was limited and so intertwined with that on the other questions that we decided to explore into them only as they impinged on the latter.

Note

1. For a balanced discussion of the gains and losses, combinations of exploitation and opportunity, of women in different settings, see Moghadam, Valentine M., 'Development and Women's Exploitation', in Pieterse, Jan Nedreveen, ed., *Emancipations, Modern and Postmodern*, special issue of *Development and Change*, vol. 23, no. 3, July 1992, Sage Publications on behalf of the Institute of Social Studies, The Hague, pp. 215-55.

3

Movements and Organizations of Peasants and Rural Workers

Most studies undertaken within the framework of the UNRISD Participation Programme have looked at movements and organizations of peasants and agricultural workers. This was for a number of reasons.

First, peasants, rural workers and those that are generally designated under the term 'rural poor' constitute the largest group of excluded people, though their relative importance is rapidly dwindling, particularly in Latin America, as a result of long-term trends in rural-urban migration and the increasing conversion of the most impoverished groups into a displaced floating population. It is also the group where results of systematic exclusion and dependency are most dramatically visible, particularly in moments of crisis.

Secondly, peasants, rural workers and rural communities constitute a priority 'target' or clientèle for many outside agents and interlocutors – the state and its numerous agencies, political parties, revolutionary vanguards, non-governmental organizations and international organizations and agencies – who attempt to promote the organization of peasants or rural workers or intend to mobilize them in a multitude of different 'participatory' projects, schemes, movements and organizations.

Thirdly, the Participation Programme of UNRISD historically evolved as a corollary to previous research on the 'Green Revolution' and as a complement to the Institute's Foodsystems Project. Quite naturally it therefore placed peasants and rural workers at the centre of its inquiry, at least in its initial stages. This bias was also reflected in the original concept of the Participation Programme. As has been discussed in Chapter 1, the 'long march' image was coined to represent the long and painful passage from the traditional rural subsistence community to a new individual identity within a modern profit-oriented economy and society, a passage which leads traditional rural producers and artisans through many forms, levels and phases of exclusion, fatal for many as there is no room and function for them in the new society. The struggle for participation was seen as the struggle by peasants and rural workers and communities over the 'terms of incorporation' into this new economy and society.

Such a conceptualization of rural participation proved useful in all UNRISD studies as it contained the notion of dynamic change of the larger society and was thus able to accommodate the rapid evolution of the rural scene within which participatory efforts occur. In most rural areas of the world, traditional agrarian societies and systems of production have indeed been undergoing rapid transformations that have led to new and more unstable forms of exclusion of ever larger segments of the rural population. As the modern state or capitalist market economy extends with the opening of communications and trade to include ever more remote areas, pre-capitalist self-provisioning forms of production and land-use are giving way to capitalist mechanized and export-oriented production systems. Traditional systems of livelihood support and social security are breaking down. New struggles flare up over increasingly valuable and scarce land that can now bring in potentially higher yields. Tenants, share-croppers and marginal farmers are increasingly pushed off the land. Many of them attempt to extend production into marginal and remote lands, such as tropical mountain and rain forests and semi-arid or arid areas, which not only leads over time to ecological disaster but brings them into conflict with those tribal and nomadic populations whose traditional livelihood depends on these lands. Others constitute a swelling army of landless workers. In one sense, most of these are redundant in the new capitalist system of production. In another sense, of course, they further the new systems by keeping rural wages low and assuring an abundant supply of labour at peak seasons. Many try to migrate to the urban areas or abroad; and many end up joining the rapidly swelling ranks of a migrating, or rather floating, semi-rural/semi-urban lumpen proletariat. They become 'wage hunters and gatherers' as Jan Breman has called them.[1]

Within this general setting we witness a vast number of attempts to organize or mobilize peasants and rural workers, purportedly to allow them to defend their interests, to fight against their exclusion and to regain some measure of control over their livelihood. In a minority of cases probably, the initiative comes from the peasants and rural workers themselves, when oppressive anti-participatory structures have been softened or have temporarily broken down as a result of revolutionary political change at the national level, or out of desperation when conditions become too unbearable. They then may spontaneously get together and join forces to fight for ownership or secure access to land, for fairer prices on the market or fairer wages, for better access to public services – essentially to fight for their livelihood and their dignity – or they may attempt to pool their resources and savings in order to free themselves from dependency on moneylenders, traders and local bureaucrats. While such action usually takes place at the local level, there are examples where the organized peasantry, profiting from a generally weak state and political system, has been able to establish itself as a political force at the national level, as was the case at various moments in Bolivia.

As is the case with most participatory movements, movements of peasants or rural workers are rarely self-initiated and even when they are they will not go very far on their own. Interlocutors of all kinds will rapidly enter the scene to advise, guide, direct, help, represent, study or simply exploit the participants and their group or movement, which will, willingly or not, enter into alliances with other social forces or with the state.

The principal outside agent with which peasants have to deal is of course the state and its multiple agencies and organizations. Relations between poor peasants, rural workers and the state are mostly antagonistic and exploitative, and at times paternalistic. The state is urban based, and central governments usually rely for their political support primarily on urban areas. The state may seek the support of the traditional landed élite or the new agrarian bourgeoisie, and may temporarily wish to gain the support of the peasantry as a whole, organized in nationwide associations. In some cases, state action includes ambitious attempts to reorganize the whole rural sector and system of production on the national level (as in Cuba after 1959, in Nicaragua after 1979, in China after 1949 or in Peru under the Velasco government), or attempts to organize the peasantry nationwide as a political force and basis of support for a given party or régime (as was the case in Mexico in the 1930s or in Colombia with the birth and rise of the National Association of Peasant Smallholders – ANUC). In such historical moments peasant movements and organizations can take on new force and may come to play an important political role at the national level, and the balance of power among social groups and forces may temporarily favour greater state support for their demands. Studies from Colombia, Mexico, Peru and Bolivia show such instances. However, as Cynthia Hewitt de Alcántara writes in her introduction to one of the Mexican studies of UNRISD's Participation Programme:

> there is nevertheless an inherent contradiction in any official promotion of peasant organization by a state which, like most in the contemporary world, is primarily responsible to urban, rather than rural interests. Politically, it is most useful (and often even necessary) to support the peasantry; but response to peasant demands must not be allowed to interfere with established lines of supply (or terms of supply) between countryside and city, on which much of urban economic activity depends. In lieu of firm commitment to privilege rural over urban development, in other words, there are often sharp limits to the concessions which can be made to the peasantry. Land may be granted, if that does not alienate large private farmers to such a degree that the latter stop producing, or utilize ties with other sectors of society to paralyse non-agricultural activities or to withdraw political support from the government. Certain legal questions may be resolved, and oppressive enemies brought to justice. Perhaps most painless of all, for a state confronted with the structural contradictions of the kind just mentioned, funds can be pledged for any number of rural development projects, implying official concern for local problems without fundamentally altering the flow of goods from the countryside. Until recently, it might be added, this tactic could be internationally financed.[2]

It is only in exceptional historical cases that state power actually relies on the support of the organized masses of the rural poor who are more often seen as an obstacle to agricultural modernization and as a potential source of social unrest and of political support for opposition forces. The state will thus naturally attempt to co-opt, manipulate or neutralize spontaneous or independent movements and organizations of peasants or rural workers, or else will attempt to incorporate these latter into its own organizations or institutions. State action to organize peasants most frequently takes place at a limited local level, within regional or issue-specific organizations or associations or within development programmes and projects in which the rural poor, who are the intended beneficiaries, are supposed to participate. At this more local level of organization and participation the state and its agencies clash, co-operate or work alongside many other social actors and self-appointed do-gooders who all attempt to organize and mobilize the peasants and rural poor for their own often contradictory motives: rival political parties in search of political support among the peasantry; revolutionary movements attempting to prompt the peasantry into playing its 'historical role' as an ally or substitute of the revolutionary proletariat; non-governmental organizations, development workers and aid agencies who, disillusioned with previous strategies and recipes, turn to rural grassroots organizations as promising alternatives; trade unions, social scientists, international organizations and many more. The proclaimed purpose of these manifold activities and interventions around the rural poor is to improve their lot and contribute to their development; non-avowed reasons behind these interventions are often quite different and attitudes of outside agents and actors range from benevolence or genuine commitment to the cause of the rural poor to cynical manipulation. The rural poor themselves are rarely, if ever, consulted about the usefulness of such interventions or the form and direction that these actions and organizations should take.

The general difficulties and ambiguities inherent in the relation between participatory groups and movements and outside agents and interlocutors are discussed in Chapter 8. It seems that such difficulties are particularly acute when interlocutors and allies have to deal with movements and initiatives of peasants and rural producers. Misunderstandings between organized peasants and outside agents, which in many cases ultimately lead to the failure of the movement or initiative itself, arise naturally from different motivations and perceptions of the reasons and goals of the initiative. Above all, however, they seem to result from the difficulty of most interlocutors and outside agents in understanding the complexity of the rapidly evolving rural scene and from their basic inability to understand the peasants' own inherent rationality, their characteristics, and their motivations to organize and engage in participatory actions and organizations, or to refrain from it.

A first difficulty resides in the increasing differentiation and fragmentation of the 'constituency' of such participatory initiatives: the 'peasants', the 'rural workers and producers' and even more so the 'rural poor'. These terms embrace today a variety of social groups and subgroups with widely differing interests and different perceptions of their actual and desired role in society. Landless labourers, marginal farmers, tenants, share-croppers, middle farmers, rural artisans and tribal groups have obviously different and often contradictory immediate and longer-term interests. They may all join initially in a participatory movement, struggling for access to or ownership of land, for example, but their interests diverge as soon as some have actually received land. Studies in Colombia and elsewhere have shown that the profound heterogeneity of its constituency was one of the main reasons for the decline of a peasant movement which was not able to sustain the initial participatory momentum once a first set of commonly agreed objectives had been reached. Studies in Thailand also show that the fragmentation of the rural poor, accentuated by clientelistic tactics of the élite, presents a major obstacle to collective action by the excluded even in the case of objective identity of interests. The complexity of this problem is increased by the fact that many peasants are simultaneously smallholder, labourer, artisan and trader and may themselves pursue contradictory interests at different times. This is difficult to understand for development workers, union organizers, party militants, government bureaucrats and social scientists who all join in their complaints that peasants and peasant groups behave and act at times in apparently 'irrational' and 'illogical' ways, ways which seem to go against their own interests, and who fail to comprehend that what appears as peasant apathy or passivity is in fact an active, deliberate response which makes sense within the rationality of the peasants' own survival strategies.[3]

The fact is that the peasants' rationality, their perception of interest, of opportunity, of risk and of time factors differ radically from those of their mainly urban or literate and educated counterparts. The following attempt to characterize peasants represents a crude generalization. It should nevertheless help to draw attention to the conceptual gulf that often separates them from those attempting to organize or interact with them on behalf of the state or other social actors.

For the vast majority of peasants, and for the rural poor generally, the one and overriding concern is to provide a secure livelihood for themselves and their families. This is a task involving for most of them a continuous struggle against the vagaries of nature, against landowners, moneylenders, traders, tax collectors, policemen and often against their colleagues, neighbours and in-laws who all may try to profit from their weakness and vulnerability, particularly in times of crisis. It is a struggle which is never definitively won but starts again, season after season, and for rural workers often day after day, and which forces them to resort to multifarious survival strategies where risk minimization is usually more important than output or even profit maximization. It requires flexibility and pragmatism – the ability to seize any opportunity from wherever it may come, if possible without taking excessive risks, for in the absence of savings and assets this may be fatal. By definition peasants are concerned with land, with water, with pastures and animals, thus with the local. The national is usually beyond their immediate frame of reference and action, and thus beyond their reach, and so is the state which appears as a somewhat abstract entity that takes concrete expression in the form of lower-level bureaucrats, tax collectors, soldiers, policemen and, at elections, passing politicians in search of votes. While at the local level relations of power, control and alliances make immediate sense to peasants this is much less the case at the national level where political developments are *a priori* beyond their reach and imagination, hence their willingness to rely on intermediaries when action extends to that level. Peasants are used to a dependent relationship – with nature (and God and the cosmic forces behind it), with the state and its authority, and with the 'big people', i.e. the wealthy, the educated, the learned, those who know, who have seemingly unlimited resources and who have relations higher up. It is not unusual for peasants to be bound to them through client relations which provide a minimum of security in times of crisis. By necessity peasants will attempt to avoid 'problems' and conflicts, and seek accommodation rather than confrontation. Peasants' consciousness of time differs also in many ways from that of their urban counterparts. For the former, time is not so much a malleable entity to be organized and controlled but rather an immutable fact beyond their control. Each action of humankind and nature will come at its time and take its necessary time and there is not much to be done about this. Also, while peasants' consciousness of the past – their historical memory of their place within nature and society – extends far back and affects in many ways their present actions, decisions and behaviour, their perspective of the future tends to be short: relevant time spans are agricultural seasons or the gestation periods of animals.

These characteristics are rough generalizations, many of which apply mainly to peasants with some family access to land, whether as owners, tenants or share-croppers. They apply only partially to permanent workers on traditional *latifundios* or to casual labourers hired by the day, and even less to rural wage workers in modern capitalist agro-enterprises.

At the same time, historical evidence from many parts of the world shows that peasant societies, when they encounter intensified impoverishment, exploitation, cultural shocks, or loss of minimum security for life and livelihood, generally arising from warfare or the economic strategies of landlords or the state, can generate movements to which the above generalizations do not seem to apply. Such movements can propagate themselves over relatively wide territories and become extremely violent in their tactics, aiming at the wholesale elimination of hated classes and structures of domination. They sometimes incorporate messianic or millennial myths that look to an imagined natural order of social equality, sometimes fall under non-peasant ideological control, sometimes launch into pogroms against ethnic or religious scapegoats. Such uprisings have been few considering the prevalence of peasant exploitation throughout history. In practically all cases they have either been brutally crushed or have provided opportunities for non-peasant allies to achieve power. The UNRISD researches did not deal directly with upheavals of this kind, but it is evident that as possibilities they have entered into the fears of the élites and the hopes of revolutionary counter-élites in such countries as Bolivia, Colombia, Peru and India. In countries in which the urban population is now a majority, as in most Latin American countries, the élite distrust of peasants as a potential source of 'barbaric' violence has naturally diminished, while distrust of the semi-urban slum population has in part replaced it.

Much more commonly, as stated above, the immediate and overriding interests of peasants remain local and focused on the provision of a secure livelihood for themselves and their families. They will on their own engage in participatory movements and actions primarily if this security of livelihood is threatened or has broken down, or else if the opportunity arises to improve it by gaining increased access to or control over resources or regulative institutions. To own land, or to gain secure access to and use of land for cultivation, is often the primary objective around which peasants organize or are mobilized. This may however be insufficient to guarantee their livelihood, as studies in Thailand and Mexico have shown. As long as controls over inputs such as seeds, fertilizers, water and machines, over credit and over marketing of the produce remain in the hands of private traders, agribusinesses or public institutions, these latter can so totally control the whole production process that even landowning small farmers are completely at their mercy, with little more say than agricultural workers. This is the case at least in a context where markets and purchased inputs have come to be important. A secondary objective of collective peasant action often thus becomes to gain access to inputs and credit at the right moment and under reasonable terms, and to exert some influence over the terms and prices at which the produce is sold. Collective savings schemes and collective or co-operative buying and marketing arrangements may be set up to reach this goal. Studies from northeastern Thailand have shown that in extreme cases, where no advance can be made towards these secondary objectives, groups of poor peasants, and in some cases whole villages, may attempt to withdraw temporarily from the market by abandoning the cultivation of commercial and export crops and concentrating on self-provisioning. The idea is to pursue this strategy until they have gained sufficient collective strength and staying power to 're-enter' the market economy at a later stage under new terms of incorporation, to be negotiated this time from a position of greater strength. Similar cases of 'temporary strategic retreats' have been advocated, or have actually occurred in some West African countries.

While the struggles of poor peasants and rural workers tend to take place primarily at the local level, they do extend in some cases, as we have seen, to regional and national levels. Experience shows that in all such cases problems arise rapidly in the relationship between the leadership of the movements and the rank and file. While the latter's concern and interest is and remains basically local, the leaders' perspectives are increasingly oriented towards the struggle of power at the national level, and they will be tempted into various relationships and alliances with other social actors at that level. Also, as the size of the movement or organization increases its leadership tends to become itself a bureaucracy defending its own interests and privileges rather than those of the rank and file. Relations and tensions then tend to become trilateral, between the base, the leaders and the state or other external actors and interlocutors, and possibilities of misunderstandings and reciprocal manipulation increase.

Most of the studies carried out as part of UNRISD's Participation Programme have addressed the questions raised above. They have looked at participatory movements of poor peasants and rural workers at different levels and from different standpoints: studies in Mexico, China, Peru and Nicaragua have looked at attempts by the state to organize the peasants at the national level within the framework of overall national policy; studies in Colombia and Bolivia have examined peasant participation within large-scale national movements, while studies in India and Thailand have looked at attempts at peasant participation at the more local level within more or less favourable or hostile overall social and political environments. Studies carried out simultaneously under other auspices, such as the ILO project on the participatory organizations of the rural poor (PORP), have concentrated more on peasant participation in the form of grassroots movements and have implicitly raised the question of the relevance of such movements at the macro-level.

It is of course difficult, and of doubtful value, to make generalizations about peasant participation based on comparisons of such different processes, taking place in so many different contexts. Some cross-comparisons will nevertheless be made in the following brief presentation of summaries and main findings of some of these studies. The results of other studies will be summarized in other chapters in Part II, such as that on interlocutors, on the institutionalization of participation and on new social and popular movements.

Peasants, the state and bureaucracy in Mexico

In Mexico, a long revolutionary struggle in which peasants took part, sometimes with their own leaders and objectives, together with workers, various regional élites and armed factions, had by the 1920s destroyed the *hacienda* system with its monopolization of land and practices of debt peonage, allowed the re-establishment of peasant communities with access to land, and ushered in a period of unprecedented 'participatory' experimentation. By the 1930s this struggle had led to the formation of a party, eventually called the Partido Revolucionario Institucional (PRI), holding a practical monopoly of political, though not economic power. The peasants have since 1938 been formally one of the three organized sectors (along with workers and middle classes) of this dominant party, and this through the Confederación Nacional Campesina (CNC). The Mexican agrarian reform was one of the results of this long and violent revolutionary struggle, at the end of which the organized peasantry constituted a significant element in the balance of power at regional level in many areas. Pursued by nationalist and populist governments more or less committed to the peasant class and going through many stages and shifts in government policy, this land reform eventually redistributed more than 80 million hectares of land to over 3 million landless peasants who were organized within a new type of land tenure known as the *ejido* system.

Under the *ejido* system the government granted land as collective property to organized groups of petitioners. Holdings were generally cultivated by individual families and were inheritable, but they could not legally be sold nor rented (though the renting of *ejido* land to private agricultural entrepreneurs has become a widespread practice, particularly in the irrigated districts). Government agencies exercised a good deal of control over cultivation and *ejido* activities, partly through legal responsibilities for supervision (sanctioning elections, transferring rights to usufruct land and administering justice), partly through control over credits, agricultural inputs, technical assistance and marketing of crops.

Mexico thus has a long experience of formal peasant participation in national political life, under relatively stable rules, of collective approach to agriculture and of intense interactions between peasants and state technocratic and bureaucratic agencies. At the same time, economic development has proceeded within a capitalist framework and led to an increasingly concentrated and unequal distribution of wealth and income. Agrarian reform was not, except by part of the revolutionary élite during the 1930s, conceived as an alternative to the development of capitalism; initially it was an institutional response to the demand of armed groups of landless, and later it became a political measure which, by providing access to land and boosting the internal market, contributed to integrate the peasants with the development of capitalism. The state and the PRI assumed the dual and ambiguous role of representative of the poor peasant class and of intermediary between this class and the economically dominant forces, i.e. primarily the new agrarian bourgeoisie. This latter emerged in the post-revolutionary decades from remnants of the old landowning class, modern capitalist farmers and groups which controlled in conjunction with the state the technical, financial and commercial aspects of agriculture, and drew increasing strength from association with transnational capital. They are not formally represented in the ruling PRI but are in close contact with the state through their own organizations. The *ejido* thus played a contradictory role, as an apparatus of the state and as an organism for peasant representation and struggle.

The corporatist strategy of the Mexican state provided it with an effective system of control over the peasantry both at national and at local level. The official peasant organization has generally acted as an instrument of the national power structure into which its leadership has been incorporated. At the local level, state jurisdiction over *ejidos* and effective control over production processes led to an easy extension of patterns of corporate control, often within the framework of client relations, over local units of peasant organization. Periodic dissident movements were contained by combinations of concessions, co-option of their leadership and repression. However, independent organizations continued to emerge and acquire tactical sophistication in taking advantage of the state's real need to maintain a measure of peasant support. Corporatist control was never complete and became increasingly frayed during the 1970s.

The researches sponsored by UNRISD in Mexico have focused on these generally ambiguous relations between state and peasants and are contained in two main reports.[4]

The first study examines the interactions between the state, the peasantry and the agrarian élite during a period of intense struggle over land in the wealthy agricultural areas of northwestern Mexico in 1976. It shows the contradictions that emerged when the government, under President Echeverria, tried to alter its policy during part of the 1970s, changing from an emphasis on bureaucratized control to the stimulation of peasant initiative and attempting to resume land distribution on more than a token scale. The change in government policy was a reaction to a wider agrarian and general crisis, an upsurge in uncontrolled peasant unrest and movements and a corresponding loss of legitimacy of the official CNC. The state responded with an agrarian-collectivization programme, channelling vast resources to the *ejido* sector and allowing the peasant movement to open up channels of expression, which seemed to lead to a rupture of the traditional *de facto* alliance between the state and the agrarian (and industrial) bourgeoisie. The different fractions of the élite, when faced with the threat to their privileges, status and property, when exposed to land seizures and other challenges from the rural poor and the landless, closed ranks and vigorously defended their interests. When the crisis came, the state, which seemed to vacillate for some time, changed policy and sided with the élite. An end was put to land distributions, *agrarismo* as a political trend was weakened, the official peasant associations were used to stop land invasions and check the momentum of the struggle, and threats and repression were used where necessary to contain continuing peasant unrest. Studies of peasant movements after 1976 show an increasing vitality of mobilizations of peasants outside the framework of the official CNC and relatively independent of the state and political parties. From the time of the land reform of 1976 to the mid-1980s, the independent peasant unions of the Yaqui valley, Sonora, created an impressive structure of agro-enterprises and had the highest wheat yields in Mexico. They provided a widely-known example to small farmers in other parts of the country. For a time, in the better-off and relatively more commercial agricultural regions, and partly to offset the loss in its capacity of control through the official peasant organizations, the state intensified its direct intervention in the management of production through regulatory agencies, state enterprises and development banks. (In poorer regions with a majority of Mexico's peasant producers, these remained a captive clientèle of caciques, merchants, and moneylenders).

The second study concentrates on one specific aspect of this, namely the state's control over *ejido* production through the operations of the Rural Bank, the Banrural. The Banrural, initially the Banco Ejidal, was originally created to support and promote land reforms and peasant participation, but gradually changed course over the years. 'From being an institution which fostered the development of a strong smallholding agriculture, capable of maintaining itself, it became the cornerstone of a plan for a particular form of nationalization of the smallholding sector, under which the Bank gradually began to take over *ejido* production'.[5] From early on the Bank had prevented the *ejidos* from starting their own accumulation process and creating their own subsistence funds and established thereby their continuous dependency on the Bank. By using its powers to grant or withhold credits the Bank effectively took over control of production by deciding what to sow, how to cultivate, what inputs to use and when and how to market the produce. In the La Laguna area that was studied, credit advances became wages in all but name and the beneficiaries of land reform were reduced to 'landed employees of the Bank'.

The Mexican studies demonstrate the ambiguous results of formal incorporation of a peasant movement into the political power structure, and also the dependence of a successful militant organization on weakness or tolerance of the state. In this case, contrary to what we will see in Colombia with ANUC and in Bolivia with the *sindicatos*, nationwide peasant organization enhanced the legitimacy of the state and led to more state control over the peasants rather than *vice versa*. The prominent tactic employed in this case of state-manipulated participation was, first, to prevent or co-opt independent peasant organizations and, secondly, to promote vertical ties between separate local or sectoral popular organizations and the state and prevent horizontal ties between peasants and other groups of the excluded that might lead to a broader mobilization of power challenging the state. Moreover, the state's flexibility in shifting between tactics of concessions, co-option and repression meant that autonomous or rebellious peasant movements (generally localized) could help the system avoid excessive rigidity without threatening its overall stability.

The Mexican studies indicate, as mentioned earlier, that secure ownership or tenure of a plot of land, while remaining a central demand of more militant peasant organizations, may itself do very little to strengthen peasant capacity to participate autonomously and make decisions concerning livelihood – a point also emphasized in the research findings in Thailand. Controls have shifted to private agribusiness and public credit institutions – backed up of course by local forces of public order. The agribusiness and credit institutions practically dictate to the peasants what they are to produce and what inputs they are to use and they monopolize processing and marketing of the products. The peasant's inability to survive without credits and supplies of seeds, fertilizers and other inputs leaves him in a position hardly more autonomous than that of a wage labourer. The public agencies and institutions are often not only paternalistic but also inefficient, due to the high costs of bureaucracy and their unreliability in supplying credits and inputs on time and in good quality.

The Mexican studies confirm that bureaucracies relied on by the state to transmit and implement policies and provide services acquire a momentum of their own toward self-serving and self-aggrandizement. The tactics of the Rural Bank in La Laguna of splitting up *ejidos* so as to deal separately with small weak groups, of co-opting leadership or of keeping accounts so complicated or confused that peasants would be unable to understand them seem to have responded originally to government purposes of terminating collective agriculture and bringing the *ejido* sector under close control. Later, however, the Bank's tactics stood in the way of attempts by the central authorities to encourage peasant initiative and to apply public resources more efficiently to the objective of raising food production. For example, documented efforts by the Banrural to prevent *ejido* members from accumulating capital of their own and thus overcoming dependence on annual credits from the Bank seem to have served the interests of the Bank bureaucracy but not those of the state, nor, of course, those of the peasants.

Finally, it should be kept in mind, as an example of the confounding of expectations that will be discussed in Chapter 9, that Mexican agrarian policies and the challenges confronting peasant organizations have changed radically since the mid-1980s. Recent reforms have removed any restrictions on renting *ejido* land, and most restrictions on selling it (although the *ejido* as a community is at least in theory to be supported and preserved). The structure of state control over the *ejido* is now being dismantled. Even the better-off *ejidatarios* who previously had access to public credit and marketing services are likely not to have such access today. The state is pulling out of the countryside. Thus, the grave problem confronted by independent regional peasant organizations since the late 1980s has been that macro-economic restructuring and the intention of reforming corrupt and manipulative state institutions such as the Banrural have left small producers without the basic support structure they required to farm profitably.

Peasants and revolutionary régimes in China, Nicaragua and Peru

The results of studies carried out in these three countries will not be discussed in full here. Research in China has been limited to a preliminary short field investigation;[6] research in Nicaragua has been carried out as a corollary to the UNRISD studies on the country's food system; and research on the peasant question in Peru was part of the wider studies on the institutionalization of participation and on the national popular movement. The main findings of these studies will be discussed in Chapters 6 and 7. We will limit ourselves here to a few reflections on these findings that are particularly relevant to the question of peasant participation.

In China poor peasants constituted an important component of the revolutionary struggle that brought the Communist Party to power in 1949, and in Nicaragua parts of the peasantry played an important role in the basically urban-based revolution that swept away the Somoza government in 1979. In China, the peasantry participated in a popular war of liberation by providing an inexhaustible source of manpower for the Chinese Red Army, by organizing local militias and support groups, and by supplying the Army with food and other necessities. The war was characterized both by authoritarian military structures of command, and by a high degree of spontaneity and participation in decision-making, at least at the local level. The socialist transformation of relations of production carried out in the early years after the revolution corresponded to a genuine demand of the landless and rural poor tenants and led to an institutionalized form of collective agriculture and peasant participation that reproduced in itself the earlier contradictory characteristics of authoritarian control from above – the Party in this case – combined with a considerable amount of local decision-making power, leaving room for much creativity and spontaneity. This local participatory space, which extended primarily to questions of production and economics and not, as a rule, to political or ideological issues, was of course not so much a result of deliberate government policy but rather of the local party and state bureaucracy's inability to enforce strict control and compliance with periodically changing general policies, and of its reluctance to translate these policies into concrete measures in a context of periodic changes in party direction where excessive identification with any one line was risky. The extent to which this participatory space, which varied according to regional conditions, was used by local peasant communities and units depended to a large extent on the quality of the local peasant leadership and on the historical experiences of collective struggle and the peasants' memory thereof. These factors – quality of leadership and political sophistication and confidence in collective action – both based on previous experiences of collective struggle, determined to a large extent the vitality of local units and their resilience in the face of arbitrary bureaucratic interference and contradictory authoritarian commands from above. The short comparative study between different communes and production units carried out by the UNRISD mission singled out the quality and experience of local cadres and peasant leaders as one of the key factors responsible for success or failure of local development and for the more or less participatory nature of this development.

In Nicaragua the political force that brought about revolutionary change was not a tightly organized and experienced party as in China but a loosely structured front – the Sandinista National Liberation Front (FSLN) – in which some peasants, mostly farm workers from west coast agro-export estates, participated with many other popular organizations and operated with much spontaneity and local autonomy. The participatory nature and style of operation dominant during the revolutionary war was *de facto* carried over to the post-revolutionary period, and in time a tripartite division of power emerged at the local level between leaders of peasant and rural workers' associations, state bureaucrats and cadres of the FSLN. The functioning of this is discussed in Chapter 6. The space for local participation of the peasantry was thus much larger here than in China, and grassroots organizations played a correspondingly important role in the plans for land reform and restructuring of the agricultural economy which started in 1982 with a national mobilization drive. At the national level, peasant participation in policy-making was bolstered with the formation in 1981 of the National Union of Farmers and Cattlemen (UNAG) which grew to incorporate more than half of the country's agricultural producers and became one of the country's most powerful mass organizations.[7] The sudden increase in armed incursions since 1983 appears to have initially reinforced the participatory capacity of peasant communities in many areas by leading to an acceleration of land expropriation and distribution and to the creation of armed defence co-operatives.[8] The general situation of the peasantry, however, became increasingly difficult in the following years. Standards of living of significant sectors of the peasant population were negatively affected due to the disruption of rural social services, a prolonged deterioration of domestic terms of trade between 1980 and 1987 and generally falling levels of production and marketable surplus. The ensuing weakening of peasant support for the revolution and pressures from the increasingly strong agricultural producers' association led the government in 1984 and 1985 to adopt a series of policy measures designed to correct previous planning imbalances that had favoured the urban and state sectors, to shift domestic terms of trade in favour of peasant producers, increase the quantities of goods and services reaching rural producers and accelerate again the process of land distribution.[9] The increasing level of hostilities made the application of these measures difficult and uneven. As the armed conflict intensified and escalated into a virtual civil war the general situation became increasingly confusing and local realities of peasant participation and involvement on one side or the other increasingly contradictory. It remains to be seen to what extent peasant co-operatives, often still armed, and rural worker and peasant associations will be able to maintain relatively high levels of autonomy and participation after the change of régime that took place in mid-1990.

The scope for comparison between the Chinese and the Nicaraguan experiences is of course limited by the differences in size, in the social and political context and the wider international context within which these developments took place. Some general trends can nevertheless be compared and lessons be drawn. Both China and Nicaragua provide insights into the complex tensions that exist between a central authority – government, party or both – and organized peasant communities in a post-revolutionary setting where peasant participation is officially advocated and institutionalized. Not only do the fundamental conceptions of peasant participation and its goals differ between these two main actors, and this increasingly so as the government/party establishes its central authority and assumes responsibility for running the country as a whole, but it appears that the central government or party authority is likely to adopt a distinct anti-peasant and anti-smallholder bias in its policies. This bias, reflected above all in economic development policy but also in the distribution of social services, is generally pro-urban, pro-state sector, pro-industrial, pro-export crop or production-oriented, or any combination of these, and is likely to neglect the interests of smallholders and rural workers even if these groups are acknowledged as important partners in the revolutionary alliance. Political and ideological debates and preoccupations at the centre will also increasingly focus on central power politics and long-term aims of the revolution and not give due attention to the immediate social and political contradictions faced by the peasantry at the local level. Organized peasants and rural workers are likely to react against this neglect in various ways, ranging from withdrawal of political support from the state and possibly alliance with opposition forces to localized acts of rebellion against state bureaucrats and party cadres or attempts to intervene openly in central party and state politics through a national organization representing their interests. Withdrawal from the national market economy into subsistence economy and semi-autarky is usually not an option available to them within a post-revolutionary society where the whole rural sector is incorporated into a planned economy.

To see these tensions between the peasantry and the state in a post-revolutionary setting in terms of such a simple dichotomy represents a gross oversimplification as in reality many more social actors each pursuing their own interests participate in and influence the outcome of this contest. As we have seen in Nicaragua, the state and party were themselves composed of several different actors, at least in the early years, which made tensions tripartite and more complex as the possibility of temporary alliances and counter-alliances emerged. Add to this the presence of a strong and hypertrophic state and party bureaucracy which comes to defend its own interests divorced from those of the state, the party or the peasants that it allegedly serves; of traditional local or regional élites or of opposition parties or forces which may enter the power struggle legally or through armed incursion or rebellion, and the tensions inherent in these state-peasant relations become even more unmanageable. Finally, to complicate matters even more, in a post-revolutionary setting the peasantry itself is divided into many different groups having different and often contradictory interests – migrant and landless rural workers, smallholders, members of co-operatives or state farms and newly emerging market-oriented middle peasants – as was the case in Nicaragua from the beginning and as is increasingly the case in China today.

The differentiation of the peasantry into groups defending contradictory interests, the irrelevance of national politics (and ensuing party sectarianism) to real peasant issues, and the struggles of the peasantry against bureaucratized and technocratic controls emerge also as important problems from the studies carried out in Peru.[10] As is explained in Chapter 6 below, Peru was between 1968 and 1975 the scene of a unique effort at social revolution from above undertaken by a military government advised among others by theorists of participation and community mobilization. This effort included one of the most systematic agrarian reforms in Latin America, aimed at replacing both the traditional *hacienda* system prevailing in parts of Peru and the export-oriented capitalist plantations dominant in other parts by variants of co-operative agriculture under varying forms of state management or supervision. The peasantry, initially passive or suspicious of the reforms and the new organizational forms promoted from above – which corresponded to the ideas and level of consciousness of government theorists (who themselves had highly contradictory views), but certainly not to those of the peasants – gradually took advantage of the spaces for participatory organized action that had been opened and struggled to modify the reforms in directions corresponding to their own perceived needs. The divorce between participatory policies defined at the centre and the concrete needs and perceptions of the local peasants, which led to a rapid imposition of more or less homogeneous participatory structures on a diverse social and political reality that in many cases was neither ready for nor adapted to it, was very much the result of the fundamental inability of government theorists and national politicians to understand the functioning of traditional economic subsistence systems and survival strategies of the rural poor.

After 1975 a changed military government, under pressure of economic difficulties and suspicious of the implications of awakening militant popular participation, modified or abandoned many of the reforms and participatory initiatives and embarked on policies that contributed to bring about a rapid deterioration in popular standards of living. Though rural poverty increased, peasant struggles receded as previous tenure reforms had removed the landlords as a readily identifiable common adversary. Struggles became localized, setting different groups of peasants and rural workers against one another in their demand for the abandonment of the bureaucratized co-operative system and for the division of land into individual holdings. Also increasing numbers of impoverished peasants migrated to Lima and other cities in search of new sources of livelihood, a trend accentuated since the 1980s with the rise of the Sendero Luminoso and conditions of increasing insecurity in rural areas.

Peasant conflicts and movements in Colombia

The investigation of peasant conflicts and movements in Colombia centres on the rise and decline of the Asociación Nacional de Usuarios Campesinos (ANUC), the most important organized peasant movement in Colombia up to the present, and on the relations between its trajectory and the changing national political and economic setting.

The history of ANUC divides into several distinct stages: (1) Government-fostered formation and growth as part of a wider strategy for agrarian reform, economic modernization, and controlled incorporation of the masses of the rural population into the national economic and political system (1966-70). As a semi-official organization ANUC brought together in the space of two years 800,000 peasants of all kinds, an astonishing feat after the tremendous social disorganization and divisions of the peasantry that many years of civil war – La Violencia (1946-66) – had brought about. (2) Autonomous mass mobilizations mainly for the enforcement of peasant claims to land through organized land seizures (1971). (3) The volte-face of the new government, subsequent split in the movement and cóntinuing but decreasingly successful struggles for land accompanied by discrimination against the movement and repression of land seizures by government and landlords, political radicalization of the main wing of the movement, inability to cope with changes in the economic situation and with the increasing differentiation in livelihood among the rural poor, and, finally, accelerating loss of membership (1972-78). (4) The reversal of tactics by the leadership, attempts to rebuild the organization through co-operation with public agencies, reunion with the government-controlled wing of the organization and participation in national politics through the established major parties (1979 to the present).

The investigation was undertaken in close collaboration with ANUC itself and resulted in a number of published and unpublished reports.[11]

The reports deal with a wide range of questions that are important to rural participatory movements in other countries and in many ways confirm results from other UNRISD studies undertaken in Peru, Bolivia, Thailand and particularly in Mexico. In some respects the dramatic rise and fall of ANUC in Colombia parallels the experience of the Mexican agrarian conflict that came to a head in 1976 (discussed above). In both cases, the perceived interests of a political régime temporarily coincided with those of important segments of the poorer peasants and to some extent landless rural labourers. In both cases, support from state institutions enabled the peasants to mobilize on a larger scale and more militantly than could otherwise have happened, and brought about real gains for some groups among them. In both cases the peasant mobilization stimulated a counter-mobilization from organized landowners who obtained support from the propertied classes in general, the political establishment, and the major media. The support of the régime proved vacillating and lacking a sufficiently clear rationale and strategy to overcome the counter-offensive. In each case, the advent of a new president brought near abandonment of the mobilization policy and of support for significant changes in land tenure, a return to previous policies and practices of manipulation, co-option, control and repression of peasant organizations.

Some of the questions discussed in the reports from Colombia, and some of the conclusions that emerge, include the following:

1. Except in revolutionary situations, the rise of peasant movements from localized self-defence and protest to wide mobilization depends heavily on support or at least toleration from the state and its agents. However, action by the state to call into being or support a vigorous movement of the rural poor, with the objective of mobilizing support for a strategy unwelcome to propertied classes and generally to forces dominant in society, has unforeseeable consequences. There is indeed no way in which the government can guarantee continuing and consistent support of the movement that it has initially encouraged. This is for several reasons.

First, the purposes of the régime controlling the state in supporting or tolerating such mobilizations are hardly ever identical with those of the peasant movement. Different parts of the state apparatus, perceiving different interests and loyal to different forces in society, may moreover be expected to work at cross-purposes. While some, who may precariously hold important positions, may advance the policy with great vigour, trying to bring about irreversible changes in the face of growing opposition, others may deliberately sabotage the policy. As was the case in Colombia, main supporters of the policy and of the peasant movement are often technocrats without power of their own and with excessive faith in their own capacity for planning and their right to exercise paternalistic controls over the movement.

Secondly, the mobilization of the rural poor whenever it threatens to change control over the means of production or the distribution of wealth will call forth rapid counter-mobilization from those sectors and social forces that stand to lose or fear disorder. This counter-mobilization will find powerful allies within the state, particularly in the armed forces, in the organs that influence public opinion and in the legal system with its bias toward the defence of private property. The government is likely to give in to the combined pressure of this counter-offensive, or to fall from power. In both cases the results will be a purge of those agents of the state in favour of the previous policy and confrontation between the peasant movement and an increasingly hostile state apparatus.

In the case of ANUC, for example, in the early years of the movement the government agrarian reform institute encouraged land seizures and followed them up by opening proceedings for expropriation and distribution of land. Later, under new leadership and new government directives, the same institute excluded peasants taking part in such seizures from rights to apply for land, while military and police forces combined with the landowners in the forcible eviction of the squatters. At the same time the agrarian reform institute and other government agencies offered services to co-operating peasants, those aligned with the pro-government co-opted wing of the movement, while ANUC became completely unable to function as a channel for negotiating with these agencies and obtaining government services for its members.

2. Interventions in peasant and generally popular movements by political organizations and groups that view the peasants in terms of their ideologically defined roles in revolution rather than in terms of the peasants' perceived needs and capabilities are likely to have equally unforeseeable consequences. In the Colombian case, the movement's break with the government and the traditional parties forced it to look elsewhere for allies and advisers. The intellectuals and ideologists who intervened led the movement into continual factional struggles that had little to do with peasant interests and into increasing isolation from the political and economic factors that were changing the real conditions for peasant struggle and participation. The complexity of these relations between the peasant movement and interlocutors in the Colombian case is discussed below in Chapter 8.

3. The debilitating consequences that diversity in the forms of livelihood, in regional and local conditions and in perception of adversaries among the rural population, combined with different rates and kinds of change in the course of the struggles, have on the unity and continuous strength of a peasant movement. In Colombia, a broad front of different rural groups could be achieved for only a short time in the first years when ANUC simultaneously pressed for redistribution of land, additional and more reliable services for small farmers and greater security for colonists in the eastern part of the country. Originally, this multisectoral character of ANUC gave a strong boost to its rise as a movement. Although the struggles centred on land seizures, the invasions of the landless peasants were accompanied by significant mobilizations and strikes conducted by *minifundistas*, colonists and Indians. Even then, though, great local and regional diversity and partial isolation of internal regions were a major obstacle. Later, and particularly after 1971/72 when ANUC began to experience government hostility instead of support, it was unable to represent effectively at the same time the interests of peasants still struggling for land, of peasants who had secured land and needed credits and public services, and of landless labourers who needed better wages and job security in capitalist agriculture and urban industries. Contradictions were more acute in some regions than in others, and their class content was also different. As one of the authors writes, 'despite ANUC's efforts to articulate the interests of the various class sectors, these differences set the stage for an uneven development of the peasant movement. Disparities in demands, organization, and politicization hindered the crystallization of shared attitudes and caused continuous internal contradictions. Against this background, ANUC's inability to handle the day-to-day demands of the peasants led to a progressive loss of support at the grassroots level.'[12] State concessions to wealthier peasants, migration to work in Venezuela and the new opportunities offered by the rise in the marijuana cultivation and drug trafficking, diluted peasant militancy in ways that the movement could neither foresee nor understand within its radicalized political orientation.

4. The changing nature of relations between the leaders of the movement and the rank and file, evolving through the tumultuous history of ANUC from client relations (in the early years) to more egalitarian relations (from 1971 to 1973) to bureaucratic and conflictive relations after 1974, and the

inability of the peasant members of ANUC to control the leadership except by withdrawal when the leaders' tactics ceased to make sense to them. In the early years after the split of the movement and the reversal of government policy the leadership of ANUC was not only drawn from among peasants and rural workers, but remained in close contact with the rank and file who maintained effective control over their leaders.[13] As leaders drawn from local peasant organizations or from school teachers and other professionals in contact with the peasants rose in the organization and associated increasingly with political and intellectual allies and interlocutors, they entered the political culture of the ideologists and came to look on the peasants as a mass to be manipulated for higher purposes. Especially after 1974 and the third congress of ANUC, the style of its leadership became increasingly bureaucratic and exclusionist. Under the influence of the left, the ANUC leadership engaged in what they believed was a decisive struggle for national power, whereas the central problem of the rank and file was a concrete day-to-day struggle to resist the power and impositions of the landlords and the state. This misperception illustrated the increasing social and conceptual gap between the leaders – who had joined the 'urban world' of politics – and the rank and file and contributed to the loss of grassroots support. The rank-and-file peasants may not have been able to oppose reasoned arguments against the neglect of their perceived interests, but when they saw that these were neglected they withdrew.

5. The ineffectiveness of efforts by technocrats of the government agrarian reform institute, in the early years, and later by progressive intellectuals backed by funds from abroad, to convert settlements originating in land seizures and expropriations into models of co-operative agriculture. In general, excessive paternalism, inadequate understanding of local conditions, and hampering of efforts by local groups to act autonomously resulted in poor performance by these settlements, and helped to discourage wider initiatives in co-operative peasant agriculture.

In conclusion, ANUC, like other movements of the hitherto excluded that were studied, has had bitter experiences from the reversal of state policy, the inability of state programmes to meet their commitments, the effectiveness of counter-mobilization by their adversaries, and shortcomings of their would-be allies in providing effective support and realistic guidance. After two decades of struggle results include improvements in the situation of some peasants who gained land, varied and contradictory changes in livelihood for the rest of the rural population, and continued overall dominance by large landowners, with a pronounced shift among them from traditional landlord-tenant relationships to modern capitalist agriculture. The outcome has been equally remote from the expectations of the government initiators of peasant organization, the Marxist ideologists, the progressive intellectuals, the state bureaucrats, and the peasants themselves during their period of mobilization.

Peasant movements and ethnicity in Bolivia

In Bolivia, 'Indian' Aymara- or Quechua-speaking peasants constitute the majority of the country's rural population. Participation in a nationalist revolution in 1952 enabled these groups to expand rapidly their previous efforts at organization, force through changes in land tenure that eliminated landlord dominance in much of the country, and set limits to the economic, political and cultural dominance of Spanish-speaking urban minorities. The massive land seizures following the revolution were essentially an autonomous phenomenon carried out by peasants who had organized spontaneously in ways the government and parties did not expect. Given the weakness of the Bolivian state, the government and parties had to deal with the peasantry, now organized nationwide in peasant unions or *sindicatos*, as a real force in the national power structure. The state, unable to maintain a continuous bureaucratic presence throughout the country, increasingly left the handling of local affairs to the *sindicatos*. The rural *sindicatos*, which often coincided with traditional Indian community structures, became an instrument of local self-government and grassroots participation and the major channel through which the peasants related to the state, political parties, labour unions and even development programmes. At the same time, the government and political parties consistently attempted, often with success, to co-opt peasant unions by incorporating their leaders into the regional and national power structure.

The *sindicatos* have recurrently been subject to governmental and other institutional pressures and interventions within a conflictive and frequently changing national political context. Especially during the past decade, the rural *sindicato* has undergone considerable changes in leadership, organization and goals in its previous strongholds. It has also emerged in new settings and has had to deal with new problems and demands. In zones along the tropical frontier, for example, *sindicatos* have functioned as organizations of colonists demanding land concessions and various services from the state. In some areas they protected peasant coca producers, and in zones of sugar and cotton agro-industry, such as in Santa Cruz, *sindicatos* have mobilized temporary migrant wage labourers, mainly Quechua-speaking highland peasants.

Two separate but complementary investigations were carried out in Bolivia, one on peasant movements and the state in general, the other on the struggles of the Aymara and Quechua peasantry from 1900 to 1980. The first investigation[14] examines the emergence of peasant organizations

in a historical perspective as part of wider processes of political mobilization in Bolivia and relates these processes to a number of issues concerning
persistence and change in ethnic identity. A first series of studies deals
with peasant revolts and mobilizations before the 1952 revolution, starting
with the great Aymara and Quechua rebellion in 1780/81. The historical
studies show how important the contributions of peasant resistance and
organization have been in Bolivia in changing national political conditions
and in the gradual weakening of the *hacienda* system. They also show that
from early on peasant rebellions and movements in Bolivia contain simultaneously elements of class, nationalist and ethnic struggles. At times one
factor or the other may be dominant, but all three considerations are usually
present to some degree. This is a particular characteristic of the Bolivian
peasant movement, which gives it unusual strength and resilience in the
face of changing political contexts and adversaries. The following studies
deal with the 1952 revolution and land reform, the creation of rural
sindicatos reflecting growing class consciousness of the peasantry, and
the subsequent gradual disintegration of the peasant movement into clientelistic politics as a result of processes of political co-option and of internal
leadership struggles. The ebb and flow of these post-revolutionary confrontations between the peasantry and the state is studied both in the
Quechua areas of the Cochabamba valley and in the Aymara-speaking
zones of the Altiplano. In these latter areas, the emergence of peasant
women's organizations, linked to the *sindicatos* but advancing demands
of their own, is studied, as are the increasing political importance of
affirmation of Aymara cultural identity and the rise of alternative clusters
of *sindicatos* rejecting government co-option.

The Bolivian studies touch on questions that recur in the other studies
on peasant movements in Latin America and are in part discussed elsewhere. In particular they throw light on the sometimes stimulating but
usually inhibiting effects of efforts by the state and political parties to
co-opt and manipulate these movements for their own ends, on the
vulnerability of the movements to such tactics and on the counter-tactics
available to them to obtain benefits from the state or defend themselves
against co-option or party/state-induced factional struggles.

After 1952 peasant *sindicatos* and their leaders were brought rapidly
into the mainstream of party politics and became involved in internecine
party conflicts. Increasing factionalism within the Nationalist Revolutionary Movement (MNR), the urban-based mass party that led the revolution
and formed the following governments, led to increasing rivalries among
peasant leaders linked through clientelistic ties to different wings of the
MNR and resulted in some cases in violent clashes, such as the one
between factions centred in the localities of Cliza and Ucurena in 1959.
The peasant movement reached what was probably its lowest point, a kind
of institutionalized dependence comparable to some features of Mexican

state-peasant relations, under the auspices of the so-called 'Military-Peasant Pact', the populist military dictatorship of General Barrientos. The transformation and reconstitution of the peasant movement in subsequent years in the Aymara regions was closely linked to a re-assessment of the relative weight of class and ethnic factors as the basis for the struggle and to the actions of a new leadership of young, urban and educated Aymaras.

On the whole, the *sindicatos* have coped with the frequent and violent alternation between more or less repressive but generally weak military governments and weak democratic governments through flexible tactics and changes in national leadership, following aggressive leaders and tactics when the government was in no position to repress them and collaborating formally with military régimes in exchange for limited concessions when this seemed prudent. Continuity at the local level of union activity was probably greater than at the national level, but the studies are not very informative on the real participation of rank-and-file *sindicato* members in bringing about changes in leadership and tactics.

An important contribution of the Bolivian study lies in its examination of relations between peasant mobilization and ethnic identity. In its original formulation UNRISD's Participation Programme had envisaged the study of ethnically defined participatory movements and situations. Indeed it recognized ethnic identity as a widely present cause of exclusion and discrimination, often intermingled in complex ways with other factors of exclusion. It also became apparent that ethnic identification and differences play an increasingly important role as the source of conflict at various levels, and that ethnic identity can have an important impact on the constitution and development of popular and participatory movements. In most of the cases studied under the Participation Programme the researchers did not feel, however, that ethnic and other forms of social cleavage were sufficiently important to warrant separate treatment; the corresponding issues were subsumed under an analysis of class-related conflict. In the study of grassroots movements and non-party political formations in India, discussed below, ethnic differentiation was studied as one of the factors having both mobilizing and demobilizing effects on participatory movements of the excluded. The one case where ethnic and cultural differences were discussed as a central issue in the participatory argumentation between the excluded and the state is Bolivia. Also, based initially on the Bolivian experience, a regional sub-debate on the role of historical consciousness and ethnicity in popular movements took place in Latin America. It seems important to consider this issue in some more detail here.[15]

Ethnicity, and ethnic and cultural identities among the excluded, are particularly important issues in the case of Bolivia. The non-dominant ethnic groups, the Aymara- and Quechua-speaking Indians, represent a majority of the rural population, and ethnicity interacts in complex and at times contradictory ways with questions of class differentiation and of national identification and affirmation of citizenship rights. Also, the ethnic component has acted as a powerful catalyst in the resurgence of a genuine peasant movement after its long period of decline, particularly among the Aymaras. The more explicit affirmation of cultural identity among the latter has since the 1970s begun to enter significantly into the political discourse of peasant organizations, although there are divergent groups and leaders and the future evolution and relationships of ethnic identification, class identification and national identification are far from clear.

The most vigorous recent effort at wider union of peasant *sindicatos* started with a new Aymara-based leadership and community membership in the form of the Katarista movement. The new organization addressed itself not only to a wide range of specific demands of government relating to peasant livelihood (prices, transport, credit, marketing) but also to specific cultural needs of peasants as Aymaras. The crucial agent in this resurgence of a militant Indian movement was a group of young educated Aymaras, who had been exposed in the cities to anti-Indian racism. They radicalized and gave new strength to the Indian peasant movement, adopting the symbol of Tupac Katari (thus the name of the movement), the legendary leader of a massive Indian revolt against Spanish domination in the late eighteenth century. The young Aymara leadership was both participant in the movement and, to some extent, interlocutor of the wider peasant movement; they thus internalized some of the ambiguity inherent in the relationship between interlocutors and popular movements. It is important to note that the new stress on cultural and ethnic demands of the movement was basically the result of the surfacing within the old Indian peasant movement of this new leadership of young educated members from the urban community who experienced discrimination and tended to develop an identification with Indian movements outside Bolivia. In contrast to this the rural Aymara majority was disposed to integrate ethnic with peasant self-identification in their organizational tactics and alliances. Organizationally the new Katarista movement struggled to maintain an independent stance *vis-à-vis* government and political parties, while formally associating itself in 1978 with the Bolivian Worker's Central, the main trade union organization from which the peasant *sindicatos* had long been estranged. The movement showed, particularly in its early stages, a profound distrust of existing parties, be they from the right or from the left, and proclaimed its intention to create its own political organizations outside the existing political system. This radical stance, which corresponded probably more to the new leadership's reading of past manipulation of the *sindicatos* by the political establishment than to the concrete preoccupations of the peasant *sindicatos*, proved difficult to maintain. In the early 1980s the movement split on the question of support for presidential candidates and alliance with political parties.

The interaction between the new urban Aymara intelligentsia, the Aymara residents in La Paz and the rural *sindicatos* in the Altiplano also brought a new dimension to the struggle: emphasizing the cultural identity and heritage of the Aymaras – through the building of cultural centres and the use of radio programmes – the new leadership revived the historical memory and consciousness of the Aymara people, thereby providing legitimacy to the struggle and inspiring confidence in its ultimate success. The role that this historical memory and consciousness has played in the development of the Indian peasant movements in Bolivia is the theme of the second investigation that was undertaken.[16] The study attributes the different trajectories of the movements of the Quechua-speaking peasants of the Cochabamba area and the Aymara-speaking peasants of the La Paz area in part to the 'short historical memory' of the former and the 'long historical memory' of the latter. That is, the former think back mainly to the 1952 revolution and the gains made through union organization and agrarian reform, and thus are more prepared to participate simply as rural producers in alliances with national political forces and in bargaining with the state. The latter are more resentful of forms of ethnically based discrimination and paternalism that re-emerged following the nationalist ideological effort of the 1952 revolution to replace 'Indian' by 'peasant' identity as a means to national integration. This resentment stimulates and is stimulated by the 'long historical memory' of oppression by the Spanish-speaking minority and uprisings against this oppression since the eighteenth century. The study criticizes the 'élitist' reluctance of the left political parties and movements in Bolivia to recognize the importance and legitimacy of cultural diversity and demands for real equality and suggests another kind of 'long historical memory' influencing these élites: a subconscious fear of being overwhelmed by the 'Indians'.

Participation in rural Thailand

Rural Thailand presents quite a different picture from the other cases examined so far. Peasants have never constituted a political force on the national level in Thailand, and there are practically no visible organized participatory efforts of the rural poor that go beyond small-scale local actions. This is in spite of the rapidly deteriorating situation of the rural poor that is a result of the profound economic changes that have taken place over the past 25 years in the rural sector. A previously relatively homogeneous peasantry with a fairly secure subsistence base producing mainly rice for the market has been fundamentally transformed by the introduction of new export crops such as sugar, maize, cassava, tobacco, jute and pineapple, the introduction of new inputs and by a new articulation with world markets, notably through the establishment of transnational agribusiness corporations. This has substantially benefited a minority while leading to a crisis of livelihood for the great majority of rural producers. The simultaneous incorporation of wider areas in the modern consumer-oriented national economy, with the concomitant rise in indebtedness, and the increasing shortage of cultivable land in the plains areas and the valleys has accentuated this trend. The result for a majority of rural producers is increased insecurity, indebtedness, greater dependence, increased relative disadvantage and, for some, absolute misery.

There has not been, during this time, a comparable or corresponding change in social and political institutions. Despite changes in the composition of ruling groups, the country has shown a remarkable degree of overall institutional stability during the past 50 years. In the twentieth century, Thailand has experienced no formal or political colonialism, no change of dynasty, no mass popular, nationalist or republican movements; and it has kept a high degree of linguistic and religious homogeneity. For 50 years the military has, for nearly all periods, been the controlling factor in national politics, and political parties are poorly developed nationally. These factors have led to a weak institutional development of 'civil society'. Government (often militarily led), bureaucracy, state, nation, monarchy and Buddhist religion are commonly perceived as a whole. This gives the state (and associated institutions and powerholders) a monopoly of legitimacy rarely found to such a degree. Under such conditions, there is relatively little legitimate or claimable space, whether institutional, legal or even of language, for the expression of criticism and for more democratic, alternative or participatory ideas and organizations.

The investigations sponsored by the Participation Programme in Thailand have aimed to document and contribute to a popular history of organized and everyday efforts made since the late 1970s by and on behalf of the rural poor to enhance their livelihood and social power. Efforts studied included both official government-sponsored co-operatives and farmers' associations as well as a range of more autonomous often small-scale actions by the rural poor themselves. The studies throw light on a number of questions regarding possibilities for peasant participation in a basically anti-participatory and repressive environment, some of which recur in other field studies of the programme in Latin America.[17]

Officially instituted co-operatives and farmers' groups in Thailand, which in practice are primarily concerned with the provision of credit, have been largely ineffective in resolving the problems of livelihood of the rural poor who, *de facto*, are usually excluded from access to institutional credit. These and other forms of officially sponsored development and community organizations tend to be managed by and to benefit principally a small minority upper stratum at village and sub-district level. These findings are not new and confirm those of previous UNRISD research on the Green

Revolution and on co-operatives which found that rural development programmes do not benefit the poor except when social structures permit it and/or when the poor are mobilized to appropriate and retain a share of the benefits. Rural co-operatives tend to reproduce the power structure of the village or local unit in which they operate, and therefore tend to increase, rather than decrease, rural inequality. Also, official farmers' groups and community organizations in Thailand tend to be single-purpose groups with discontinuous activities, unable to link with other organizations, and dominated by official, bureaucratic priorities, regulations and mentalities.

Above all, official farmers' groups in Thailand have not been able to prevent the increasing dependence of small farmers and to address what these farmers identify as the overwhelming problem of livelihood, namely the 'problems of the market'. While the majority of the rural poor indeed still have some access to land, in most other respects they have decreasing control over other strategic factors of production and over the labour process. In a development similar to the one affecting Mexican *ejido* farmers, controls have shifted to private agribusinesses that dictate to the peasants what they are to produce and what inputs to use, and that monopolize the processing and marketing of the product. As one small Thai farmer said, 'It is like working for wages on your own land.' Furthermore, the agribusiness corporations can leave the farmers stranded, and often do so, when a shift in international markets makes their product no longer profitable. Though problems of land and land rent are real problems, particularly for the steadily increasing number of near-landless and landless, the main problem as identified by the poor farmers is the problem of the market – low product prices, high input prices, expensive and/or unavailable credit – and their inability to influence it.

More autonomous and participatory organizations set up by the rural poor in Thailand have addressed this main problem and taken the form of credit unions or savings groups, rice banks or buffalo banks, fertilizer banks, medical savings schemes and production and marketing groups. Given the overall anti-participatory nature of Thai rural society, most of these actions have been small-scale, usually localized and unable to establish horizontal links with similar efforts elsewhere. As Turton states in the overview report of the Thai studies, many such efforts of poor farmers to organize themselves collectively in defence of their livelihood appear as 'desperate strategies for short-term survival. They may be seen, at least, as ways to avoid even more desperate and socially harmful or undignified options, such as recourse to beggary, prostitution, the selling of children to Bangkok sweat-shops, crime and drug addiction, or migration to city slums to work as rag-pickers and scavengers.'[18]

The study of more successful participatory groups showed that no particular form or formal purpose of organization was inherently limiting or enabling. Rather, their success depended on adopting goals, forms of activity and linkage, style of working, learning and leadership that were in marked contrast to the characteristics of official organizations. As had been seen in other case studies, such as in China, the quality of leadership proved crucial. In almost all cases the energy and quality of work of a very small number of poor farmers' leaders, and sometimes of associated volunteers and community organizers from non-governmental organizations, were crucial for the successful self-organization of the rural poor. More successful groups had not only developed multiple survival strategies, usually based on a combination of various activities that provided a stimulus to continuous action and an array of defensive possibilities, but had also increased self-confidence and understanding of their critical situation, decreased dependence and fear, and forged wider horizontal and vertical links.

The studies in Thailand put a particular emphasis on the analysis of what the Participation Programme originally called 'structures and ideologies of anti-participation', namely those structures that resist the participation of the non-élite elements in decision-making and those ideologies which are created, or rather 'secreted', by dominant classes to maintain existing power monopolies and forms of exploitation.[19] In their attempts to organize, poor farmers met with a complex range of constraints from powerful local interest groups and from processes of administrative, political and cultural control. These constraints combine into a highly repressive and coercive ensemble including an ideological set of control mechanisms that lead, on the level of the excluded, to a veritable 'culture of subordination'. The study analysed the complex overlapping and interpenetration of commercial, administrative and political agencies and institutions, official and non-official, formal and informal, legal and illegal, explicit and covert. Also identified as crucially problematic were coercive forms and processes of surveillance, accusation and intimidation, variously backed by both informal and legal sanctions and also extreme physical sanctions in a context of rural violence. Severe limitations on organization were also imposed by a number of factors accentuating the fragmentation of poor farmers, and in part already discussed in the Latin American studies: increasingly varied types of economic activities and intensification of labour processes, clientelistic tactics and tactics of selective rewards/punishments by local élites, and, paradoxically, the multiplication of institutions and channels of aid and resources that compete for the rural poor. The studies in Thailand have shown particularly well how the local power structures and other forces of coercion and control that are operative at the local level are closely linked to, and often based upon, those at the national and international level.

Later studies testing the UNRISD approach to participation, carried out in Thailand between 1983 and 1985, confirm the conclusions summarized above, although overt government attitudes had changed significantly in the interim. 'Participation' through sponsorship of local organizations became a main theme in rural policy, with some positive results, but without reversing trends towards greater differentiation within communities, deterioriation of the livelihood of the majority of peasants, and vulnerability to external economic and political power centres. In practice, 'participation itself is used to mean semi-compulsory joining of official schemes in the name of giving villagers a say in their own lives'. Required attendance at meetings and contributions in labour become a serious burden to the poor peasants, while 'decentralization of power in the name of participation ... merely serves to decentralize inequality and reinforce or reshape, rather than replace "non-rational" aspects of power and economic relations.'[20]

The Thai studies also throw some light on general tactics available to and adopted by peasants and invite some comparisons with Latin American cases. The results from the UNRISD participation studies suggest generally that only on comparatively rare occasions do peasants and rural workers, alone or allied with others, openly and violently confront the state and agrarian élites, and attack the system of domination as a whole. In extremely anti-participatory societies in Asia, where state legitimacy is generally high and in some countries quasi-sacrosanct, it is only when peasants reach a desperate situation of increased exploitation and impoverishment, and when the state's legitimacy has weakened as a result of obvious malperformance or the presence of an open political challenge, that their organized efforts go beyond local action. They then often become extremely violent and are directed against the system of domination as a whole, resembling the medieval jacqueries or the many historic Chinese peasant revolts. In Latin America some of this desperation may also be present, but the anti-participatory system seems more permeable and the state itself, or non-peasant political parties or movements seeking control of the state, have now and then given the peasants precarious openings to organize at national level in pursuit of their own interests.

Everywhere, in Latin America and in Asia, however, by far the most common form of peasant participation and tactics are situated on the middle-ground between passivity and open collective defiance. Attention has increasingly focused in academic work on such 'everyday forms of peasant resistance' as a less visible yet more appropriate and common form of minimal peasant participation.[21] As James Scott wrote, one may plausibly group under the term 'everyday resistance' all 'the ordinary weapons of many subordinate groups – ranging all the way from clandestine arson and sabotage, to footdragging, dissimulation, false compliance, pilfering, slander, flight, and so forth'.[22] Such forms of peasant resistance are less visible and confrontational, and more individualistic, and they require less co-ordination then the more open acts of collective defiance. They often represent forms of self-help but typically avoid any direct symbolic affront to authority and are generally underwritten by a 'sub-culture of resistance'. They are more constant than the more visible open forms of struggle and 'may, cumulatively, have an appreciable impact on class and authority relations in the countryside'.[23]

Participation in rural India

The Participation Programme has sponsored two separate but related studies in India on local and micro-political movements attempting to articulate and defend the interests of the poor.[24] These movements, so it is argued in the studies, have resulted from the conjunction of two processes characterizing the present situation in India, namely the deepening crisis of livelihood for the poor, and a seeming weakness both of the state in stimulating development and of political parties in helping to articulate and channel the discontent. The studies have focused on a variety of non-governmental and non-party efforts to organize different social groups for collective action: landless labourers, tribal groups, urban workers and women. The main findings of these studies, as well as the specific context of the Indian state and economy in which these movements have emerged, are discussed in Chapter 8. Some of the findings that relate more particularly to peasants and rural workers and provide links to some of the other cases discussed so far are briefly summarized here.

The social struggle in the Indian countryside can be seen as a tripartite one between the former feudal landed élite, the new middle-class and capitalist/kulak upper-class peasants, and the poor peasants and agricultural workers, with the tribal groups, known as *adivasis*, being both part of the last group and constituting a fourth group on their own. The state has consistently played these social forces one against the other, through co-option, repression, selective favouritism and manipulation, aiming to maintain a a certain level of peace and stability and to prevent excessive violence in order to ensure conditions for continued growth of agricultural production.

In the course of these encounters class lines are often blurred. Large peasant agitations in Tamil Nadu, Karnataka and Maharashtra were thus led by rich farmers defending their demands against the state but carried by mass participation of poor peasants and agricultural labourers. For many of the latter participation in these agitations represented a desperate fight for survival which could ultimately result in some token benefit; others joined because of client links with rich farmers, or following appeals for caste unity. Also, co-operatives, which are usually controlled by middle-class and upper-class farmers, are used by these latter to break the power of the former feudal élite and high caste moneylenders, and in this struggle they enlist the support of poor peasants and the landless by appealing to peasant unity that would transcend class. Powerful factors of fragmentation make class action by the rural poor difficult in India: patron-client relations, the differential incorporation of the poor into the modern economy and the multiple divisions of the rural poor along caste, linguistic, religious, regional and other communal lines which often cut across classes.

Poor peasants, agricultural labourers and above all tribal groups have increasingly felt that established political parties and their mass fronts cannot cater to their needs, and that dovetailing their demands to those of rich farmers, a strategy often even supported by communist parties in India, brings benefits to the rich but none to them. Hence the numerous attempts to form their own organizations and movements, attempts supported by radicalized sections of the mainly urban middle classes who felt increasingly alienated from the traditional left parties and other 'macro-organizations of the poor'. The UNRISD studies have documented several such local movements of the rural poor, as has the Rural Employment Policies Branch of the ILO.[25] All the studies underline the great potential of such grassroots initiatives of the rural poor for initiating a participatory learning process, for liberating their creative energies and for collective empowerment. At the same time they show the vulnerability of such initiatives to manipulation by interlocutors, their often excessive dependence on a single charismatic leader, and their limitation to local issues and to a local scope of action which leaves them without sufficient clout to negotiate their interests with national parties and the state at higher levels. The question to what extent such grassroots initiatives can be of relevance at the macro-level, and to what extent they constitute a viable alternative to traditional approaches to participation and development will be discussed in Chapter 10.

The Indian studies have not focused in particular on ethnicity or other communal factors that influence participatory actions by the excluded. Since a number of participatory movements studied were *de facto* tribal movements – at least at the origin – the studies do nevertheless touch on some interesting questions regarding the relation between class and ethnicity and the mobilizing or demobilizing effect that ethnicity can have on participatory actions of the excluded. The tribal groups in India, or *adivasis*, constitute the poorest of the poor, experiencing not only exploitation and exclusion as a class but also as an ethnic group outside the main social and religious systems of Hinduism and Islam. Non-tribal groups have increasingly encroached on their traditional lands, and their traditional systems of livelihood support have been threatened or been destroyed by exploitative forest and mining policies and large hydraulic projects. Being literally excluded, i.e. not part of the dominant social system, and thus legitimately 'exploitable' in the eyes of many non-tribal people, the tribal communities have, on the other hand, not suffered as much from the multiple fragmenting forces that operate in wider Indian society. Their strong sense of community and tradition of collective problem solving has given them a definite advantage over other groups of rural poor. It is thus not surprising that many local grassroots initiatives and movements have emerged among tribal groups. The studies also show that collective historical consciousness, expressed in the glorification of past struggles or of historical leaders vested sometimes with magical powers and representing the legitimacy and continuity of the struggle (a characteristic also present among the Bolivian Indian movements), is much stronger among tribal groups than elsewhere. On the other hand, this strong sense of ethnic group identity, which facilitates in initial stages the emergence of participatory movements of rural poor, easily acquires exclusionist and xenophobic traits which blur class analysis and prevent the extension of the initial movement at a later stage of its development to non-tribal sections of the rural poor.

Notes

1. Breman, Jan, *Wage Hunters and Gatherers*, Oxford University Press, New Delhi, 1993.

2. Rello, Fernando, *State and Peasantry in Mexico: A Case Study of Rural Credit in La Laguna*, UNRISD, Geneva, 1987, p. xvii.

3. See the Prologue to the Participation Programme's Thailand study, written by Mary Hollnsteiner Racelis, in Turton, Andrew, *Production, Power and Participation in Rural Thailand*, UNRISD, Geneva, 1987, p. xiv.

4. Rello, Fernando, op. cit. in n. 2, and *Bourgeoisie, Peasants and the State in Mexico: The Agrarian Conflict of 1976*, Geneva, UNRISD, 1986.

5. Rello, Fernando, op. cit. in n. 2.

6. See Stiefel, Matthias and Wertheim, Willem, *Production, Equality and Participation in Rural China: Reflections on a Field Trip in September/October 1979*, Zed Books and UNRISD, London and Geneva, 1982.

7. See Utting, Peter, *The Peasant Question and Development Policy in Nicaragua*, UNRISD Discussion Paper No. 2, Geneva, 1988.

8. See Marchetti, Peter, ed., *Co-operativas y Participacion Popular in Nicaragua*, unpublished manuscript, UNRISD, Geneva, 1985.

9. See Utting, Peter, op. cit. in n. 7.

10. The findings from the Peruvian studies are contained in Ballon, E. and Tovar, T., *The Development of Popular Movements in Peru, 1968-1982*, unpublished manuscript, UNRISD, Geneva, 1985; and Franco, Carlos, ed., *El Peru de Velasco*, 3 volumes, CEDEP, Lima, 1983.

11. Zamosc, León, *The Agrarian Question and the Peasant Movement in Colombia: Struggles of the National Peasant Association, 1967-81*, UNRISD and Cambridge University Press, Geneva and Cambridge, 1986; Rivera Cusicanqui, Silvia, *The Politics and Ideology of the Colombian Peasant Movement: The Case of ANUC*, UNRISD, Geneva, 1987; Izquierdo Maldonado, Gabriel, *Peasant Popular Participation: Rise and Fall of the Peasant Movement in Manati*, unpub-

lished manuscript; Molano, Alfredo, *Relatos de la Violencia*, unpublished manuscript, UNRISD; Escobar, Cristina, *Trayectoria de la ANUC (1966-1982)*, unpublished manuscript.

12. Zamosc, León, op. cit. in n. 11, p. 207.

13. See a discussion of this in Parra Escobar, Ernesto, 'ANUC: A History of Peasant Participation', Postscript to Rivera Cusicanqui, Silvia, op. cit. in n. 11.

14. Calderon, Fernando and Dandler, Jorge, eds., *Bolivia: la Fuerza Historica del Campesinado*, UNRISD and CERES, Geneva and La Paz, 2nd revised edition 1986.

15. The role of ethnicity in participatory movements and organizations is further discussed in Chapter 9. Some results from the regional sub-debate on historical consciousness and ethnicity, with contributions from Bolivia, Chile, Colombia, Ecuador and Peru are contained in Rivera Cusicanqui, Silvia, *Collective Memory and Popular Movements*, UNRISD, unpublished draft manuscript, 1984.

16. Rivera Cusicanqui, Silvia, *'Oppressed but not Defeated': Peasant Struggles among the Aymara and Qhechwa in Bolivia, 1900-1980*, UNRISD, Geneva, 1987.

17. Most research findings and reports from Thailand are in Thai. An overview of the findings in English is available: Turton, Andrew, *Production, Power and Participation in Rural Thailand*, UNRISD, Geneva, 1987.

18. Ibid., p. 76.

19. See Pearse, Andrew and Stiefel, Matthias, *An Inquiry into Participation: A Research Approach*, UNRISD, Geneva, 1979.

20. Hirsch, Philip, *Development Dilemmas in Rural Thailand*, Oxford University Press, Singapore, 1990, pp. 210 and 218.

21. See Scott, James C. and Kerkvliet, Benedict J. Tria, eds., 'Everyday Forms of Peasant Resistance in South-East Asia', *Journal of Peasant Studies*, vol. 13, no. 2, Jan. 1986.

22. Ibid., p. 1.

23. In his overview report on the UNRISD project on 'A unified approach to development analysis and planning' Marshall Wolfe placed such forms of popular action within a range of participatory tactics, from everyday forms of resistance and withdrawal to participation in national politics and attempts at revolutionary transformation of the state. See Wolfe, Marshall, *Elusive Development*, UNRISD and ECLA, Geneva, 1981, pp. 158-61.

24. Most findings from the Indian research are contained in Sethi, Harsh and Kothari, Smitu, eds., *The Non-Party Political Process in India: Uncertain Alternatives*, unpublished manuscript, UNRISD, Geneva, 1985, and Dasgupta, S., *Understanding Social Reality*, unpublished manuscript, UNRISD, Geneva, 1983.

25. See Rahman, Anisur, *Some Dimensions of People's Participation in the Bhoomi Sena Movement*, UNRISD, Geneva, 1981; Rahman, Anisur, ed., *Grassroots Participation and Self-Reliance*, Oxford and IBH Publishing Co., New Delhi, 1984; and Ghai, Dharam, 'Participatory Development: Some Perspectives from Grassroots Experiences', *Journal of Development Planning*, no. 19, 1989, pp. 215-46.

4

Urban Wage Workers and their Organizations

Workers in industry and comparable occupations (mining, transport, electrical power, construction) have been central to developmentalist as well as Marxist conceptions of social transformation, and also to populist tactics for mass mobilization. Their relation to production and their concentration in large groups with common interests in wage levels, job security and working conditions, confronting readily identifiable adversaries and interlocutors, have shaped a long history of 'organized efforts'. A voluminous literature of research and polemic has accumulated on the emergence of an industrial working class in the Third World and on its potential roles as revolutionary proletariat or 'committed' industrial labour force.

To an important extent historical precedents and ideological expectations deriving from the long-industrialized societies have shaped the organized efforts of wage workers elsewhere. National and international union federations in these societies have entered into systematic relationships with unions in the Third World, giving them an international perspective and a type of interlocutor not present in other popular organizations except for political parties. These relationships have been important sources of material support, technical advice on organization and defence against repressive governments, but have also contributed to divisiveness deriving from the Cold War and rivalries between Marxist, Social Democratic, Christian Democratic and other tendencies in the international union organizations.

In much of the Third World by the 1970s, and particularly in Latin America, the industrial working class was not excluded from 'control over resources and regulative institutions' to nearly the same extent as other categories of the urban and rural poor. After long struggles much of it was organized in unions with some bargaining power *vis-à-vis* employers and some ability to influence the policies of the state. Class consciousness and confidence in future growth in numbers and organizational power were pronounced, although working-class leaders and ideological guides tended to exaggerate these factors through their idealized images of the 'proletariat' and its vanguard role. Other currents of opinion tended to exaggerate the gap between the organized workers, as a relatively privileged and conformist minority, and the poorer and more insecure majority of the people.

The national role of the organized working class was also 'institution-alized' in various ways that involved co-option of the leadership, sectarian struggles for control of unions, and abrupt shifts from inclusion to exclusion or *vice versa* with changes of political régimes. In some countries during different periods the union movement (or its leadership) achieved formal recognition as a component of governing coalitions (Argentina, Bolivia, Chile, Mexico) or as a mass base of support for parties contending for political power (Brazil and Peru). In general, unions were able to do more for their members through their negotiations with the state than through their negotiations with employers.

During the 1970s and early 1980s the vicissitudes in relations between working-class organizations and governments became more pronounced. Military régimes in Argentina, Bolivia, Brazil, Chile and Uruguay violently repressed unions or restricted them by decree to narrow and localized functions, while trying to sever their previous links to political movements and mobilizing ideologies. In these cases, unions became more dependent on their international interlocutors for bare survival. Elsewhere promotion-cum-manipulation of unions combined with state repression of autonomous 'organized efforts' predominated (Guyana, Mexico), or unions became more 'feudalized' through struggles for control by rival political factions (Peru).

Meanwhile, various shifts in national economic policies and in international markets and financial flows brought about changes in the composition of the working class that disrupted its capacity for organized defence of jobs and wage levels:

• State-protected import-substitution industrialization fell into discredit. With reduction or elimination of protection of such industries, employment in them fell sharply; the rise of certain export-oriented industries compensated only partially and belatedly for this (Argentina, Chile). Falling world prices of certain minerals combining with modernization of mining techniques reduced the numbers of employed miners, in Bolivia by more than two-thirds.

• While numbers of stably employed manual wage workers stagnated or declined, the numbers and trade union militancy of white-collar employees (public functionaries, teachers, health workers, bank employees, etc.) continued to increase up to the early 1980s, so that the centre of gravity of the trade union movement shifted away from the traditional 'proletariat'. More recently the shrinking resources of the state and campaigns of debureaucratization and privatization have curtailed the ability of unions in these sectors to defend the interests of their members.

• Within the industrial sector, production of semi-finished goods by transnational enterprises able to shift production from country to country according to relative labour costs and employing mainly women without previous organizational experience became more important.

• With the curtailment of opportunities for 'formal' industrial employment, the importance within the economically active population of various categories of practically unorganizable activity rose sharply: the self-employed, workers in small 'informal' enterprises able to survive only by evading labour protective regulations, home piece-work by women and children.[1] Since many working-class families had to fall back on such activities, generally carried on by members other than the previous bread-winner, the dividing line between the industrial working class and the urban poor or 'informal sector' became less distinct.

• With the onset of economic crisis in the early 1980s wage and salary levels fell by as much as 50 per cent, even for workers and employees able to keep their jobs. In a good many countries, high rates of inflation have since further eroded wage levels. Unions have lost most of their capacity to protect their members' jobs and wage levels.

• As developmentalist faith in industrialization and Marxist faith in the eventual triumph of a revolutionary proletariat weakened simultaneously, the organized working class became deprived of previous utopias or sources of faith in a better future.

• At the same time, paradoxically, the union movement in several countries has been able to build on its organizational tradition to survive repression, generate new leadership and objectives, and take a leading part in the struggles for redemocratization.

Four of the research projects sponsored by UNRISD (in Brazil, Chile, Guyana and Peru) deal, primarily or secondarily, with struggles of the organized working class under the difficult conditions summarized above.

Social struggles in São Paulo, Brazil

The loosely co-ordinated researches carried out in Brazil by the Centro de Estudos de Cultura Contemporanea (CEDEC) in co-operation with UNRISD[2] had a double focus: on the struggles of workers in the major industries of the metropolitan area of São Paulo to achieve autonomous union organization and reverse a long trend of intensified exploitation; and on the efforts of the masses of the population, through local solidarity, to improve their access to shelter and urban services and to resist the continual rises in costs of living generated by Brazil's chronically high inflation. In São Paulo these two kinds of struggle have been more closely intermeshed than in most Brazilian or other Latin American cities and their historical evolution has been somewhat different. Here the growth of industry and industrial employment was continuous and dynamic up to the economic crisis of the 1980s. Thus, a high proportion of the São Paulo families seeking shelter and services have been families of industrial workers rather than self-employed, 'subproletarians', or members of a heterogeneous 'informal sector'. In this respect, São Paulo is at the opposite extreme from Lima, where industrial workers have been a declining minority within the low-income population.

Up to 1964, the workers of São Paulo as well as the rest of urban Brazil enjoyed a certain kind of 'inclusion' as dependent allies of populist régimes, enrolled automatically in unions promoted and supervised by the state. The state entrusted these unions with extensive social welfare responsibilities and substantial funds to meet the responsibilities, but imposed wage settlements in preference to union bargaining with employers. After the military coup of 1964, the redistribution of political power and the economic-political strategy of the dominant forces inhibited practically all organized efforts by the workers to advance their interests as wage earners, city dwellers and citizens. Intensified repression followed a wave of strikes in 1968. Up to the late 1970s legal provisions and a leadership imposed from above confined unions to very narrow functions. Real wage levels were deliberately lowered, legally guaranteed job security was eliminated, strikes were prohibited, and legal political parties were barred from competing for mass support by advancing issues of livelihood and social rights.

Shelter for the rapidly expanding numbers of workers' families continued to be left to practically unregulated private initiative. Up to the 1950s most workers lived in rented slum housing (*cortiços*) close to the factories. 'Clandestine' subdivision of privately owned land and sale of small plots to workers then became common and continued on a rising scale up to the recent past. The buyers generally built their own houses as best they could. At present, half the dwelling units of São Paulo are estimated to be of this type. Neither the public authorities nor the land speculators assumed responsibility for streets, transport networks, water, electricity or sewerage for the new settlements. The tactics of land speculation produced a chaotic and sprawling pattern of urban growth, with vacant areas deliberately left between settlements to be placed on the market later at higher prices, after pressure on municipal authorities from the earlier settlements had forced the expansion of urban services.

This pattern of growth has appeared in a good many other Latin American cities, but its relative importance is greater in São Paulo than elsewhere. The co-ordinator of the researches summarized here emphasizes that it is one of the principal dimensions of 'expoliation' of labour in São Paulo. It places on the worker heavy burdens for land payments, legalization of title, building materials and labour; leaves the family in an unhealthy environment deprived of normal urban services and amenities for long periods after settlement; and necessitates exhausting and expensive daily journeys (four hours on average) between home and work.

However, the relative stability and homogeneity of the owner-occupied neighbourhoods and the impetus to co-operate to provide their own basic services or negotiate for them with the authorities have been conducive to vigorous neighbourhood organization. In recent years, such organized efforts have been further stimulated by the church-supported movement of 'base ecclesial communities'. Neighbourhood associations could survive and even exert some influence through political channels when unions and workers' parties could not.

When militant union activities reappeared at the end of the 1970s and culminated in a series of major strikes, the solidarity and material support of the neighbourhoods were decisive for the success of the strikes, while the militancy of the unions under new leadership also helped to invigorate the neighbourhood struggles. The authors of the research findings argue against viewing the neighbourhood associations as merely auxiliaries to the workers' movement proper: in settings such as São Paulo, the struggles against 'urban expoliation', i.e. against an environment threatening the well-being of the worker's family and the very reproduction of the labour force, are just as important as the struggles over wages and working conditions.[3]

The co-ordinator of the studies has pointed out that the researchers, unavoidably concentrating on one kind of organized effort or the other, in separate physical environments, had serious theoretical and methodological difficulties in capturing the complexities and changes over time in relationships between struggles and demands, sometimes fragmentary and isolated, sometimes merging in broad popular movements. He emphasizes that the major mobilizations and expressions of solidarity have emerged in spite of settings that are inescapably demobilizing through the exhausting daily routine and continual urgent problems of livelihood and shelter that face the workers and their families.

During the early 1980s, economic crisis wiped out the gains made by São Paulo industrial workers through strikes at the beginning of the decade and further reduced the capacity of the authorities to respond to demands for urban services. Unemployment and underemployment, previously of minor importance in São Paulo, rose sharply, and inflation ran far ahead of nominal wage gains. The widening gap between incomes and land prices, even in 'clandestine' sub-divisions, began to change the characteristics of the struggle for shelter. Squatter settlements (*favelas*), also previously of secondary importance in São Paulo, began to come to the fore. In these, relations with unions are much less important, since most of the settlers are in unorganized occupations or self-employed. Since then, conditions have fluctuated but in a context of recurrent threats of unemployment, hyperinflation and government adjustment policies striking at levels of consumption and public services. The main response of the working-class movement seems to have been to organize politically, behind a party that won the mayoralty of São Paulo and in 1989 came close to capturing the Presidency of Brazil. The São Paulo working-class movement has thus shown remarkable capacity to advance from local and class issues to leadership in a broad national movement but confronts the contradiction between popular demands and economic and other constraints that will be discussed in Chapter 9.

Trade unions and the state in Chile

Chilean society by the 1970s was predominantly urban, and the proportion of wage earners in the economically active population was higher than in any other Latin American country apart from Argentina and Uruguay. The country had a long experience of militant trade union organization among mining, industrial and transport workers, and to a lesser extent among public employees. Trade unions were linked to competing Marxist and other political parties rather than subordinated to authoritarian-populist régimes, but generally maintained organizational unity in spite of party rivalries. Unions were accustomed to intervene in national policy formulation and legislation with some effectiveness. During the 1960s groups hitherto excluded, particularly rural workers and the urban 'informal sector' began to organize and respond to similar political appeals. The electoral victory of the 'Popular Unity' coalition in 1970 opened the way to more varied participation, including worker management of industries and farms, and seemed to make the 'transition to socialism' promised by the government an immediate possibility. Contradictions appeared between the expected unity of workers in support of this transition and their real predisposition to grasp at perceived immediate advantages, particularly after the régime encountered severe economic difficulties, but the organized workers enjoyed a large measure of 'control over resources and regulative institutions'.

The violent seizure of power by a military régime in 1973 suddenly reversed previous trends, with a shock to popular consciousness undoubtedly greater than in other settings in which working-class organization and political democracy had shallower roots. The new régime outlawed the aspiration to socialism along with all party-political activity, sharply depressed workers' levels of living through price increases, wage freezes and curtailment of job security, and left the trade union movement with a merely formal existence. Unions were cut off from previous party-ideological orientation and deprived of rights to collective bargaining, strikes, representation of workers' interests *vis-à-vis* the state, and internal union democracy.

In 1978, after some vacillations of government policy and a limited revival of union activities, the régime promulgated a 'Plan Laboral' that restored rights to internal union election of officers, collective bargaining at the level of individual enterprises, and strikes. It imposed conditions on these rights, however, that ensured that unions would remain fragmented, barred from contact with political forces, and able to represent their members solely through bargaining with individual employers over wages. The Plan was partly a response to threats by unions in the industrialized countries to boycott Chilean exports, but was consistent with the neoliberal doctrines of the régime's economic advisers.

The research sponsored by UNRISD in Chile was designed to assess the tactics actually adopted by unions and the alternatives open to them under an authoritarian régime and within the rules of the game prescribed by the 'Plan Laboral'.[4] The research was initiated during a period when both the economic setting and the Plan seemed to be responding as expected by the government and continued into a period of deepening crisis. It made use of systematic discussions with people active in the labour movement and tried to ensure that the findings would be accessible and useful to them. For this purpose the researchers prepared a summary version of their report for circulation within the unions. They also opened one of the Participation Programme's regional sub-debates in which social scientists concerned with problems of trade unions and authoritarianism in Argentina and Brazil as well as Chile took part.[5]

The most obvious conclusion to emerge was that the 'Plan Laboral' did accomplish its purposes within the repressive national political framework as long as the economic policy was associated with growth, no matter how inequitably distributed the fruits of growth might be. The unions found no alternative to working within the very narrow margins afforded by the Plan. Strikes generally taught the lesson intended by the authors of the Plan that workers could gain nothing from them. The minority of militant union members could do no more than maintain a minimum of solidarity and class-consciousness among the workers in the face of the extreme individualism, consumerism, and competition for jobs deliberately fostered by the economic policy. However, the maintenance of organizational continuity took on new importance once economic and political crises discredited the régime.

The unions gained greater autonomy from the ideological guidance of the (outlawed) political parties, and this might have lasting consequences. Most of the unions were able to work together in the limited space open to them for discussion of tactics and for protests against government policies. They were able to take advantage of support from the international trade union federations. These were sometimes indispensable in hindering the intensification of repression and in helping exiles, and were probably major sources of funds. At the same time, the Chilean unions managed not to succumb to the divisive tactics of their international interlocutors, committed as these were to different contenders in the international power struggle.

Up to 1981 the new rules of the game functioned within a context of economic growth and government self-confidence. Then economic crisis struck, marked by bankruptcy of many enterprises, a drastic slump in production and unemployment of more than 30 per cent of the labour force. This shock left the unions even less able than before to bargain effectively with employers or to influence the government on their members' behalf. The government did mitigate the impact of the crisis on the poor by expanding public works employment at subsistence wages; at its peak in 1983 such employment absorbed 13 per cent of the labour force. The unions had no voice in the extent or terms of such programmes and resented them as tactics to depress wage levels and replace previously sacked public sector workers.[6]

At the same time, the crisis opened up possibilities lacking since 1973 for mass mobilization and pressure for major political changes. The unions' preservation of Chile's long tradition of working-class organization enabled them to take the lead in this, in conjunction with the reviving political parties and informal associations of the urban poor. During 1982 and 1983 demonstrations of hundreds of thousands of people were organized but later declined without having brought about a change of régime. The economy recovered, largely through improved export markets, unemployment fell, and the political parties regained their leading role in negotiating an end to dictatorship.

Since the electoral victory of a broad democratic coalition at the end of 1989, the unions face a situation in which authoritarian domination and manipulation have disappeared, but in which, as in other parts of Latin America, the traditional industrial bases of the labour movement have declined in relative importance, unorganized sectors of wage labour, particularly in commercial agriculture, have grown, and large numbers of workers have been forced out of wage labour into heterogeneous survival strategies. Union efforts to advance long-repressed worker demands for recovery of previous income levels clash with the requirements of an export-oriented economy. The socialist utopia that inspired previous working-class mobilizations has lost plausibility, and has practically disappeared from the programmes even of the parties that call themselves socialist. The state is in no position to reverse the processes of 'privatization' that have shrunk the public sector and limited government capacity to respond to worker demands for subsidies and services. Such constraints loom before unions and other popular movements in a good many countries today, but the Chilean historical trajectory makes it particularly acute, and it is far from clear how the 'collective memory' of the union militants will interact with a democracy of diminished expectations.

Workers in the bauxite industry of Guyana

In Guyana, since the achievement of independence in 1966, political competition has followed ethnic lines, with groups of African and of Asian-Indian descent concentrated in different occupations and supporting two rival major parties. The party relying on the former ethnic group has held a practical monopoly of political power and has pursued, rather erratically and with economically disastrous results, policies of national self-sufficiency and state socialism.

The study undertaken in Guyana deals with a setting fairly common in the Third World and quite different from that of industrial workers in large cities: that of an extractive industry in which wage workers are concentrated in partial isolation from the rest of the society, confronting a single employer, private or public, who is responsible for meeting many of their basic needs outside the work relationship and even for maintaining public order. Such settings are conducive to strong union organization, generally achieved after protracted struggles against paternalism and repression. The industries are generally important to the state as sources of foreign exchange, giving their organized workers considerable bargaining power but also exposing them to state intervention. They are also particularly vulnerable to shifts in external markets and prices, which may produce sudden prosperity or wipe out their livelihood and organizations altogether.

The study in question, of workers of the Demerara Bauxite Company, was carried out by a Guyanese social scientist, himself formerly a welder in the bauxite industry.[7] The company, which was nationalized in 1971, was at the time of the study the sole employer of several thousand workers living in a demographically stable, ethnically homogeneous, relatively isolated community. The workers had been unionized since the 1940s.

The government, the company, the union and the workers were involved in complex struggles and misunderstandings before and after nationalization. The government was understandably concerned to avoid interruptions to production, since bauxite accounted for about 40 per cent of Guyana's export earnings. It was also concerned to safeguard its traditional support from the bauxite workers in Guyana's ethnically divided politics.

The company management was anxious to dissociate itself from the dictatorial tactics of the previous foreign ownership and encourage limited forms of worker participation, but could not escape from paternalism and preoccupation with productivity.

The union leadership had become bureaucratized, sluggish in dealing with worker grievances, and determined to cling to office.

The workers, while the highest paid in Guyana, were diffusely dissatisfied with working and living conditions, with the management, and with the union. This led to continual struggles against the union leadership, first through an ethnic nationalist movement, then through a dissident union grouping, and finally through an opposition political party. Since the government interpreted these struggles as threats to its own dominance, it protected the union leadership and repressed dissidence. The workers, unable to bring about changes in management or union leadership in spite of participatory rhetoric from these quarters, reacted by frequent wildcat strikes, non-co-operation and petty sabotage. Productivity remained low.

The study emphasizes the consequences of mutual misunderstandings and distrust in a situation in which the basic interests and intentions of all parties should have been compatible. Despite continual discussions of means to improve labour-management relations, 'the workers remain uncertain about the company's, the union's, and government's real motives and plans for workers' participation in decision-making. The result is predictable. In their efforts to strike a "balance" between the apparent linguistic confusions, the workers must constantly wade their way through a stream of rumours, half-truths, misinformation and simple ignorance.' The researcher concludes that promises of more participation within anti-participatory structures will not help, and that a solution depends on 'the democratization rather than the bureaucratization of the decision-making process' for development policy as a whole, so that the competing forces can gain the ability 'realistically [to] appreciate the limitations and possibilities of power-sharing'.

After the period of the study, in the early 1980s, the bauxite workers' union did achieve independence of the ruling party, and joined the Indian sugar workers' unions in strikes protesting against shortages of basic foodstuffs. However, these broader organized efforts have faced a context of deepening economic crisis, failure of nationalization policies, and persisting tactics of repression.

Trade unions and popular movements in Peru

In Peru, one of the studies sponsored by UNRISD dealt with workers' organizations in conjunction with a wide range of social and popular movements as they evolved during the 1970s and early 1980s.[8] Chapter 6, which discusses questions of institutionalization, deals with other dimensions of this study. Here ideologists and activists had looked to the urban 'proletariat' as a revolutionary vanguard or spearhead of an emerging 'national popular movement' since the 1920s, but wage workers in organizable enterprises, including plantations and mines as well as urban industries, were a relatively small part of the labour force. Trade unions emerged in a context of struggles for control between political factions and alternating toleration, co-option and repression from governments.

The Velasco régime (1968-75) tolerated trade union organization, and unions grew rapidly during this period, but it did not incorporate the unions into its schemes for institutionalized participation, for reasons indicated in Chapter 6. Most unions remained under the control of opposition political forces, and by the mid-1970s relations between unions and government were highly conflictive. As the economic situation worsened, the unions engaged in vigorous but ineffective efforts to protect job security and wage levels. They were able to mobilize broad support outside their ranks in several national general strikes, but these were followed by dismissals and blacklisting of activists. Employment in modern enterprises continued to decline, and so did real wages.

Throughout the period, efforts to unify the labour movement persisted and succeeded to some extent in mass mobilizations and general strikes, but efforts by political parties (APRA, the Peruvian Communist Party, various other Marxist factions) to maintain their control over specific unions and federations also persisted, and this involved an 'enormous confusion' between the attributes of unions and parties and a sort of 'feudalization' of the unions, with competing parallel unions in many branches of industry. According to the researchers:

> party struggles led to an overpoliticization of union leaders, taking them beyond the concrete situation and practice at the grass roots level and giving rise to a radical *'ideologismo'* and *'finalismo'* which bore little relation to reality. As an immediate consequence, trade union leaders became distanced from their social bases. The latter became marginalized from the discussion, since for them it lacked real meaning and content. ... These limitations were particularly serious in a situation where the trade union movement's actions revolved primarily around workers' immediate grievances. ... The discourse of the 'classist' union leaders did not attract the support of wider groups among the popular classes. And it was only with great difficulty that they were able to obtain grass roots support for the struggles of other social groups. This explains the enormous importance of the national stoppages and the tremendous difficulties the Peruvian working class experienced in becoming a force which could give some direction to society. Trade union practice at this time was clearly influenced by the reduction in class struggle to a struggle at the level of production, assigning 'interests' to different classes and overlooking the enormous variety of social relations in Peruvian society. ... Political parties, because of their own prevailing conceptions, idealized the role of the proletariat as a member of a 'vanguard class' and thus attempted to organize it so that the party could fulfil its own historical role. In the short term, the parties on the left managed to direct the radical activities of the unions under their control against the government. The workers for their part accepted the left's perspective and its approach to labour relations, because it seemed an effective approach in the context of a military dictatorship, in which trade union gains depended more on pressure and direct mobilization than on negotiation.

During the 1970s and early 1980s, the numbers of public employees, schoolteachers and university-educated youth seeking white-collar employment increased considerably as a result of the expansion of state responsibilities and of education. The numbers of private employees in commerce and banking also grew. These trends partially offset declines in the working-class base of the labour movement. The white-collar groups were subsequently as much affected by falling real incomes and blockage of further job opportunities as were the manual workers, and joined in their protests. Teachers, in particular, engaged in some of the hardest-fought strikes, which took on national dimensions and were particularly effective in mobilizing wide support from their communities. Strikes of bank employees and public employees in general were also recurrent. Thus, groups that the Marxist left had classified as 'petty bourgeois' figured increasingly in union militancy, as in most parts of Latin America.

By 1983 there were in Peru only one million fully employed wage workers, out of an economically active population slightly over 6 million, of whom 500,000 were wholly unemployed, 3 million under-employed, and 1.5 million self-employed. Of the fully employed wage workers, more than 200,000 worked in 'informal sector' enterprises that paid less than the legal minimum wage and disregarded all labour regulations. More than 400,000, working in small factories, in commerce and in services, belonged to unions with no capacity for collective bargaining. Fewer than 400,000 belonged to unions with some capacity for such bargaining, and only about half of these worked in the large modern enterprises where such bargaining was most likely to be effective. Employment in the modern sector was continuing to decline.

By this time, under a democratic political régime but in a context of free market policies, unmanageable external debt and declining production, neither pressure on the government nor collective bargaining with employers could produce results, and the unions found that the preceding history had left them impotent:

> 'Classism' in this context revealed itself more as a principle of sectarian radicalism than as one of class solidarity. As the crisis developed the workers began to realize that the relative security they had achieved as wage earners during the 1970s was drawing to an end. ... Industry no longer provided a means for the integration of migrants into the city. And as unions were no longer able to help fulfil people's basic needs, the unions gradually lost their previous identity, which to some had appeared to be already consolidated.

*

These summaries of four research findings do not by any means cover the range of working-class organizational experiences in Latin America, let alone those in other regions of the Third World. The huge industrial unions of Argentina and Mexico, for example, with their complex involvement in populist régimes, and the combative tin miners of Bolivia, have followed quite different paths. The summaries do, however, suggest certain common problems in the wage workers' quest for control of their own organizations and for choice among the different potential roles of these organizations.

The unions must try to advance the interests of their own members through bargaining with employers and through pressures on the state for favourable legislation, social services and subsidies, and employment-promoting public investment policies. They must try to 'organize the unorganized' wage workers and white-collar employees.

However, their efforts in these directions clash, more than might have been expected during the more optimistic years of economic development, with the stagnation or instability of national economies and labour markets, continually weakening the traditional strongholds of unionism and throwing up new categories of unorganized. They also clash with currents of disillusionment and resentment toward the 'welfare state' that have gained influence in all classes, and with a conviction on the part of most governments that the laws of the world economic system and the sources of their political support restrict them to a narrow range of 'adjustment' policy options, ruling out significant income redistribution toward wage workers and significant expansion of the social services of most interest to these workers. Moreover, if the unions concentrate on the immediate interests of their own members, they are accused of hampering economic recovery and harming the poor for the benefit of a not-so-poor minority.

Therefore, the union movements cannot avoid trying to take a leading role in multi-class coalitions aiming at a redistribution of political power and thus of the policy options accessible to governments. The examples of Brazil, Chile and Peru show that they can, in specific conjunctures, assume this role effectively and even heroically, but only for short periods and thus far without accomplishing many of the objectives of the mobilizations. Then political parties recover the role of protagonist, with their own potentialities and dangers. In Brazil, the new union movement generated its own political party, which achieved national importance but only local electoral success. In Chile, the pre-existing parties of the left reappeared, but more pragmatic and disposed to compromise than previously, thus no longer disposed to fight for working-class hegemony. In Peru, the sectarianism of the political parties left the unions split and exhausted, without immediate hope of recovery.

In all these cases, the myth of the vanguard proletariat and the objective of socialism have had ambivalent consequences, strengthening working-class confidence in its own future but committing it to unrealistic tactics and ends unintelligible to most workers. One consequence of the worldwide loss of credibility of socialism, to be discussed in more detail in Chapter 9, has been to leave the working-class movement bereft of an inspiring utopia. While peasant movements have suffered from judgements going back to Marx, dismissing their organizational capacity and looking to the disappearance of their way of life, workers' movements have probably suffered from over-estimation of their potential, making them the favoured target of non-proletarian ideologists determined to control this potential.

Notes

1. In Argentina, probably the most industrialized country in Latin America, the percentage of industrial workers among wage earners fell from 25 in 1950 to 11 in the 1980s. In Greater Buenos Aires the percentage of self-employed in the labour force rose from 18 in 1976 to 24 in 1982 . See Palomino, Hector, 'El Movimiento de Democratización Síndical', in Jelin, Elizabeth, ed., *Los Nuevos Movimientos Sociales*, vol. 2, Centro Editor de América Latina, Buenos Aires, 1985.

2. Most of the findings of the researches on which this summary is based have been published in Kowarick, Lúcio, ed., *As Lutas Sociais e a Cidade: São Paulo, Passado e Presente*, Paz e Terra, São Paulo, 1988. An English version of this volume has been published as: *Social Struggles and the City: The Case of São Paulo*, Monthly Review Press, New York, 1993.

3. In Greater Buenos Aires, a metropolitan area with industrial growth previously comparable to that of São Paulo, the patterns of working-class settlement through sub-divisions and land purchases have been somewhat similar, and there have been long traditions of neighbourhood organization as well as strong trade union organization. However, mutually supportive links between the two kinds of organized effort seem to have been slight up to parallel mass mobilizations in the last stages of the military régime around 1982. See Garcia Delgado, D.R. and Silva, Juan, 'El Movimiento Vecinal y la Democracia', in Jelin, Elizabeth, op. cit. in n. 1.

4. The findings have been published in Barrera, Manuel; Henriquez, Helia; Selamé, Teresita, *Trade Unions and the State in Present Day Chile: Collective Bargaining as an Instrument of Popular Participation*, UNRISD and CES, Geneva and Santiago, 1986.

5. See Barrera, Manuel and Falabella, Gonzalo, eds., *Sindicatos bajo Regímenes Militares: Argentina, Brazil, Chile*, UNRISD and CES, Geneva and Santiago, 1990.

6. The World Bank, *World Development Report 1990, Poverty*, Oxford University Press, New York, 1990, p. 119.

7. Quamina, Odida, *Mineworkers of Guyana: The Making of a Working Class*, Zed Books, London, 1987.

8. Ballón, Eduardo and Tovar, Teresa, *The Development of Popular Movements in Peru, 1968-1982*, unpublished manuscript, UNRISD, Geneva, 1985. Quotations on the following pages are drawn from pp. 185-8 of this manuscript.

5

Social Movements of the Urban Poor

It is well known that the rapid urbanization of Third World countries and the emergence of agglomerations of unprecedented size have brought new patterns of 'exclusion' and hence new kinds of 'organized efforts' to overcome them. The phenomena associated with urbanization have been varied and contradictory, and since the 1950s demographic and sociological research findings, polemics and policy prescriptions have generated and then demolished successive stereotypes. Controversies have continued over distinctions between the urban working class or 'proletariat' and the urban poor, conceptualized or labelled as 'marginals', 'sub-proletarians, '*pobladores*', etc. As information has accumulated and the urban settings themselves have continued to change and expand, generalizations have become no easier.

The key issue around which 'organized efforts' outside the work setting have taken place has been shelter. As the urban agglomerations have expanded without effective planning or land-use controls, the predominant trend in low-income housing has been from centrally-located slums to peripheral squatter settlements and from rented tenement quarters to self-built dwellings. The natural focal points for organization and co-operation have been the securing and defence of land for settlement; mutual aid in house-building; and combinations of organized self-help and negotiations with the authorities in obtaining water, electricity, sewerage, paved streets, public transportation, markets, schools, health services and police protection.

In cities in which wage-earners in industries and related occupations have predominated, as in Buenos Aires and São Paulo, peripheral settlement has taken place mainly through the unregulated sale of building lots by speculators, as we saw in Chapter 4. Here the initial issue stimulating organization is likely to be defence against fraud in the sale of land and pressure on the seller to meet promises or legal obligations to pave the streets, lay on mains water and provide other services.

In other cities, as in Lima, organized or unorganized occupation of vacant land has predominated. Here the initial issues are the planning and execution of the occupation, followed by self-defence against eviction and pressure on the authorities to grant secure tenure. Tactics have been worked out over several decades of successful and unsuccessful land occupations, and in some cities specialized organizers acting for personal advantage have become important.

In both types of settlement, organizational participation is likely to decline once tenure is secure, but the struggle to obtain infrastructural improvements is a long-term source of cohesion. Later, during periods of economic downturn and depressed labour markets, neighbourhood co-operation in setting up workshops, pooling of resources and external aid for soup kitchens, and co-operatives for food-buying may come to the fore.

While organized wage workers are likely to predominate in the first type of settlement and 'informal' or self-employed groups in the second, there can be no consistent dividing line. Where housing is scarce and land prices high, where publicly-owned waste land can be occupied at only moderate risk of eviction, or where wage levels have been depressed, the majority of workers may live in settlements that originated in land occupations. In cities in which the first type of low-income settlement predominates, the second is usually also present (*villas miseria* in Buenos Aires, *favelas* in São Paulo) but has been more identified with extreme poverty and groups exposed to ethnic or other discrimination.

The popular associations that derive from the problems of shelter and community services thus overlap in membership with the trade unions to varying degrees in different settlements and cities. They are naturally much more localized, responding to specific problems and the characteristics of the leadership that happens to emerge in each neighbourhood. Neighbourhood associations are not limited to settlements of the poor, and conflicts between neighbourhoods over allocation of public services and other questions are common.

According to most researchers, except in times of land occupation or defence against eviction, only minorities participate actively. Since men spend more of their time working outside the neighbourhoods – and frequently in long and exhausting journeys to and from work – women are prominent among these minorities.

There have been a good many initiatives toward the formation of citywide and nationwide federations of urban neighbourhood associations, some coming from the associations themselves, some from the state, from political parties, or from non-governmental organizations, but these seem generally to have been shortlived and ineffective in co-ordinating the struggles of their affiliates.

When neighbourhood associations have brought themselves to the attention of the authorities – as sources of pressure for allocation of public resources, sources of political support or opposition, and of local 'development' through aided self-help – the authorities have commonly tried to 'institutionalize' them through procedures for legal recognition, rules for election of officers and other aspects of their functioning, and formal ties with municipal authorities and national agencies responsible for public order, urban planning, and so on.

In countries such as Brazil and Chile, urban neighbourhood associations have been able to survive and provide some services to their members during periods when trade unions and political parties have been silenced. However, they are subject to permanent insecurity from the changing attitudes of successive régimes (promotion, manipulation, repression, neglect) and to frustrations from dealing with a multiplicity of bureaucracies as sources of inhibiting regulations or of aid with strings attached.

Neighbourhood groupings, in their efforts to obtain a hearing from the authorities, may resort to political clientelism, vote-bargaining, mass demonstrations or 'representative violence' (street barricades, occupation of public buildings, burning of buses, looting of shops) depending on their judgement of effectiveness in a given political conjuncture, their own level of mobilization, and the violence of the price rises or other threats to livelihood to which they are reacting.

They encounter promises of aid and efforts at control by Marxist, populist and religiously-inspired political movements, but seem to respond more to the likely effectiveness of such interlocutors than to their ideological appeals. In a good many instances they deliberately try to keep their distance from political parties, because of risks of factional division within their own ranks, or the danger of being identified with a defeated party, or general distrust of national politics and disillusionment with past experience of politicians' promises. They cannot do without allies, but non-political voluntary organizations often seem to be the most acceptable.

The visibility of the peripheral settlements, their rapid increases in size and numbers, and the supposed revolutionary potential of their poverty have made many of them targets for an excessive number of would-be guides and helpers, as well as researchers, some trying to improve their lot within the existing economic and social order, others trying to mobilize them to overthrow it, still others trying to help them to renounce their economic and psychological dependence on it. A study of such efforts in Lima, where they have proliferated more and over a longer period than in most other cities, was entitled ironically, *De Invasores a Invadidos* (from 'invaders' [of land for settlement] to 'invaded' [by researchers and advisers]).[1]

In recent times, with obviously wide variations in different cities and countries, urban population growth has continued to outrun the supply of new housing and infrastructure, while commercial and industrial expansion have continued to invade the older low-income residential areas. The feasibility of creating additional settlements has become narrower, both for lack of accessible land and because of more effective controls by the authorities. Overcrowding has naturally increased within the existing settlements and in a good many cities a drifting homeless population is becoming more numerous and visible. At the same time, previous sources of livelihood have become more precarious, and previous aid from the state (subsidized food prices, provision of water, electrical power, schools and clinics) has contracted, whether through deliberate policies of promoting market prices and privatization of services or through the state's shrinking ability to raise funds. While the previous focuses of neighbourhood organization on shelter and services have remained important, new focuses on livelihood and mutual aid for survival have come to the fore.

Informal economies, present in the low-income settlements since their beginning, have expanded and diversified during periods of economic growth as well as stagnation. The former make the informal activities more profitable, the latter make them more inescapable as survival strategies. Much of the activity really consists of highly competitive petty capitalism, surviving through sub-subsistence wages and evasion of all regulations. It is partially integrated with and exploited by the 'formal sector' of the economies, including transnational enterprises, through home piece-work, sub-contracting of industrial inputs and distribution through street vendors of goods mass-produced in 'formal' industries. At the same time, and partly through the efforts of such allies as the base community movement, part of the informal sector takes the shape of small producers' co-operatives, vendors' associations, etc., sometimes composed of unemployed former wage workers, or workers excluded from industrial employment because of past union or political militancy. 'Organized efforts' in the informal sector can be expected to have contradictory objectives in their encounters with the authorities: first, to evade, resist or repeal bureaucratic regulations that hinder production and marketing; secondly, to obtain technical aid, credits, and subsidies from state agencies or NGOs. While the earlier neighbourhood associations, focusing more on shelter and services, have been extensively studied, information on the 'organizations for economic survival', as Chilean researchers have labelled them, is only just beginning to appear. Some of their allies and supporters look on them as seeds of a new economic order, and they coincide with widespread cultural preferences for self-employment over wage labour. It is probable, however, that most of the participants enter into them as survival strategies that would be abandoned if better opportunities should open up. In a good many urban settings, intensified poverty, the curtailment of public social services, traditions of neighbourhood co-operation, and the availability of some external aid have combined to stimulate the emergence of a wide range of efforts for 'social survival', co-operative buying of foods, child-care centres, soup kitchens and mothers' groups distributing milk and other supplies received from NGOs or the state. As in the case of the organizations for economic survival, judgement of the potential of these activities depends on the values and hopes of the observer.

The position of young people in the low-income neighbourhoods or urban peripheral settlements is particularly problematic, and previous forms of organized action have only limited relevance to their needs. Their access to wage employment is even more restricted than that of their elders, so that few of them can belong to trade unions. Existing political parties, even the most radical, are in a poor position to offer them either inspiring utopias or attractive careers. In a few settings, the explosive growth of free public university enrolment offered minorities among them a hope of upward mobility as well as socialization through student movements, but this outlet is now being blocked by cuts in university budgets and the lack of white-collar job opportunities. The possibility of combining the formation of a new family with occupation of land for a new home is smaller than before, so that most of the youth must continue to live with their parents or on the street.

Association through sports or rock music, the formation of sub-cultures influenced by the mass media, various forms of delinquency and drug addiction seem widespread phenomena but their relative importance is not clear. Authoritarian governments have generally treated young people as a potential menace; and in some settings of mobilization against such régimes, particularly in Chile, young people from low-income settlements have been the most combative and persistent protestors, with no visible organization nor direction from political movements. In general, the past trajectory of 'organized efforts' in urban settings, and what is known of the present circumstances of young people, give hardly any basis for assessing the kinds of 'organized efforts' that will be accessible and relevant to them in the future.

A few of the researches sponsored by the UNRISD Programme, and some others influenced by it or addressing similar concerns, can be drawn upon to suggest the range of interactions of urban neighbourhood movements with the authorities and with various allies and inter-locutors in specific settings. This discussion unavoidably overlaps with the last chapter on urban workers' movements and later chapters on institutionalization, social movements and interlocutors.

Neighbourhood associations in Greater Buenos Aires[2]

In Greater Buenos Aires, for the first half of the twentieth century the largest and most prosperous metropolitan area in Latin America, urban expansion proceeded mainly through land subdivision and purchases by middle- and working-class families. From an early stage, *sociedades de fomento* (promotional societies) were organized in the new settlements, mainly to negotiate with municipal authorities over services. Traditional *fomentismo* operated as 'an interest group that based its action on the use of institutionalized channels, on contacts with the public administration and on a technical knowledge of urban questions acquired in long years of negotiation with the authorities'.

Fomentismo avoided political activism and ties with parties or trade unions, although many of its members belonged to one or the other. It coexisted in the neighbourhoods with many other local associations: of housewives, pensioners, shopkeepers, sports clubs, popular libraries, etc. Its relations with successive régimes varied from co-option to strict regulation in order to keep it localized and non-political. In general, as neighbourhoods became consolidated and problems of services lost urgency, active participation in the societies declined. In some of the poorest neighbourhoods, including squatter settlements, less formalized but more combative and participatory movements appeared, but they could exert less influence on the municipal authorities. These movements, unlike the *sociedades de fomento*, were usually aided by the Catholic Church at parish level.

Beginning in 1976, the neighbourhood associations underwent a series of shocks that transformed their predominant orientation. First, the 'deindustrialization' policy of the new military régime brought about a rapid rise in unemployment and insecurity. Secondly, the régime privatized a wide range of public services, or decentralized them to the municipalities without giving the latter resources to meet their new responsibilities. Thirdly, the régime suspended activities of political parties, trade unions, and other popular organizations, leaving the neighbourhood associations almost the only channels for open collective activity. Fourthly, the elimination of rent controls and a drive to eradicate the squatter settlements that housed more than 200,000 people in Buenos Aires city sent a flood of low-income families seeking shelter into the peripheral municipalities.

Altogether, the sudden loss of employment prospects and services that had been taken for granted 'modified the values and beliefs of the urban culture', eroding faith in the future. Reactions differed according to social strata: 'Among the very pauperized it promoted social disintegration and apathy. In the newly marginalized, on the contrary, it multiplied their efforts to change their situation through collective action; the declining middle-classes were also included in this latter attitude.'

Neighbourhood associations began to undertake many kinds of self-help activities, including co-operatives, and to struggle against the land speculation that had been unleashed. Penetration and control of the associations became more important to the parties and trade unions, looking for ways of maintaining their presence in the societies, and to the municipal authorities, looking for ways to meet the responsibilities placed on them by decentralization of services and withdrawal of federal government financing.

The increasingly varied activities of the neighbourhood associations and their rethinking of the traditional non-political non-confrontational approaches came to a head in 1982, in the last stages of the military régime, when the municipal authorities of Buenos Aires province announced major increases in already heavy property taxes, in a setting of deepening economic depression and defeat in the war over the Malvinas. Mass demonstrations, organized by the *sociedades de fomento* along with the more specialized neighbourhood groupings, occupied the main plazas of the municipalities. After attempts at repression failed, the provincial authorities had to resign and the new taxes were not enforced. At this point the reviving political parties became even more determined to control the neighbourhood associations, partly out of concern for their own representativeness, partly out of fear that the mass expression of protest, after a long period in which normal institutional channels had been blocked, might reach a level of confrontation that would endanger their tactics of negotiating a transition from military rule while recovering their previous hegemony in the political system.

The poorest neighbourhoods and squatter settlements did not take part in the mobilization over taxes, but the success of this struggle opened the way to new mobilizations for land, particularly among the groups expelled from the *villas miseria* of the central city. In one such effort, an organized land occupation involving about 20,000 people succeeded, after resisting attempts at eviction between 1981 and 1984, in achieving state expropriation of the land and distribution to settlers on favourable terms. Church groups, unions, professionals, human rights activists and political parties helped in the struggle. The settlers' Co-ordinating Commission and advisers were determined to achieve a habitable settlement with modern infrastructure and secure tenure instead of reproducing the squalor and insecurity of the *villas miseria*. The leaders also evolved generally effective although precarious tactics to obtain maximum support from the political parties while avoiding co-option or factionalism among themselves. The struggle of San Francisco Solano thus resembled the more successful organized efforts of squatters in Latin American urban agglomerations in which this type of settlement has predominated, such as Villa El Salvador in Lima.

The reports summarized above end with the relatively optimistic period of redemocratization of the early 1980s. Since then, it is well-known that very high rates of inflation and deteriorating levels of popular consumption have continued, with the democratic régime unable to restore the social services eliminated in 1976. It is not clear to what extent organized efforts aiming at neighbourhood self-help and co-operation have been able to cope with these conditions. Meanwhile, desperate unorganized protests involving the looting of food markets have intermittently come to the fore as in other urban settings of Latin America.

Favela organization in Brazil

Neighbourhood associations in working-class districts of owner-occupied housing in São Paulo were discussed above in relation to the revival of a militant trade union movement at the end of the 1970s. Squatter settlements (*favelas*) were of minor importance in São Paulo until very recent years, when declining real wages, unemployment and rising suburban land prices began to force a higher proportion of low-income families to adopt this form of struggle for shelter. *Favelas* have been important in most other large Brazilian cities since the early stages of urbanization, however, and they have been intensively studied. The researches sponsored by UNRISD included comparative investigations of *favela* growth and organization in the cities of Rio de Janeiro, Brasilia, Curitiba and Fortaleza.[3]

These studies describe a transition from slow and unorganized infiltration of vacant land by squatters to organized land seizures, with increasingly complex relationships between the squatters and the external forces trying to help or manipulate them, including political parties, religious movements, municipal authorities and the press. In these cases, relations with unions were secondary or lacking, since most of the settlers have been in unorganized occupations. Under the populist régimes up to 1964, the *favela* dwellers exerted appreciable influence as sources of votes and participants in mass demonstrations. Under the military régimes, on the contrary, forced eradications became common, and efforts at organized self-defence were harshly repressed. In the early 1980s, redemocratization opened up wider spaces for organized action and for seeking allies, and the settlers have responded to these. As elsewhere, however, economic crises and inflation have intensified the poverty of *favela* populations and reduced the likelihood of significant responses from the state to demands for services and subsidies.

Organizations for economic survival and mass mobilizations in Chile[4]

In the cities of Chile, settlements originating in clandestine land subdivisions, in unorganized occupations of waste land, and in large-scale organized land occupations have all been important in the struggle for shelter. From the late 1960s to 1973, land occupations took place in a setting of competitive mobilizations stimulated by political parties, religious and other allies, and even by some public agencies. With the coming to power of a military régime conditions changed as abruptly as in Argentina and Brazil. Previous settlement associations were repressed and settlements deriving from recent land occupations were eradicated.

Later, between 1979 and 1983, the Ministry of Housing embarked on a systematic policy of eliminating shantytowns from the more prosperous municipalities of Greater Santiago and relocating their residents in municipalities that were already more densely populated, with less adequate revenues, and thus with less capacity to support public services: a 'territorial relocalization of poverty'. About 172,000 persons were relocated in this way.

In 1982, people living in low-income settlements, mainly of self-built housing, known as *poblaciones*, were estimated to number 1.2-1.3 million out of a total population of 3.7 million in Santiago province; in 11 out of 32 municipalities they constituted a majority. The heterogeneity of the settlement population as well as its segregation from the better-off zones of the metropolis were increased by the forced resettlement, which disintegrated previous community ties. Under these conditions, the renewal of localized 'organized efforts' assumed two dimensions: a 'defensive communitarianism' and a striving by the *pobladores* to 'relink themselves to a process of global social cohesion', i.e. to assert their right to belong to the Chilean nation.

The communitarian dimension was strengthened by the ideology of the only allies able to act openly, the religious movements. In a very difficult situation, with previous expectations of 'increasing control over resources and regulative institutions' suddenly shattered, new local groupings became important not only in providing services but also in creating 'a certain institutionality to compensate for social disintegration'.

In the earlier years of the military régime, organizational activities had a short-term outlook, on the supposition that the régime would be transitory. A central purpose was to help in the economic survival of experienced working-class leadership that had been expelled from employment, and this naturally involved only small minorities among the *pobladores*. By 1980 it was more generally recognized that changes in the economic structure had permanently weakened unionism. Organizations for economic survival acquired longer-term perspectives and became more necessary with the economic slump of 1982 and the beginning of mass protests. At that point, the presence of leaders with pre-1973 organizational experience and strongly-held convictions became better able to make itself felt.

Strong leadership was needed to compensate for a realistic perception of weakness among the *pobladores*: they preferred to follow the lead of forces with more potential organizational strength and national influence: Church, unions, students, political parties. Interviews did not reveal any perception of autonomous power as *pobladores* or any disposition to think of their organizations as 'anticipatory microsocieties', as their communitarian allies might have hoped. The ideal of trade union vanguard action remained influential, but the younger *pobladores* had hardly any contact with real unions.

The thinking of the mass of *pobladores* and of their strictly local leadership, on the one hand, and that of the leadership in intermediate-level organizations linking the local groups, on the other, differed considerably. The former were more defensive and survival-oriented, concerned about the dangerous consequences of radicalized mass action. Two ideological models could be distinguished: 'revolutionary populism' and 'promotional or integrative populism'. The two ideologies competed for influence but also mingled in real tactics. The fact that the leadership responded to two logics, from bases and from the political parties, made for vacillation between giving priority to a general strategy and giving priority to 'social work' activities.

In practice, during 1983 and 1984 the *pobladores* became the most combative element in a broad mobilization including large parts of the middle and working classes, but they gradually became isolated and more vulnerable to repression as militancy in the other classes declined, probably in part because of uneasiness at the implications of violent mass action from the lower depths. The metropolitan and intermediate leadership of the *pobladores* went from a phase of ideologically-based over-confidence to one of rethinking and recognition of the limitations on their representativeness.

While the study cautions against over-estimation of the level of political consciousness among the *pobladores*, it also emphasizes the importance of continuity in ideas of social justice legitimizing their struggles, influential among them since the 1960s, and also the importance of support movements as sources of tactical advice and continuity throughout cycles of organizational rise and disintegration. Various of these support movements first looked to the trade unions, then decided that the *pobladores*, through the extremity of their exclusion and their possibilities of struggle against this exclusion, deserved priority. The discussion below of 'interlocutors', will return to the question of the influence of such support movements on categories of the urban poor that have many unsatisfied needs but lack a central issue on which to focus their organized efforts.

From *barriadas* to *pueblos jovenes* and beyond in Peru

Urban social movements in Peru are discussed below in relation to the unique pattern of 'institutionalization' in 1968-75 and the later hopes of aggregating local 'social movements' into a 'national popular movement'. For present purposes, it deserves emphasis that urban neighbourhood organizations, most of them originating in organized land occupations, have had a particularly long and varied history in Peru. They have had complex and shifting relationships with successive governments, without ever encountering the degree of repression characteristic of the military régimes in Argentina, Brazil and Chile. Tactical experience gained through encounters with the authorities is extensive. The settlements have dealt with many kinds of would-be allies and mobilizers, and have been subject to continual sociological and journalistic investigations. A few settlements, most recently Villa El Salvador, have become internationally famous for their organizational achievements. The efforts of external interlocutors to define the central problems and prospects of the settlement population have probably been even more vigorous and varied than in Chile. At the same time, the settlement population has had to cope with a particularly deep and protracted crisis of the national economy and with a continual influx of rural migrants, most recently impelled by insecurity in the countryside. The capacity of public authorities to maintain normal urban services is particularly precarious, as is the capacity of the low-income population to feed itself. Thus, outstandingly vigorous popular traditions of self-help organization and ingenuity in survival strategies confront increasing strain from the economic and political environment.

A *barrio* movement in Caracas[5]

In Venezuela, the political and economic setting for urban social movements has differed in important respects from those of the countries discussed above. Since 1959 two political parties have alternated in power through free elections. At the level of discourse, one of these parties, COPEI, has insisted on 'participatory democracy', but in relatively abstract terms deriving from Christian Democratic doctrines. The other party, Accion Democratica (AD), has, more pragmatically, identified itself as social democratic. The practice of both parties in power, however, according to the researcher, has been centralizing and technocratic. State control of huge resources from oil exports combined with 'the heavy autocratic heritage of a century and a half of dictatorship, has generated an authoritarian democracy and a model of state that is paternalistic, centralizing and concentrating of powers, and thus eminently and structurally anti-participative'. At the same time, until recently, the state has been able to support a wide range of social services and subsidies, including public housing, for low- and middle-income groups, wage employment has been abundant, and wage levels have been far above the average for Latin America. Trade unions have been relatively large and vigorous, but subordinated to party control. At the same time, a high proportion of the rapidly growing population of metropolitan Caracas has lived in squatter settlements.

During the 1970s, failure of the state to cope with the social needs and expectations of the population in such settlements, administrative inefficiency, and ambitious urban planning under the Ministry of Housing that called for the eradication of a number of large and well-established squatter settlements, generated a rapid growth of local associations for self-defence.

The settlement under study dated from 1959 and originally housed about 1,200 families; two-thirds of the family heads were wage workers. Up to 1973, the settlement enjoyed reasonable stability and the residents had invested considerable efforts in improving the physical setting. The decree calling for its eradication began a struggle lasting for ten years and ending in partial victory for the families; they achieved resettlement in satisfactory public housing rather than in temporary camps. However, this result dissolved their organization, since they were distributed among different housing projects. Ironically, new squatters immediately occupied their locality, thwarting the Ministry's plan to convert it into a park.

The neighbourhood organization deliberately avoided alliance with political parties but made use of the support of the elected representatives of whichever party was in the opposition to publicize its demands. It had only very limited contacts with local organizations conducting similar struggles in other squatter settlements. External aid and advice came mainly from church organizations and from the schools of social work and medicine of the Central University; these allies were welcomed as not threatening co-option or factionalism. Tactics ranged from legal petitions and endless negotiations with the authorities to seizure of new public housing and barricading of streets when petitions were disregarded. Experienced and combative local leadership was crucially important to the struggle. With hindsight, participants thought that their reliance on such leaders had been excessive and demobilizing when leaders departed for one reason or another.

Notes

1. Rodríguez, Alfredo, Riofrio, Gustavo, and Walsh, Eileen, *De Invasores a Invadidos*, DESCO, Lima, 1973.

2. See García Delgado, D.R. and Silva, Juan, 'El Movimiento Vecinal y la Democracia: Participación y Control en el Gran Buenos Aires'; González Bombal, M. Ines, 'Protestan los Barrios (El Murmullo Suburbano de la Política)'; and Fara, Luis, 'Luchas Reivindicativas Urbanas en su Contexto Autoritario. Los Asentamientos de San Francisco Solano', all in Jelin, Elizabeth, ed., *Los Nuevos Movimientos Sociales*, vol. 2, Centro Editor de América Latina, Buenos Aires, 1985. The quotations in the following pages are drawn from this book.

3. The findings of these researches were not included in Kowarick, Lúcio, *As Lutas Sociais e a Cidade: São Paulo Passado e Presente*, Paz e Terra and UNRISD, São Paulo and Geneva, 1988, since this publication focuses on São Paulo. See for example: Valladares, Licia, *A Luta pela Terra no Brazil Urbano: Reflexões em Torno de Alguns Casos*, UNRISD, unpublished manuscript.

4. This summary relies on the findings of researches carried out between June

1985 and December 1986 by a Chilean institute, ILET, among 'organizations of economic survival', youth organizations and intermediate and metropolitan co-ordinating bodies. See Campero, Guillermo, *Entre la Sobrevivencia y la Acción Política: las Organizaciones de pobladores en Santiago*, Ediciones ILET, Santiago 1987. See also Hardy, Clarissa, *Organizarse para Vivir: Pobreza Urbana y Organización Popular*, Programa de Economia del Trabajo, Santiago 1987; and Chateau, Jorge and others, *Espacio y Poder: los Pobladores*, FLACSO, Santiago 1987.

5. The following summary is based on research making use of the concepts of the UNRISD Programme along with a wide range of theories of the state, participation and urban social movements. It focuses on the experience of one low-income settlement in Caracas to explore the discrepancies between government discourse, policy and praxis, and their 'encounter' with organized efforts from below. See Fadda, Giulietta C., *Participación: Discurso, Política, y Praxis Urbana. Caracas (1973/1983)*, CENDES/Universidad Central de Venezuela, Caracas, Diciembre 1987.

6

Institutionalization of Participation

The term 'institutionalization' implies, at a minimum, an intention on the part of the state to set rules for the game for participation. The state then encourages or protects certain kinds of participation by certain groups and discourages or prohibits other kinds of participation by other groups. All states do this to some extent, with widely differing efficacy and coherence. At one level, 'institutionalization' refers to the constitutional framework for pluralist democracy: elections, referenda, legal protections of rights to voice opinions, etc. At another level, it refers to the regulations and bureaucratic entities dealing with non-governmental organizations such as trade unions and co-operatives. The preceding chapters of Part II have discussed a wide range of instances in which popular movements have interacted with state efforts to institutionalize them, through changing combinations of promotion, bargaining, co-option, conflict and repression.

This chapter is concerned with institutionalization in a narrower sense, i.e. with régimes that have deliberately promoted and channelled organization of the 'hitherto excluded' for their own ends and on a national scale. The régimes in question have generally come to power through revolutions or coups and have looked to institutionalized participation as an alternative to pluralist democracy, at least for the short term and as a means of changing the distribution of power in society. Four of the studies carried out for the UNRISD Participation Programme (in China, Mexico, Nicaragua and Peru) dealt with institutionalization in this sense, and one unsuccessful research initiative, in Grenada, throws some additional light on the question. Although for various reasons the UNRISD Programme was unable to initiate studies in Africa, in subsequent years one of the authors of this book had the opportunity to study in the field the Tanzanian experience, which constitutes the most prominent and long-standing example of institutionalized participation in the continent. Its interest lies both in its specificity – its African character and content – and in the similarity of contradictions that emerged with those observed in the Latin American countries.

In general terms, the researches confirmed the enormous importance of state policy for the 'organized efforts ... of the hitherto excluded', but also threw into relief the deficiencies and contradictions of 'institutionalization' guided by ideological preconceptions and administered by bureaucracies. Such institutionalization has at times escaped from the control of the institutionalizers and has contributed to eventual empowerment, but it has more generally involved mobilization of the excluded for ends they had no part in deciding, reduced them to apathetic conformism, and left them vulnerable to sudden changes of régime or of official goals and tactics. Moreover, the economic constraints under which the régimes have found themselves and the claims of other priorities have usually kept them from translating institutionalized participation into significant material gains for the most impoverished groups. As was discussed in Chapter 2, the use of the term 'participation' for such policies has brought it into discredit among some advocates of more autonomous efforts.

It would be pointless to recommend that governments refrain from participatory initiatives because of the likelihood of distortions of popular strivings. It can be assumed that such initiatives will continue under changing names and justifications, and that agents of the state, would-be allies of the 'hitherto excluded' outside the state, and activists among the latter can all learn something from past experience.

The main contradictions within the more authentic and less ephemeral state efforts to institutionalize participation seem to be the following:

1. Authoritarian-paternalistic, clientelistic and 'participationist' approaches by different power-holders and functionaries generally clash and generate policy ambivalence within a given régime. The partisans of the third approach commonly find their share of power too precarious for their purposes. This contradiction emerges with particular clarity in the trajectory of the Velasco régime in Peru, as discussed below.

2. Contradictions emerge within régimes between policy-makers (divided among themselves) and the bureaucratic machinery available to execute the policies. The former are commonly unable to enlist positive participation by the latter in the design and application of policies or to understand the roots of bureaucratic non-co-operation. These include: self-protectiveness from the consequences of identification with controversial policies that may be reversed by a new régime or minister; inability to change authoritarian-paternalistic attitudes to clientèles; bureaucratic alliances with economic interests or political factions hostile to the policies, etc. The main remedy proposed has been to train the functionaries, but training alone can hardly overcome the more deep-seated reasons for non-co-operation.

3. The expectations of the régime concerning the benefits of participation are generally in partial contradiction to those of the groups expected to participate. The long-standing gap between governmental hopes of social peace and social services supported by the beneficiaries, on the one hand, and popular hopes of more generous subsidies and better services as a reward for 'participating', on the other, typical of community development programmes, has persisted. Even when the proponents of participation working within the state have been mainly social scientists, their understanding of the cultures and sources of livelihood of the target groups has commonly been inadequate, as those active in the Velasco régime in Peru have since admitted. Popular understanding of the state has been equally limited, and has generally been coloured by collective memory of efforts by previous régimes to enlist participation, efforts later reversed or abandoned. Both parties have been unable to grasp the internal heterogeneity of the other.

4. The overtly non-partisan objectives of state initiatives contradict the propensity of governing political parties to manipulate them so as to reward their own followers and block benefits for their adversaries. In some cases, a dominant party achieves a long-term monopoly in the use of this tactic. In others, parties belonging to reformist coalitions compete among themselves for sources of patronage and electoral credit. In either case, state-institutionalized participation risks falling back into clientelism.

5. The participatory initiatives of a given régime are bound to clash with initiatives of other forces that consider the régime's efforts fraudulent or contrary to their vision of the future. Some of these forces aspire to seize control of the state, others to help the organizations of the excluded achieve maximum autonomy from the state and national political parties. This contradiction leads to others: infiltration of the dissident forces into the régime's programmes and efforts by the régime to purge such infiltration; and dependence on state subsidies and services by local associations whose mentors are ideologically opposed to such dependence, etc.

6. Within revolutionary régimes that rely on the mobilized support of groups previously excluded or exploited, different contradictions emerge, in addition to some of those summarized above. On the one side, the régime needs, for its own survival as well as its values, to strengthen a wide range of participatory organizations and create new initiatives (such as literacy and public health campaigns). It must hope that these organizations and initiatives will bring immediate benefits to the participants, and thus confirm their loyalty. On the other side, its hold on power may be precarious, the resources at its disposal are generally meagre, its ideological preconceptions limit its understanding of the groups expected to participate, and its weaknesses in economic management combined with a hostile external environment may make it unable to prevent economic deterioration particularly damaging to the groups on whose support it relies. Other priorities (defence, maintenance of production for export, guaranteed rules of the game to encourage industrialists and farmers to invest and produce) stand in the way of responses to the aspirations of the previously excluded groups and make their expression of these aspirations seem dangerous. Contradictions between the régime's anxiety to control everything and its aspiration to delegate power to popular organizations are inevitable. Such contradictions may lead to regimented consensus in

the name of participation; or to vacillations in the régime's attempts to satisfy incompatible objectives; or to evolution of the 'participants' into competing pressure groups.

Peru 1968-1975

The experience of planned institutionalization of popular participation that evolved in Peru between 1968 and 1975 should be particularly rich in lessons for intellectual-ideological groups that aspire to institutionalize participation from within a state apparatus that they can influence but not control. UNRISD sponsored a comprehensive study of this episode by social scientists who had taken a leading part in it,[1] as well as a study under different auspices of the conflictive popular movements that competed with and then replaced institutionalized participation during the 1970s. The latter study will be discussed in the next chapter.

In 1968, the leadership of the armed forces, which had just taken power through a coup, found common ground with a circle of intellectuals and social scientists.

The former were preoccupied by threats to 'national security' deriving from the alienation and extreme poverty of the majority of the population. They saw a combined danger of helplessness in the face of exploitation by transnational interests, military inferiority to traditional rival countries, and popular support for revolutionary guerrilla movements.

The latter were convinced of the necessity for a transformation of Peruvian society, a break with historical processes they found incompatible with social justice or national autonomy. They considered that most paths to reform or revolution were blocked by international dependence, oligarchic power, ineffectiveness and corruption of the national bourgeoisie and middle classes, fragmentation and lack of realism of the Marxist parties. They concluded that the armed forces were the only actors capable of transforming Peru under existing circumstances.

Policy-making took place under various constraints:

• Competition for influence within the armed forces involving a 'participationist' group headed by the Chief of State, General Juan Velasco Alvarado; ultra-nationalist officers; centralizing leftist officers looking to the Cuban model; and traditional military men.
• Competition for popular influence with the Marxist parties and Apra, a populist party with a disciplined following and long tradition of militancy. The parties were not suppressed but were excluded from any role in policy-making, and their criticisms reinforced a pervasive popular distrust of government programmes.
• Determination by the régime to achieve intense local participation

without permitting national mobilizations or giving any voice to trade unions or political parties.

One of the authors of the study sums up the paradoxical combination of authoritarianism and participation as follows:

> The revolutionary process was possible thanks to a high degree of concentration of power. The régime did not accept control mechanisms, did not negotiate with its adversaries and, rather, questioned their very existence. The authoritarian character of the régime was a necessary condition of the revolution, because one cannot carry out in relatively short historical periods profound alterations affecting decisively the interests and existence of dominant classes, through policies of negotiation and compromise. [However,] the secrecy of the decisions in which a very small number of persons participated prevented a broad debate, ... and, above all, made impossible the direct participation of the popular organizations in decisions that responded to old aspirations, drastically limiting the generation of a revolutionary climate.
>
> From this incomprehension of politics as an inescapable dimension of human life ... there derived a series of consequences disastrous for the revolutionary process: the frequent lack of understanding of strikes; the rejection of criticism, especially that coming from groups whose ideology and reading of reality contradicted the régime's image; the disregard of the conflictual essence of every process of political and social change, etc.

Moreover, in spite of the predominance of social scientists in the civilian group trying to shape participatory institutions, they were hampered by inadequate understanding of the functioning of the economic system and also 'of the ancient survival strategies used by the poorest and most marginal groups in the Andean region and the urban groupings adjacent to the great cities'. These shortcomings were not remedied during the seven years of the experience, while the civilian group struggled to impose its own vision.

The régime embarked on reforms through various institutions dealing with different sectors of the population. In each case, the contradictions between participation and dictation; inadequate understanding of the social actors involved, including the bureaucracy; and inability to control the economic environment led to results different from the hopes of the military as well as the civilian advisers.

Agrarian reform. Throughout the country, large holdings were expropriated and reorganized into co-operatives under varying forms of state management or supervision. This represented the most lasting achievement of the régime, eliminating permanently the power of the landed oligarchy. The scale of the reform, its suddenness, and the institutions it created clashed with the prevailing outlook and level of consciousness of the peasants. However, as one of the directors of the reform points out, if the régime had tried to precede the reform by adequate conscientization and training, the political conditions would probably have changed before the process could begin and the opportunity would have been lost.

The implementation of the reform was marked by:

• A strong contradiction between rural diversity and the homogeneity and rapidity of the reform process, which applied a single basic scheme to widely differing regional and cultural realities. Moreover, the reform introduced a model of modern enterprise self-management that 'responded to a cultural evolution that had not taken place in Peru'.

• A separation of two mechanisms for local decision-making: the mechanisms for productive-technical tasks, staffed by managerial and technical personnel; and the mechanisms for peasant participation, consisting of peasant delegates to an assembly and various councils. This sometimes produced a confusion or invasion of functions between the two mechanisms. It also hindered the workers' proposals for cultivation techniques, etc., based on experience, from reaching the technical management, and made for a bias toward the abandonment of traditional farming methods.

• A multiplicity of bureaucratic institutions that confused and divided the peasants. The very participatory aspirations of the régime intensified this problem. Municipal, judicial, educational, security and other entities were already invading attributions of the traditional community authorities. Now the agrarian reform functionaries, SINAMOS, the Ministry of Education, development committees, etc. created their own mechanisms for participation. 'Frequently, in the public offices the participation process was viewed as an obligation of the popular organizations to be present in all the institutions that each state entity was creating in line with its own needs. Moreover, each state organism tended to create and encourage popular organizations to serve as its interlocutors in the rural setting.'

SINAMOS. The Sistema Nacional de Movilización Social, set up in 1972 to integrate and expand activities already under way, was the most ambitious initiative of the participationist group in the régime, and may also have been the most frustrating. SINAMOS assumed very broad and varied functions for the promotion and technical support of urban as well as rural popular organizations. Its first frustration derived from its initial composition, 'integrating' eight pre-existing public agencies with more than four thousand functionaries, many of them uninterested in participation and with a range of statutory responsibilities that prevented flexibility. The second frustration derived from the régime's placing of military officers in most of the key positions within SINAMOS. As the more authoritarian tendencies gained ground within the régime, the military presence became increasingly inhibiting, and it became more evident that 'it was a small minority among the civil and military groups and persons exercising important roles in the power structure that sustained and supported the participation policy in all its breadth and consequences'. At the same time, the authoritarian tendency, expressing itself in 'vertical, legalist and rigid behaviour' was not limited to conservative sectors of the régime. Some high-level civilian and military authorities identified with leftist positions were equally authoritarian.

Educational reform. The régime decreed sweeping changes in the educational system aimed at 'education for participation'. However, 'full participation ... supposed a high degree of integration of the society, which was precisely the objective of the reformed education; this integration was non-existent in Peruvian society'. The participatory mechanism set up for education competed with mechanisms set up for various other reforms and with private participatory initiatives. Meanwhile, the reform was crippled by active opposition from the teachers (under anti-régime leftist union leadership) and passive opposition rooted in bureaucratic inertia. Administrative decentralization only complicated these forms of opposition, by shifting struggles over promotions, etc. from the central to the regional and zonal levels. Instead of motivating the teachers and functionaries to 'participate', the new regulations came to be seen as 'an oppression equal to or greater than their economic penury'.

Mass communication media. The régime was chronically frustrated by opposition from the mass media, controlled by capitalist or 'oligarchic' interests. In 1970, it expropriated two daily newspapers and turned them over to co-operatives. In July 1974, it took over the remaining dailies and arranged for transfer of control to popular organizations. With the change of régime in 1975, direct state control soon replaced the 'popular' initiative, and the newspapers finally reverted to private ownership in 1980. Control of radio and television was never attempted, although these media reached a wider public than the newspapers. In any case, control over the printed media did not go far toward a solution of the problem of explaining the participatory objectives of the régime in terms accessible to the general public:

It was a question of reaching the majorities. ... The intention was praiseworthy, the results were less so. The reason lies in a repetition of the errors committed by the intellectuals in so many other change processes. Writing for the people is not writing about the people nor making polemics on differences in concepts and ideologies the central theme of the daily press. ... The absence of reflection on the ways in which the reforms were actually advancing, disarticulated and out of step, brought it about that many journalists, including those openly committed to the process, disregarded how the public actually received their journalistic production. Among the opposition to the régime, the rejection of this production was perfectly understandable, but the middle sectors very rapidly experienced saturation and boredom, while the popular sectors were simply unable to follow what, for them, were esoteric debates (above all, for their language and level of abstraction) on the fine points of participation and the eventual dangers of authoritarianism.

Pueblos jovenes. Not long after the military régime took power it rechristened the squatter settlements that surrounded Lima and several other cities as *pueblos jovenes* (young towns) instead of *barriadas*. The new name symbolized recognition of the legitimacy of these settlements of the urban poor and an intention of helping them advance through their own organized efforts. From the beginning this policy encountered the usual ambivalence between support of participation, identified mainly with SINAMOS, and the concern of the Ministry of Interior (which supervised municipal administration) to exclude or control potentially subversive local leadership.

The reactions of the people of the *pueblos jovenes* to the new situation depended on the past history of each settlement and on the degree and kind of leadership already present. All of them welcomed material and technical aid from the state. The accompanying participatory mechanisms might be welcomed, passively and noncommittally accepted as just another ephemeral government scheme, or violently rejected, in the case of settlements led by the Marxist left – in which case the régime's 'authoritarian reflexes' often responded with repression. Gradually, strengthened neighbourhood associations, easier access to state organisms, and visible basic services projects made most of the groups in question more favourably disposed toward the régime, but also raised their expectations. They pursued these expectations through their traditional forms of action, and also through joint strategies arrived at by discussions between community leaders and sympathetic functionaries of SINAMOS and other public agencies. Before this process could settle down to a stable new institutionalization of relations between the *pueblos jovenes* and the state, the onset of economic crisis, conflicts within the régime and the loss of influence by the advocates of participation combined to inhibit further progress.

Industrial communities and social property enterprises. From the beginning, the régime envisaged workers' participation in the control of enterprises as an essential component of the future of Peru, but its approach was more gradual than in some other areas of reform. Its main instrument was a 1970 decree law providing for the acquisition, through profit sharing, of up to 50 per cent of the ownership of enterprises employing more than six workers by 'industrial communities' consisting of all stable workers and employees; these communities would participate in management and distribution of profits. The employers naturally resisted or evaded the application of the law as far they could. The workers were initially taken by surprise by the scheme coming from above. Most of the trade unions, which had not been consulted, opposed it as a tactic of class collaboration. The industrial communities eventually numbered about

3,500 with nearly 200,000 members, but by 1977 they held only 15 per cent of the capital of the enterprises. By that time governmental as well as entrepreneurial attitudes had turned negative, and the possibility of transforming the control of enterprises in general had disappeared. The advocates of the experience, however, argue that it resulted in important gains in worker mobilization and education in the secrets of management and the global functioning of the economy.

The early intentions of the régime also included the linking of localized participatory organization with productive enterprises, for which the *pueblos jovenes* should have been a propitious environment. This intention failed to advance, 'not only because of the short historical space available, but also because of relative ignorance concerning the informal economy and its relations with the modern industrial sector. This conditioned a marked emphasis on organization schemes without adequate corresponding plans for development of production. In a way, this was an expression in the *pueblos jovenes* of the discrepancy between the development of the participatory conception in the government's official discourse, and its management of the global economy.'

This last assertion points to the main reason why the participation stimulated by the régime's policies was, by its close, becoming ever more conflictive rather than harmonious. Between 1968 and 1976, the sum of wages expanded by only 7 per cent while the sum of profits destined to personal consumption rose by 20 per cent. Thus income distribution became even more concentrated than before. Consumption of wage goods rose only slightly while demand for automobiles, refrigerators and television sets grew by annual rates generally over 30 per cent. Meanwhile, the transformation in land tenure was not supported by any significant investment in agriculture or by trade and price policies that might have stimulated production and investment. The majority of peasants became even more impoverished and prone to migrate to the cities.

To sum up, in Peru a group that had no power of its own embarked on a multisectoral effort to institutionalize local participation, as part of a comprehensive strategy to transform the society from above. This group and its military allies did not have nor did they seek support from a national political movement, and encountered initial suspicion from most organized sectors of the population and apathy from the remainder.

The unsparingly self-critical account by its former leading actors, from which the above pages have summarized only some of the outstanding points, suggests a number of things that might have been done differently if they had understood better the society with which they were dealing, and, above all, if they had been conscious of the requirements for an economic policy capable of dynamizing production, changing its structure, and backing up the participatory organizational initiatives with real benefits for the majority. However, they were convinced that they had to seize a unique opportunity and learn by acting. They show a lingering conviction that if General Velasco Alvarado had continued in good health and had been able to control the armed forces they would have had time to correct errors and generate sufficient popular support to make their reforms permanent. However, their rejection of pluralist political competition suggests that in such a case the participation might have evolved into routinized manipulation by the state or by a political élite, as happened, through quite different historical processes, in the case of Mexico as well as the 'real socialist' states.

Mexico: routinized institutionalization in the 1970s

In Mexico, popular participation was institutionalized as a result of a long and complex revolutionary struggle in which popular organizations took part to various degrees, together with regional élites and armed factions. The researches sponsored by UNRISD focused primarily on the relations between peasants and the state, and the contradictions that appeared when the government, during part of the 1970s, tried to change its policy emphasis from bureaucratized control to stimulation of peasant initiative and to resume land redistribution on more than a token scale. The findings from this research have been discussed in relation to other peasant movements in Chapter 3. These findings emphasized a tactic prominent throughout state-manipulated participation in Mexico, to encourage vertical ties between separate local or sectoral popular organizations and the state, and prevent as far as possible horizontal ties linking broad categories of the excluded that might lead to a mobilization of power challenging state policies.

Institutionalized participation in vertically-controlled structures seems to have had similar but more inhibiting effects in the urban population, according to studies carried out in three low-income zones of Mexico City in 1968-69, 1971-72, and 1987.[2] Some of these zones initially had vigorous local organization and leadership, comparable to those found in similar zones of large cities elsewhere in Latin America.

> Local leaders established ties with regional and national functionaries because they wished both to secure benefits for their members and extend their own spheres of influence. ... Paradoxically, local groups became less politically effective when they affiliated with revolution-linked national organizations and institutions. Also paradoxically, the groups' political effectiveness was undermined precisely when they seemed to be most effective: when they received land, public facilities and other benefits from the state. This situation developed because they were at that point subjected to political and social deterrents and controls, regulating local demand-making and political participation. [Upon affiliation with national organizations linked to the PRI,] associations which once had large and highly

active memberships became largely inactive. ... Those who continue to participate in group-sponsored activities generally do so in return for or in anticipation of favours from the group leaders. Participation has become ritualized.

At this point, according to the study, the groups in question not only lost the ability to defend their own interests in an organized way. They also became less accessible to the mobilizing and legitimizing purposes of the régime, or even to 'demagogic manipulation by dissatisfied members of the élite'.

Interest in groups affiliated with both the party and the government had already tapered off in the course of the 1960s. However, since the early 1970s residents have become even less inclined to participate in civic activities, less inclined to attend group meetings and ... less inclined to vote. ... In sum, state organizational control ... has atrophied, in part because no co-optable grassroots movements have arisen in recent years. Government-party hegemony has prevented such movements from arising, and residents no longer see any reason to organize. As a consequence, co-option no longer serves the regulatory effect of earlier years.

The study concludes that the urban poor in Mexico, like the peasants and the wage workers,

never attained institutional power on the national level, despite 'popular' grass roots political participation. ... Otherwise Mexican urban poor would be better off than their counterparts in non-democratic Latin American countries. ... Institutions such as the PRI, which regulate urban poor in Mexico, are unique to the country, but the hierarchical, personalistic, clientelistic, and class-based relations and the types of largely non-redistributive economic benefits extended to urban poor in Mexico are found in other Latin American countries as well.

For some years after the economic crisis of 1982 and the subsequent plunge in incomes and standard of living of the urban poor as well as other sectors of the Mexican population, the main reaction in the zones studied was further withdrawal from participation and higher electoral abstention. The main exception followed the 1985 earthquake, when the population of one of the zones mobilized successfully to impose its own demands for new housing over government plans for demolition and evacuation. More recently, of course, with the upsurge of opposition political activity in the presidential election of 1988, the Mexican people seem to be emerging from this long phase of pseudo-participation and apathy. This emergence encounters declared government intentions of reducing the scope of its economic and social responsibilities, moving away from paternalistic tutelage of the economy and social organizations, without renouncing the political hegemony of the PRI. The consequences for organized efforts of the hitherto manipulated sectors of the population are not yet clear.

Nicaragua since 1979

In Mexico, the state consolidated its distinctive system of institutionalized or ritualized participation over a long period of economic growth and political stability. In Peru, the intellectual proponents of participation had several years to try to apply their model within a setting that was relatively although precariously stable.

In Nicaragua, organized popular participation emerged in the course of a traumatic revolutionary war. The victorious Frente Sandinista de Liberacion Nacional (FSLN), itself a coalition of several leftist groupings, had to try to institutionalize this participation under permanently precarious circumstances and various difficulties in reconciling ideological preconceptions with these circumstances. The UNRISD Participation Programme touched on some aspects of the early stages of this process, in relation to wider research on food systems and society.[3]

The insurrection that brought the FSLN to power in 1979 was carried out by a large number of groups (of peasants, workers, women, university or high-school students, religious congregations and neighbourhood associations) operating with much spontaneity and local autonomy. While some currents of opinion in the FSLN were convinced that a genuine revolution should rely on an industrial proletariat, in Nicaragua this proletariat was relatively small and declined further in numbers and organized influence in the course of later economic difficulties. In view of the multiclass backing of the revolution and Nicaragua's external vulnerability, adoption of the Cuban model of centralized political control and socialization of the means of production was not a realistic option. It was not until eighteen months after the revolution that the first steps were taken toward conversion of the loosely-organized 'Frente' into a political party.

In the interim (i.e. between July 1979 and the end of 1980) the régime's hope of transforming Nicaraguan society turned, first, on the consolidation or creation of mass organizations covering all the forces that had participated in the revolution and on the promotion of rural and urban production co-operatives; secondly, on a massive literacy campaign that depended organizationally on creative local initiative in every rural and urban municipality. The participatory style of this campaign was repeated in subsequent health campaigns and helped to confirm such participation as a way of meeting basic social needs in a society that, even if it had not needed to divert the lion's share of public resources to defence, would not have been able to support a universalized system of social services and welfare for decades to come.

The implementation of land reform and the restructuring of the agricultural economy were the next urgent problems to be faced. Here, the intention was to reconcile as far as possible the preservation of large modern private holdings and state farms with the meeting of demands from peasants and landless labourers for land distribution. The former would be indispensable for the maintenance of high levels of agricultural exports bringing urgently needed foreign exchange; the latter for production of basic foods for domestic consumption. This dual policy, set forth in an agrarian reform law in October 1981, was initiated through a national mobilization drive, between May and December 1982, when representatives of rural workers, peasants, women, neighbourhood associations, popular education centres and the civilian militia met local representatives of the FSLN and government agencies.

In principle, land redistribution was not to be carried out through the state bureaucracy. Instead, leaders of grassroots organizations were asked to work out local plans that were then presented in meetings with representatives from other areas. Regional plans were defined and a nationwide debate about FSLN rural strategy took place.

In practice, a tripartite division of power emerged at the local level between leaders of grassroots organizations, representatives of state agencies and the FSLN. The division, and accompanying tensions, were most striking during the mass mobilization drive in 1982. While in most localities the FSLN allied itself with the grassroots groups against the state functionaries (also FSLN members), in other localities the FSLN and the state agencies aligned themselves against the grassroots groups. The tensions deriving from these different alignments, while sometimes clashing with considerations of efficiency and consistency, became significant stimuli, if not guarantees, for continuing non-ritualized popular participation. In 1982, also, all government agencies, as well as the FSLN itself, were formally decentralized. This further enhanced the capacity of grassroots organizations to control the implementation of policy.

The sudden increase in armed incursions by anti-Sandinista forces in March 1983 also at first broadened the participatory capacity of peasant communities. The need to strengthen peasant support led to a rapid increase in expropriation and land distribution along the lines already mapped out at the local level. Also, a decision was taken in early 1983 to convert co-operatives hitherto concerned exclusively with production into armed defence co-operatives.

It is well known that since the early 1980s Nicaragua has paid a very high price in economic terms as well as in human suffering for survival in the face of armed conflict and disruption of external markets. In view of other priorities the régime could not maintain its early achievements in bringing material benefits to the 'hitherto excluded'. Contradictions emerged between the participatory efforts of different social actors. The National Union of Farmers and Ranchers (UNAG) proved relatively effective in advancing the demands of landholding peasants for better food prices and liberalization of trade. The urban neighbourhood Committees of Sandinista Defence, the trade unions, and the women's organization, whose members were primarily interested in protecting popular consumption levels, lost influence and the rank and file withdrew confidence from their leaders. In the policy-making process contradictions persisted between technocratically biased planners concentrating on large-scale industrial and agricultural projects; ministries 'feudalized' by allocation to different Sandinista leaders pursuing their own priorities; decentralization objectives; and efforts to involve the mass organizations through representation on numerous committees. In these last, communication between the technocrats and leaders of mass organizations proved difficult and the latter often found mass pressure tactics more effective than committee arguments.

Participation became increasingly subordinated to crisis management, particularly after the régime in 1989 found no alternative to an economic adjustment policy that further depressed the standard of living of the majority. While some grassroots organizations and the FSLN itself remained vigorous and combative, the régime lost majority support, as the 1990 election demonstrated.

A sympathetic observer describes the more recent stages and the associated illusions concerning participation as follows:

> The belief that an adjustment programme could meet with popular acquiescence turned out to be a technocratic fantasy that cost the revolution dearly. Some of the opinion polls taken at the end of 1989 reflected a marked drop in participation in government-sponsored community development programmes, which are run by the Sandinista mass organizations. A poll taken in Managua in October, for example, showed that two-thirds did not participate in activities such as environmental hygiene, vaccinations, or community gardens. This may have resulted from government policies that used the mass organizations to control popular activity and demands whenever these threatened to go outside state channels. Increasingly, these once-autonomous pressure groups came to act as part of the state apparatus, as mechanisms of control subordinated to the FSLN. The demobilization of the mass organizations and the gradual drop-off in the level of social participation were noted at the time by Sandinistas and observers, and pointed to as indicators of the weakness of the revolutionary process. However, simply mentioning this type of problem more often than not evoked aggressive attacks from those, inside the FSLN and out, who preferred to see the world through rose-coloured glasses and interpreted any critical stance as something close to treason.[4]

Grenada 1979-1983

In Grenada, a very small (population: 110,000) and vulnerable island country, a 'People's Revolutionary Government' (PRG) based on a tightly-knit political organization came to power through a coup in 1979 and aspired to transform the economy and society through participatory methods. As in Nicaragua and Peru, the greater part of the economy was expected to remain in the private sector. The new régime initiated ambitious programmes for popular education, health and nutrition; promoted co-operatives, trade unions, a national women's organization and a national youth organization; and set up zonal and regional councils expected to discuss issues in monthly meetings.

The UNRISD Participation Programme envisaged studies in this setting focusing on the application of participatory initiatives to food production and use. For various reasons, however, an exploratory mission in October-December 1980 could not be followed up.[5] This mission found a reasonable degree of progress toward the meeting of economic and social welfare objectives, but practical difficulties in making participation a reality through continual meetings of the wide range of new organizations (e.g. absence of public transportation in the evenings).

It also found a 'wait and see' attitude on the part of some mass organizations, with particular reserve toward the Centre for Popular Education, which was responsible for a mass literacy campaign and also for overcoming apathy toward the régime's objectives. 'With the passing of time and the absence of any real political organization in the formal role of opposition, various fraternity groups and service organizations felt compelled to show public support for the PRG and its programmes. However, much of these public acclamations were empty gestures of goodwill, signifying good public relations.'

The mission's report concluded with forebodings concerning the contradiction between the régime's commitment to participatory democracy and its exercise of centralized control:

> the present emphasis on state institutions inhibits mass involvement rather than encouraging popular participation. Care must be taken to avoid any arrangement which further strengthens the central control of the revolution. Instead, any programme designed to involve the people in the decision-making process must be based on democratization rather than bureaucratization.

This contradiction was not resolved, and in 1983 the régime collapsed in a bloody struggle for power within the top leadership followed by external interventions. Apparently the people who were supposed to be participating were kept in the dark until the last moment that such a struggle was under way.

According to a later assessment, the 'relative success' of the participatory initiatives

> was due to the fact that Grenada is a micro-society of 110,000 people, making it possible to experiment with new structures that would be impractical in a larger country. In retrospect, however, it is apparent that the system of popular democracy was in some ways a deception. ... The grassroots organs were only marginally plugged in to the real power structure. While Grenadians turned out in large numbers for the meetings of the parish and zonal councils, these meetings were often top-heavy with speeches by government officials. Debate was lively on a variety of topics, yet actual policy decisions were still being made by the ... Central Committee, whose membership was not even known to a majority of Grenadians.[6]

'Real socialist' institutionalization in rural China

In the 1970s, the USSR and allied countries of Central and Eastern Europe displayed highly inclusive formal participatory structures institutionalized by post-revolutionary régimes in the name of empowerment of workers and peasants. Communist parties, elected councils at many levels, trade unions, collective farms, organizations of women, youth, intellectuals and professionals involved most of the population in voting, discussion meetings and organized activities for public purposes.

While many currents of opinion outside these countries had long questioned the authenticity of the participatory structures, they continued to enjoy considerable credit as models for mobilizing régimes in other parts of the world and supported this role through frequent international gatherings, study tours, and so on. More recent events and internal self-criticisms have confirmed that by the 1970s institutionalized participation had been reduced to ritual and manipulation, stifling of initiative, while 'organized efforts' not sanctioned by the state, such as the Participation Programme dealt with in other regions, were practically out of the question. The sharpness and incontrovertibility of the demonstration that the most highly institutionalized participation can mask the extreme of anti-participation has had consequences for social and political movements throughout the world that will be further discussed in Chapter 9.

State institutionalization of participatory structures in the People's Republic of China at this time seemed to have quite different and somewhat more promising traits. It had not hardened into bureaucratized routine as in the other 'real socialist' countries, but was experiencing successive waves of mobilization from above encountering diverse and poorly understood responses from below. Its apparent egalitarianism and achievements in transforming mentalities, social relationships and productive techniques excited the sympathies of conservative developmentalists as well as radical advocates of 'another development' and Maoist revolutionaries.

The UNRISD Programme undertook an exploratory mission to China, comprising two visits, in September/October 1979 and in November 1980.[7] The main task of the mission was to assess whether field research into popular participation as an element in rural policy would be feasible. It came during a period when the Chinese policies in which many external sympathizers had invested their hopes were changing radically, not for the first time. Unfortunately, lack of resources prevented follow-up of the research contacts then made.

Such a follow-up would have been able to trace the consequences of a shift away from highly egalitarian and also regimented participatory structures, subject to sudden changes in organization and objectives, marked by mass campaigns focusing on the exposure of real or imaginary class enemies and attributing infallibility to the Thoughts of Mao. The disastrous consequences of this model of participation have since been amply documented by Chinese as well as foreign observers.

The exploratory mission naturally could observe only small fragments of the complex and diverse Chinese rural reality, and could not foresee the directions of change. On the basis of discussions in Beijing and visits to rural communes in south-east and central China, some of which had been previously studied by one of the investigators, the mission found a greater degree of continuity and initiative at the local level than might have been expected from the agitated period through which China had just passed. Local communities seemed to retain some flexibility in applying central directives or evading them when inapplicable.

The mission concluded that the socialist transformation of relations of production, carried through in the early years after the Communist victory in 1949, seemed to have created certain preconditions for popular participation in rural China, but had also generated its own constraints on such participation. The previous monopolization of power by landowning or money-lending élites, common to most rural areas of the Third World, had been eliminated. At the same time, collectivization of land and other means of production led to the emergence of a state and party bureaucracy practically monopolizing decision-making power. In the Chinese case, localized resistance to these new élites had combined with campaigns from above, originating in power struggles within the national leadership, to generate insecurity and a great deal of violence.

The mission also concluded that collectivization of the means of production, mechanisms for distribution of food and local responsibility for social services had enabled China to ensure to each citizen a basic security of livelihood, even though this might be at a bare subsistence level. This should have freed the Chinese peasantry from constant anxiety about the provision of livelihood for their families and made it easier for them to engage in planning, discussions, experimentation, and more generally in participation in political decision-making. In the absence of such security of livelihood, in pre-revolutionary China or in other Asian countries, political participation by the rural poor was likely either to be reduced to meaningless participation in formal elections or to take the form of violent and short-lived outbursts and uprisings against intolerable social injustices.

Subsequent revelations on famine in parts of China around 1959, following the Great Leap Forward, and on the extraordinary level of inter-group violence accompanying the Great Proletarian Cultural Revolution from 1967 onwards, indicate that these conclusions were too ready to accentuate the positive side of the Chinese experience.

Chinese rural policies during the 1980s have favoured individual peasant initiative at the expense of the egalitarian as well as the mass-participation features of the previous system. These policies seem to have been highly successful in terms of increasing production, but have also permitted the enrichment of some and the impoverishment of other peasants, the emergence of a large-scale landless floating population, and deterioration of local support for social services and social security. Political control remains strong and challenging organized efforts of the 'newly excluded' are no more likely to be tolerated than before. Some observers have pointed to a new potential for unorganized violent protest, if not in the rural areas, then among the landless poor massing in the cities.

Ujamaa socialism and participation in Tanzania

Popular participation in Tanzania must be understood in the context of the ideology of '*ujamaa*' socialism and of its founder and main proponent Julius Nyerere. *Ujamaa* is a Swahili word that means something like 'friendship', 'brotherhood' or 'familyhood'. *Ujamaa* socialism, which was most forcefully spelled out in Nyerere's famous Arusha Declaration of 1967, was to revive a supposedly classless egalitarian and collectivist traditional African society that had been corrupted and distorted by colonialism and should now be restored within the setting of a modern nation-state. The *ujamaa* society was to be based on equality, co-operation, self-reliance and full people's participation.

People's participation was to be guaranteed through a one-party democratic system. According to Nyerere, the leading TANU party (Tanganyika African National Union), which had led Tanzania to independence, represented by definition the aspirations and interests of the nation as a whole and not of one specific social force or class. Assuming a basically classless and egalitarian society, other parties that could emerge would therefore not represent different social classes as they did, for example, in Europe but simply different factions. A multiparty system would thus reduce politics to sterile struggles between rival factions. A single ruling party, open to every citizen and giving room for free expression of ideas and interests, was thus in the Tanzanian case the best guarantee for free democratic choice by the people of their leaders and for democratic participation within a politically stable constitutional framework.

This vision of a classless, egalitarian and collectivist traditional African society did not correspond fully to reality. Traditional African societies, at least in some areas of present-day Tanzania, may have been collectivist but were certainly not egalitarian. Nor were they necessarily classless, though it is true that the absence of a strong indigenous middle class largely explains the lack of any real political opposition to Nyerere's *ujamaa* socialism. What is important, however, and this distinguishes the Tanzania example from others discussed above, is that socialism and institutionalized participation in Tanzania derived from an ideological vision referring to traditional social values and institutions of solidarity, to the extended family, the clan, the village and to collective property of land.

The imposition of one-party rule, however shaky the ideological argumentation, represented politically an important tactical move. It is this, and the personality of Nyerere and his successor, which must be given main credit for the unique achievement, in the African context, of lasting political and social stability and the absence of ethnic conflict. These are very important assets in meeting the challenge of pluralist democratization and economic liberalization with which Tanzania is grappling today.

During the 1960s and 1970s advocates of self-reliant and participatory styles of development looked to Tanzania (along with China) as a potential model, and the country attracted substantial aid from governments sympathetic to Nyerere's vision. The outcome, however, has been paradoxical in several respects. The main characteristics of the evolution of the Tanzanian system can be summed up as follows:

1. 'Participation' was institutionalized by the party/state from above, in an attempt to create appropriate structures for the realization of an ideal socialist society. No social or popular movements were present that would have represented real social forces: the state was so to speak the only actor and unilaterally fixed the rules of the game. This has not changed substantially over the last quarter century. It is only in the early 1990s, as a result of new liberalization policies, that a new mainly urban entrepreneurial middle class is starting to emerge.

2. Though traditional social structures and values were idealized in a nostalgic way, when it came to the adoption of concrete policies, traditional forms of social relations and methods of production were considered 'primitive' and backward, and 'modern' methods of agricultural production were centrally imposed. The state and party considered it their

legitimate function to educate the people and help them thus to overcome what was called 'the triple handicap of ignorance, disease and poverty'.

3. Even supposedly 'popular-based' institutions such as local government institutions or co-operatives were usually created, dissolved and at times reconstituted through central decisions by the state, from above, without involving the people concerned and often with little regard for their interests. People's participation in decision-making remained usually limited to minor issues regarding the concrete local implementation of policies that had been decided at the top.

4. Through successive administrative reorganizations, and ironically through a policy of decentralization, the party structures (and thus central control) gradually extended down to the lowest level of society, the ten-cell unit. Practically all forms of collective action have been officially organized and controlled and, until recently, there seemed little space for autonomous, participatory, creative forms of expression of popular interest. Also, throughout its history the Tanzanian state has intervened increasingly in the running of the economy, and this far beyond its administrative, financial and managerial capacity. This over-extension of central controls led not only to often ineffective and inefficient utilization of resources but in many cases stifled grassroots initiatives.

5. The people have generally reacted to this institutionalized participation with apathetic conformism, with voluntary compliance if this seemed to be in their best interest, or with resort to a variety of 'avoidance techniques' in order to ignore, by-pass or circumvent official directives and by-laws that don't seem to make sense or seem contrary to their interests. This has been all the easier as the state has not commanded the necessary resources effectively to follow up and police the implementation of many directives and regulations. In this last respect, real participation in Tanzania resembles that observed by the UNRISD mission in rural China.

6. The policy of top-down mobilization has thus negated official attempts to promote a spirit of self-reliance and has led, on the contrary, to a pronounced and all-pervasive 'assistance mentality'. It has also led to contradictory expectations by the party, the government and the people: while the government expects the people to take increasing responsibility for the running of social services and the maintenance of transport and water infrastructure, the people expect increased subsidies and assistance as reward for participating in the official schemes and institutions.

7. The non-participatory way in which major policy decisions seem to be taken, based on ideological arguments rather than analysis of reality, has led to the definition of unrealistic, ambitious ideological goals. It is often the pursuit of such goals and policies that has made the state gradually move from persuasion to forced implementation.

These characteristics are particularly visible in the 'villagization' policy carried out since 1967, and in the agricultural marketing policy.

'Villagization' refers to the *ujamaa* village approach that was adopted after the Arusha Declaration in 1967. The idea was to bring the majority of the rural population together in 'familyhood villages', characterized by village self-government on an egalitarian basis and significant communal activities in infrastructure building and production. Originally stress was put on gradualism, co-operative production and persuasion. The state and party were to have a catalytic rather than coercive role. As Nyerere stated, 'Viable socialist communities can only be established with willing members; the task of leadership and government is not to try and force this kind of development, but to explain, encourage and participate'.[8] Despite government incentives and promises to provide social services to *ujamaa* villages, the pace of voluntary villagization was however slow, and in 1973 the TANU party decided to accelerate the process and make villagization compulsory. As a result, between 1973 and 1976 the army was used in a major campaign to relocate half or more of the country's rural population, more than six million people, in some 8,000 *ujamaa* villages. Sources differ as to the numbers resettled and the size of the rural population.

Behind this move was the desire to draw all rural households into a uniform system of modern production and exchange, preferably for export, and to regulate and increase the transfer of revenue to the state through monopoly marketing. The relocation of the rural population in nuclear villages was also to allow the state to improve economic and agricultural support services and to extend health, education and water supply services to all villages. With the 1975 Village and Ujamaa Act these villages became the basic political and economic units of power in the country. Control over land was transferred to the village council, and collective *ujamaa* farms were introduced throughout the country.

While villagization did allow the Tanzanian state to extend social services (and party control) down to most villages, economic and environmental consequences were sometimes disastrous. This was particularly so in the areas previously characterized by scattered settlements and where for environmental reasons extensive forms of agriculture and land use had prevailed. Forced villagization put an end to seasonal migration, led to an artificial separation of crop and livestock farming, and replaced traditional, risk-conscious integrated and extensive farming with permanent and often mono-crop farming dependent on costly inputs of fertilizers and insecticides. This led to soil exhaustion, overgrazing and deforestation around villages. Moreover, the state did not have the means to ensure regular provision of agricultural inputs nor to organize the efficient marketing of the products that it obliged the farmers to grow, and the increasing rate of surplus appropriation by the state led to a growing antagonism between the peasants and the state. Collective *ujamaa* farms were increasingly unpopular as the farmers often did not receive their due share of the produce. The peasants responded by gradually withdrawing from cash-crop and collective production, in spite of new by-laws and directives trying to prevent this, and shifted increasingly to production of food crops or to non-agricultural cash-producing activities such as fishing, charcoal burning and crafts.

In the field of agricultural marketing, the state decided to replace the former co-operative societies, which it had itself created and previously encouraged, by production-based multi-purpose socialist co-operatives. State crop authorities were established which controlled not only agricultural marketing but also crop procurement, transport, storage, processing and even export operations. However, the agricultural stagnation of the later 1970s, and the inefficient bureaucratic operations of these crop authorities led the government to dissolve them in 1982 and replace them with new co-operatives. Unlike the earlier co-operatives, which had been largely autonomous, these new co-operatives were to function under party control, and for the sake of economic viability each primary co-operative society was to comprise several villages. This however was in contradiction with party-dominated political village structures, and in 1987 the party decided, against arguments for economic efficiency, that co-operatives should again be limited to one village only. Political and ideological arguments once more prevailed. Today most co-operatives in charge of food crops and oils have broken down or become inoperative and private traders and entrepreneurs have gradually taken over.

Following a dramatic economic crisis in the 1980s, the Tanzanian government embarked on 'economic survival' and structural adjustment and recovery programmes and has since 1986 entered into an agreement with the IMF. The main thrust of these programmes is to liberalize domestic trade, to give more emphasis to the private sector in both production and trade, and drastically to cut social service budgets. Not surprisingly such an approach led to political struggles within the party. The second phase of the IMF agreement, endorsed in 1989, while continuing most macro-economic policies of the previous agreement, specifically aims to rehabilitate social services. This should be achieved mainly by increasing people's participation in the financing, operation and management (not in identification, planning and design) of social service programmes.

More recently, Tanzania has been affected, like many other African countries, by a wave of democratization. Nyerere himself, having retired in August 1990 as party chairman, launched the debate about the advisability of introducing a multi-party system in Tanzania. Growing tensions and unrest are felt as the liberalization of the economy leads rapidly to new social and regional disparities. Whatever the changes that may occur in the near future, they are likely to affect significantly the scope and forms of participation in Tanzania.

*

Studies of state policies for the institutionalization of participation have been subject to obvious difficulties from the state's natural propensity to exaggerate successes and conceal shortcomings, and its ability to admit or exclude researchers on the basis of the expected acceptability of their findings. Researchers also may be prone to self-censorship, partly because of their interest in continued access, partly because of their sympathy with the aims of beleaguered régimes such as those of Grenada and Nicaragua. A comprehensive and balanced picture is likely to become feasible only after the policy or the régime has receded into history, as the study of the Velasco period in Peru indicates. The present should be a propitious time to study institutionalized participation in view of the wide range of experiences in the recent past that present governments have disowned, and that forces within these governments as well as 'organized efforts' from within the civil societies are now trying to understand so as to guard against their recurrence.

If participation really hinges on empowerment, the extent to which any state, whether under pluralist democratic or authoritarian leadership, can help groups excluded from power to achieve a share in it, thus limiting the options of the groups previously dominant, cannot be affirmed with much confidence. Institutionalization, in the sense of fixing consistent rules of the game for 'organized efforts' is an inescapable responsibility of all states. Beyond that, the most promising way forward for the state may be to encourage the popular survival strategies that are emerging in the context of democratization, decentralization, and self-limitation of state responsibilities, letting the participants institutionalize themselves as their members see fit.

Notes

1. See Franco, Carlos, ed., *El Peru de Velasco*, 3 vols., Centro de Estudios para el Desarrollo y la Participacion, Lima, 1983. Both the permanent interest of this experience and the fact that the length and late completion of the reports on the study prevented inclusion in the UNRISD publication series justify relatively detailed discussion here. All quotations in this summary are translated from the above report.

2. See Eckstein, Susan, *The Poverty of Revolution: The State and the Urban Poor in Mexico*, Princeton University Press, Princeton, N.J. First published 1977; republished with an Epilogue, 1988. The quotations in the following pages are drawn from pp. 209-10, 215 and 255 of this monograph.

3. This research was carried out by a team from the Centro de Investigación y

Estudios de la Reforma Agraria (CIERA) in Managua. Based on the Nicaraguan experience, a regional sub-debate on 'transition and institutionalization of popular participation' took place in Latin America. See Marchetti, Peter, *Guerra, Participación Popular y Transición al Socialismo*, unpublished draft manuscript, UNRISD. Results from the Participation Programme's research in Nicaragua are also contained in Marchetti, Peter, ed., *Co-operativas y Participación en Nicaragua*, unpublished manuscript, UNRISD, Geneva, 1985. Results from the Institute's research on food systems can be found in: Barraclough, Solon, *A Preliminary Analysis of the Nicaraguan Food System*, UNRISD, Geneva, 1982; CIERA, *Sistema Alimentario*, vol. 2 of *La Reforma Agraria en Nicaragua 1979-1989*, CIERA, Managua, 1989; and Utting, Peter, *Economic Reform and Third World Socialism*, Macmillan and UNRISD, London, 1992.

4. Vilas, Carlos N., 'What Went Wrong', in *Nicaragua: Haunted by the Past, NACLA Report on the Americas*, vol. XXIV, 1, June 1990.

5. The findings of this preliminary investigation can be found in: Quamina, Odida, *Food Systems and Popular Participation in Grenada*, draft final report submitted to UNRISD, February 1981.

6. Sunshine, Catherine A., 'Grenada', in *The Caribbean Survival: Struggle and Sovereignty*, Ecumenical Programme for Interamerican Communication and Action, Washington, D.C., 1985.

7. See Stiefel, Matthias and Wertheim, Willem F., *Production, Equality and Participation in Rural China*, Zed Press and UNRISD, London and Geneva, 1983.

8. Quoted by John Loxley, in *Africa South of the Sahara*, Europa Publications, London, 1976, p. 891.

7

From Social Movements to National Movements

During the 1970s many intellectual and activist advocates of popular participation looked for more hopeful alternatives to previous mobilizing myths concerning vanguard parties and classes with preordained roles, on the one hand, and state-institutionalized participatory mechanisms, on the other. They observed the vitality and diversity of the more or less organized movements that were taking shape, some of them new variants of traditional struggles for livelihood, others with quite different (ethnic, gender, religious, environmental, etc.) sources of solidarity and focuses for struggle.

Some of the movements in question were becoming rapidly internationalized, with their own 'networks' for mutual aid and proselytism; others clung to local or sectarian criteria for identity. Could the separate struggles of these heterogeneous and spontaneous 'social movements' interact through broadening experience and consciousness of common interests, so as to transform national societies in historically unprecedented ways? Or would they mainly overstrain the capacity to function of societies already semi-paralysed by unmanageable problems? In some of the discussions the groupings identified as social movements became so all-inclusive and the roles attributed to them so varied and contradictory that almost any forecast might be justified.

In Latin America and some other parts of the Third World the emphasis in consideration of social movements stayed closer to the traditional categories of 'hitherto excluded' and to objectives of redistribution of power. During these years experience of military authoritarianism was stimulating among would-be guides and allies of the excluded a higher regard for pluralist democratic procedures, human rights, the autonomy of civil society *vis-à-vis* the state, and openness to the unexpected in thinking about the future. During the 1980s, in such countries as Argentina, Brazil, Chile and the Philippines, popular mobilizations that stemmed more from the social movements than from the political parties seemed to confirm the potential transforming role of the former.

Attempts to conceptualize this potential have persisted, with inevitable contradictions between ideological propensity to prescribe for it, and recognition that the trajectory of the social movements, like pluralist democracy itself, must remain open-ended, unconfinable by predetermined 'roles' and utopias. For the present, some social movements in some settings seem to be on the rise, or completing their own kind of institution-alization. Others are waning, in some cases because they accomplished their immediate objective, such as the fall of an authoritarian government, or because the consequences of such a success proved disillusioning, or because they have been unable to help their members cope with crises of insecurity and impoverishment.

The various theoretical or ideological approaches to social movements are too numerous and complex to be summed up here. The following pages will deal briefly with one prescription akin to some of the 'organized efforts' discussed elsewhere, and then, at greater length, with another.

A current of opinion particularly influential in Brazil but present in many countries has rejected national politics and political parties alto-gether, and has looked forward to the withering away of the state rather than to popular control of it. According to a Brazilian sociologist and political leader concerned to defend the legitimacy of political parties as intermediaries between the people and the state:

> For the grassroots democrats the fundamental question is the autonomous organization of the population around concrete demands ... almost always within the reach of and with direct consequences for the well-being of concrete groups of people. These demands should be made on the Public Authority without the ostensible mediation of parties and, if possible, without delegation of responsibility to elected representatives. ... The subject of the political process becomes a 'living community': neighbours, workers in the same factory, landless tenants who measure their aspirations around the control of an area, etc. More than the rather abstract solidarity of a 'class', what is needed is the solidarity of a professional 'branch' or a specific segment of the people to give substance to the demand for democracy.[1]

Such a conception, fusing 'lay anarchism and Catholic solidarity thought', would, in principle, lead to a society composed of autonomous and localized 'social movements' practising direct democracy.

Other currents of opinion have looked to eventual coalescence of 'social movements' into 'national popular movements' as the only prom-ising path to social transformation in the interest of the dispossessed majority, while trying to avoid dogmatism in their conceptualization of this process. This current of opinion has generally accepted political parties as legitimate actors in the formation of a national popular move-ment, but has considered that the participating social movements should maintain their autonomy, guarding against party dictates and sectarian divisiveness. They have viewed control of the state and socialist transfor-mation of the relations of production as ultimate objectives of mature national popular movements, but reserved judgement as to how this might come about. They have distrusted the '*basismo*' or '*movimientismo*' of the approach referred to above as an exaggerated reaction to the shortcomings of previous political party tactics.

Social movements and the national popular movement in Peru

Although most of the researches sponsored by UNRISD dealt with social movements in the broad sense, the only study that addressed systematically the question of such movements as potential components of national popular movements concerned Peru, as did the even more systematic study of institutionalized participation in Peru from 1968 to 1975.[2] This concentration reflected the unusually extensive and varied development of social movements in Peru, the abrupt shifts in relationships between movements and state policies, the incapacity of aspiring 'vanguard parties' to dominate the movements, and the extraordinary proliferation of non-governmental institutions studying and debating questions of popular participation from different ideological frames of reference.

During the 1968-1975 period, autonomous popular organizations, particularly trade unions, grew rapidly in Peru, together with the localized organizations promoted by state agencies. Even before the close of this period, economic crisis and an increasingly repressive government reaction to protests brought about the beginning of a convergence between movements with different origins. Peru has experienced in most years since 1974 a combination of economic stagnation, high inflation, high unemployment and underemployment, 'informalization' of productive activities, deteriorating living conditions and crippling debt burdens that became general in Latin America only in the early 1980s. Under these unpropitious conditions, popular organized efforts have gone through several stages.

The first, from 1975 to 1978, saw a military régime under changed leadership abandon most of the reforms and participatory initiatives of its predecessor and respond to economic difficulties with measures depressing popular welfare. This period was one of continual struggle by unions and allied organizations to defend levels of income and employment. These struggles included several nationwide general strikes, some of them successful in terms of popular mobilization but not in forcing the government to meet their demands. On the contrary, several thousand union activists were permanently excluded from industry.

The second period, up to the early 1980s, saw a waning of militant mobilization, a shift in attention to electoral tactics, a partial unification of the left political parties, and a transition from military to elected civilian government. Then, as the crisis deepened and the policies of the elected government proved as adverse to popular interests as those of its predecessor, protests over employment and standards of living again came to the fore. Still more recently, two years (1985-1987) of apparent improvement were followed by deeper depression, culminating in a 'shock' structural adjustment programme in mid-1990 that drastically cut the already deteriorated living conditions of the urban population by freeing prices and eliminating consumption subsidies. In this last period, levels of political and non-political violence rose ominously, but mass protest mobilizations were lacking and electoral support for the left political parties fell sharply.

The DESCO study attempted to 'evaluate the process of constitution of the popular movement as a social force and the possibility of it becoming the pivot of an alternative bloc which is capable of questioning and transforming political society today'. It concluded (as of 1982) that 'it is clear that the process of constitution of the popular movement is not yet complete. ... Efforts by the popular movement to search for consensus and for spaces which allow common identities to be defined have multiplied. It appears as an increasingly heterogeneous collective, in which the difficult and long-standing phenomena of cultural and ethnic *mestizaje*, different histories and interests are explicit.' Between 1968 and 1982, 'Peru's popular sectors made a substantial contribution to the structuring of civil society. ... The challenges they have faced since then are simply enormous and their continued process of constitution depends mainly on their capacity to face up to such challenges.'

This approach can be criticized as excessively teleological, as evading the question of the constraints imposed on popular choices by the economic setting, and as reading into popular struggle intentions that are not proven to be present. According to Carlos Franco, whose Introduction to the Ballon-Tovar report reflects the point of view of the 'participationists' active in the Velasco régime,

> the obvious reference to the state by those movements and the pressure they exert on government often tend to be understood as an expression of their inclination and capacity to change the direction of the state and take over political control. Therefore the fact that many actions of the popular movements are geared to achieving a redistribution of resources, the satisfaction of consumption needs or changes in policy are overlooked. For that same reason, insufficient value is attached to the state's capacity to exercise patronage over the popular movements, subordinate them or co-opt different factions among them. A persistent methodological confusion in the analysis of popular movements contributes to this, whereby the democratizing consequences of their action are identified with the intentionality of their behaviour. ... The popular movements are soon perceived as the inherent bearers of democracy or of socialism. They are thus attributed with a level and depth of political consciousness they do not possess, or at least not to the extent suggested by the studies.

In fact, the DESCO studies provide a critical assessment of the whole range of social movements that might constitute a national popular movement, as they have evolved in recent years in Peru. This assessment hardly supports the earlier hopes.

The labour movement. The findings on the Peruvian labour movement have been summarized above in Chapter 4. In short, the social movement with the longest history of organized solidarity and the closest links with theories of social transformation gained little or nothing in terms of its members' grasp of their own potential role in such transformation, and declined markedly in organizational vigour, following a brief period in the late 1970s when it could mobilize much wider strata of the population in national strikes.

> Contrary to certain political predictions according to which a more acute crisis would bring about a greater integration of the workers through a radicalization of their struggles, the situation indicates that a crisis with the present characteristics tends rather to demoralize the worker, dilute his identification with his class, foster the desperate search for individual ways out and, in synthesis, weaken the mechanisms of integration in his condition of member of the working class.[3]

Movements of *pobladores*. After 1975, the squatter settlements on the outskirts of the major cities continued to grow in numbers and in their share of the urban population, through the same processes as earlier, of massive land occupations and struggles/negotiations with the authorities for legal recognition of tenure and for urban services. By 1980, they housed half or more of the total number of inhabitants of several cities and more than a third of the population of Lima. In that year, 741 out of 962 had received legal recognition. As was stated above, the 1968-1975 régime had made a relatively systematic effort to transform not only the social organization and living conditions of these settlements, but also their cultural image. Even in this period, the extension of recognition and services lagged behind the growth of the settlements, and the régimes after 1975 had neither the resources nor the will to do as much, so that organized struggles were continuous.

These struggles had natural links with other popular struggles. Since a high proportion of the organized workers live in settlements of this kind, relations were close between the settlements and the labour mobilizations of the late 1970s. Neighbourhood committees supported strikes in the factories and participated in demonstrations. Many workers were active in the settlement organizations negotiating with the authorities over water, drainage, transport, etc. Settlement organizations in provincial cities participated in the regional movements to be discussed below, since they stood to benefit from a fairer share of state funds for the development of these centres. Moreover, since the settlements were peopled largely by migrants from peasant communities and small towns of the Andean highlands, they were linked to these communities and to the peasant movement through more than 4,000 clubs based on place of origin.

The settlement organizations formed city-wide and departmental federations, and two rival national confederations were set up, in 1978 and 1980. According to the DESCO study, however, both of these confederations 'had to face an enormous challenge, since in 1982 they were unable to incorporate the spontaneous mass mobilizations in the settlements, nor was there a convergence of the struggles in the various districts, zones and departments. Many struggles developed in isolation, in spite of the attempts to link up. Combined with the social, occupational and cultural heterogeneity of the inhabitants of the settlements, this created great difficulties for the articulation of a clear common identity.'

Settlement organizations could usually make some progress, even if halting, toward solution of the traditional problems of land tenure and urban services, and the settlers continued to manifest the ability, noted by many observers over the years, to improve their own housing once assured of tenure. From the mid-1970s on, however, problems of livelihood became even more difficult than before, with the overall deterioration of the economy and shrinkage of openings for wage work. Among the survival strategies of the settlement population street vending became increasingly important, and with it organizations of vendors to defend their right to this livelihood against municipal regulation. Other movements, in which women have taken the lead, centred on family consumption, and like the earlier focuses for organization required a combination of collective self-help with whatever aid could be obtained from the authorities. Altogether, localized solidarity movements, mainly in the settlements but not confined to them, became more numerous and diverse; these will be discussed below.

Peasant movements. After 1975, although rural poverty became even more extreme than before, peasant struggles receded in importance and the peasants received relatively little attention from proponents of a national popular movement. One reason was that cityward migrations were reducing the peasantry to a minority in the national population; flight from the land was replacing struggle for the land. Another reason was that tenure reforms during the Velasco period had removed the antagonism against landlords that had been the main unifying factor in previous peasant mobilizations. With the failure of the (generally bureaucratized) co-operative agricultural structures promoted by the government up to 1975, struggles became localized, pitting different groups of peasants and landless rural workers against each other, in demands for division of the co-operative lands into individual holdings and disputes over entitlement to land. The two national peasant organizations, the Confederación Campesina de Peru (CCP) and the Confederación Nacional Agraria (CNA) were unable to unite owing to 'party sectarianism' and were unable to reconcile the objective interests of the better-off rural producers and the poor peasants among their members. 'They were incapable of adapting to the changes taking place in rural Peru, once their earlier forms of struggle, particularly land occupation, no longer worked.' The government's agricultural price policy, unfavourable to producers, affected directly only those able to produce for the market. The only significant mobilization during the later period, the National Agrarian Strike in December 1982, mainly involved such producers. 'The poor peasants did not participate in any significant way, due to the very nature of the means of struggle adopted.'

The rural setting came to the fore again only with the rise of the Sendero Luminoso guerrilla movement in the 1980s, and the nearly simultaneous rise of coca cultivation, enabling peasants in some zones to achieve unprecedented income levels, while at the same time exposing them to new problems of defensive organization against the state, the guerrillas and the cocaine traffickers. The Sendero Luminoso is not a peasant movement, in terms of composition of leadership or ideology, but it did give an outlet for the pent-up frustration of peasants in the most impoverished parts of the Andean highlands. In some areas, the pre-existing peasant organizations were able to resist and exclude Sendero penetration. In others they were disintegrated by competing intimidation from Sendero and the armed forces. One result was a further acceleration of flight from the land to the city squatter settlements.

Regional movements. Throughout modern Peruvian history, political and economic power have been concentrated in Lima, and the national capital has naturally received a disproportionate share of public resources. Regional and local expressions of resentment against this centralization also have a long history, as in many other Latin American countries. During the late 1970s, the government's austerity policies further reduced allocations to the regions and stimulated an unprecedentedly extensive and broad-based series of organized protests in their urban centres. These movements temporarily united interest groups and classes generally far apart. Chambers of Commerce often took the lead, and their demands were most likely to get a hearing from the national authorities. The teachers' and bank employees' unions, which had more effective national organization than other unions, were particularly active. Industrial workers' unions, organizations of *pobladores*, and in a few cases peasant unions, were also involved. 'The involvement of the popular sectors ... in the regional movements had a double aim. On the one hand, it was to demand that the state fulfil its obligations in terms of services (health, education, housing, etc.) and promote development in the region. On the other, their aim was to fight the dominant local power groups in order to increase their own share of the wealth produced in the region.'

The main tactic when the national authorities failed to respond to initial demands was the city-wide or province-wide general strike, and this naturally placed the unionized workers at the centre of the mobilization. However, leadership and sources of support were likely to change significantly in the course of the struggle. Sometimes a local commercial élite captured what had started as a broad movement and settled for concessions confined to its own interests. Sometimes a movement started by such an élite was taken over by unions and organizations of *pobladores* when the struggle attracted mass backing and became more combative.

In their composition, the regional movements seemed to represent significant advances toward what the proponents of a 'national popular movement' had in mind, but in other respects they were hardly compatible with such an ideal. They could not unite nationally since they were in competition with each other as well as with Lima for a larger share of public allocations, and this emphasis really perpetuated their dependence on a state that was less and less able to respond to such demands. Some city-based movements entered into bitter conflict with others in their claims to larger resources on the grounds that they were at the legitimate centre of a region. Moreover, they could not escape the tactics of the political parties trying to capture them as bases for eventually achieving power nationally, and this complicated their representation of purely regional interests.

The DESCO study's summing up of their experience is somewhat ambivalent: 'The regional movements, as well as the national strikes, were a significant element in the special dynamic in which the Peruvian popular movement and the social classes themselves gradually articulated and constituted themselves. In the process, regional logic necessarily conflicted with the process of forming the Peruvian nation.'

Grassroots solidarity movements. Peru, like the rest of Latin America, during the 1970s saw a proliferation of many kinds of localized groupings constituting means of expressing moral solidarity, meeting cultural and recreational needs, and coping with the deepening crisis of livelihood through reciprocity.

The DESCO study recognizes the importance of such initiatives, particularly as a means of overcoming atomized individualism in the survival strategies of the poor, as a 'liberating experience in which the collective was synonymous with struggle for life', and as a channel for the entry of women into organized participation. However, it does not go beyond this general recognition, and apparently found it hard to define the relation of these groupings to a national popular movement. Many of them are spontaneous efforts to meet basic needs collectively or negotiate and distribute aid from the authorities or non-governmental organizations, with no ambitions for wider organization. In the settlements of Lima in the early 1980s, for example, it is estimated that there were around 7,500 neighbourhood committees organized around the municipal 'glass of milk' programme in which more than one hundred thousand women and more than one million children were involved.

Other groupings, in particular the Christian base communities, combining purposes of religious revival with collective self-help, are cold toward nationwide political movements as well as the state. The one reference to them in the DESCO study shows a certain uneasiness: 'Regarding grassroots Christian communities, previously unknown to those not connected with them, for the moment it is enough to stress their vigour and clear presence within the various popular sectors. They are part of a brilliantly coherent ideological effort which has an undeniable capacity to achieve change.' Finally, the DESCO study warns against either mystifying or devaluing the grassroots groupings: 'giving way to this temptation has dangerous consequences.'

The intellectual advisers of the Velasco régime, with their preference for localized participation and their distrust of national political organization, had fewer reservations about groupings of this kind. Carlos Franco, in his introduction to the study under discussion, reproaches the researchers looking to a national popular movement for neglecting them: 'Researchers preferred to pay attention to the trade union movement and only to a lesser extent to the movement among *pobladores* and in the interior regions of Peru. The intricate range of provincial clubs, parish groups, mothers' clubs, popular dining-rooms, feminist, cultural and youth groups, etc. – that is, organizations which were not exclusively working class – receive very little attention if any.' In fact, the localized groupings, however distrustful of the state, would have to deal with its social agencies directly and separately, and thus would be more vulnerable to institutionalization from above.

The left political parties and ideologists. The main reason why some intellectuals and activists placed their hopes on 'institutionalization' under an authoritarian régime and others placed theirs on the emergence of a 'national popular movement' was the manifest inability of Marxist and other left political parties to guide and unite the 'hitherto excluded', who were showing increasing disconformity with the existing order since the 1960s. The political factions seeking popular support were, up to the late 1970s, extremely fragmented, internally quarrelsome, and predisposed to the more exotic and extreme variants of Marxism. These parties dominated or influenced different parts of the trade union movement, and to a lesser extent other movements, and in doing so introduced their own factional quarrels and frequently urged unrealistic tactics on the movements. According to the DESCO study, however, 'on the whole, there were no "vanguards" present in the actions taken by popular groups. Vanguard elements seemed incapable of understanding events. ... There was a political disjunction between the global praxis of the dominated classes and the message or discourse of the vanguard (or of the groups who pretended to be such.'

Nevertheless, there seemed to be no way in which a popular movement aiming at power at the national level could divorce itself from political party organization. After the failure of national protest mobilizations and strikes in the late 1970s popular attention turned increasingly to electoral struggles and thus to the parties. In 1980, a coalition, 'Izquierda Unida', was formed that combined the majority of the Marxist parties and factions. This considerably strengthened the electoral capacity of the left, which obtained control of the municipal government of Lima in 1983 and was able to form positive links with the unions and movements of *pobladores*. The economic crisis, however, blocked significant responses to popular demands, and at the national level successive elected governments have quickly lost popular support. The centrist party that won the presidency in 1980 with 45 per cent of the votes gained less than 9 per cent in 1985. The winner of the latter election (Apra) experienced a similar slump in 1990, along with the once again divided left parties, and the two leading presidential candidates represented variants of neoliberalism remote from the state-interventionist, socialist and developmentalist currents previously in the foreground.

The DESCO study concluded, as of 1985, that most of Peru's political factions, including the 'Izquierda Unida', had shifted toward the centre of the political spectrum. The hopes for the social movements have shifted significantly from transformation to survival and stability:

> It is absolutely clear ... that the social movements are permanent producers of society, or order. [The various movements, forming a] complex organizational fabric ... have crystallized a particular order, have established new ways of inter-relating and, and even if they do not succeed in putting together new development strategies, at least show in relation to this question an enormous vitality for survival and capacity for creation and re-creation. It is this that permits them, in some cases with more flexibility than in others, to cope with their relation to and their opposition against a state that in fifteen years has changed its orientation drastically: from promoter of solidarity to disorganizer of the society. ... The crisis represents a long moment of questioning of the former basic identities of the social movements. ... This lays bare authoritarian limits in their interior, accelerates processes of internal democratization, and questions the basic mechanisms of representation and participation, requiring that the social movements, through their organizations, recognize and incorporate their diversity so as to strengthen themselves. ... Once again, social polarization has not ended in catastrophe. On the contrary, there is a kind of reaccommodation, a quest for balance, that carries the movements toward the centre. The electoral results are a clear expression of this. [The social movements] have been strengthening and also enmeshing the fabric of the civil society as a basic factor of equilibrium, to the extent that they are the

best guarantee against the authoritarian utopia represented by Sendero Luminoso.[4]

*

The preceding pages have demonstrated the difficulty of generalizing about social movements, even in a single national setting and from a relatively unified ideological position. The category itself represents an attempt to align highly diverse phenomena behind a conception conveying hope of positive participatory societal change in a period when more structured utopias have become discredited. It has an affinity to thinking about pluralist democracy that emphasizes the 'uncertainty principle'. Discourse on social movements, however, tends to generate its own utopias of spontaneous social mobilization and transformation. It is evident that the flowering of social movements throughout the world has not come closer to solutions because of three main problems: their ambiguous relations to political parties and the state; their inability to deal with economic crises except reactively or to generate coherent and convincing economic policy alternatives at the national level; and the impossibility of reconciling the aspirations and outlooks of the whole range of social movements, many of which have diametrically opposed convictions on human rights and human destiny.

There is some reason to think that the shift in conceptualization of the role of social movements noted in Peru is more generally applicable. Social movements are transforming societies, up to a point, but their heterogeneity and the complexity of their interactions may make them predominantly sources of stability, or at least of diffusion of popular energies, rather than sources of revolutionary upheavals.

Notes

1. Cardoso, Fernando Henrique, 'Associated-dependent Development and Democratic Theory', in Stepan, Alfred, ed., *Democratizing Brazil: Problems of Transition and Consolidation*, Oxford University Press, New York, 1989.

2. This research, conducted by the Centro de Estudios y Promoción del Desarrollo (DESCO), was later incorporated in a regional project, 'Social Movements before the Crisis of South America', under the auspices of the United Nations University (UNU) and the Consejo Latinoamericano de Ciencias Sociales (CLACSO). See Ballón, Eduardo and Tovar, Teresa, *The Development of Popular Movements in Peru, 1968-1982*, unpublished manuscript, UNRISD, Geneva, 1985; and Ballón, Eduardo, ed., *Movimientos Sociales y Crisis: El Caso Peruano*, DESCO, Lima, 1986. Unless otherwise noted all quotes in the following pages of this chapter are from the unpublished DESCO study by Ballón and Tovar.

3. Parodi, Jorge, 'La Desmovilización del Sindicalismo Industrial Peruano en el Segundo Belaundismo', in Ballón, Eduardo, ed., op. cit.

4. Ballón, Eduardo, ed., op. cit., pp. 40-2.

8

Interlocutors and Allies

Schemes for participation institutionalized by the state or by political parties have naturally attributed primary importance to the recruitment, training and motivation of organizers from outside the groups expected to 'participate'. Schemes emphasizing 'conscientization' have envisaged more modest roles for outsiders, as catalysts in the group's emerging self-awareness of domination and auxiliaries in its organized efforts toward liberation. At the other extreme, some currents of opinion have insisted that outsiders have no legitimate role; liberation and transformation can spring only from the spontaneous struggles and learning processes of the 'excluded' themselves.

In fact, the available evidence suggests that outsiders can rarely if ever bring into being significant participatory efforts unless the groups in question are already in movement and looking for help, and that the personal or institutional biases of outsiders inevitably condition their capacity to work with the excluded. However, the evidence also indicates that, with the partial exception of workers' unions, organized efforts almost always from their beginnings look for allies from outside the group, or take shape from an encounter between groups in movement and activists 'going to the people'.

Interlocutors are needed or wanted as intermediaries with the authorities, as interpreters of the legal and political context that the organized efforts confront, as negotiators of alliances with other organized forces, as sources of material aid, as spokesmen publicizing local injustices and demands and, finally, as formulators of utopias giving local struggles a broader meaning and a longer perspective.

At the same time, in real social settings it is impossible to draw a consistent dividing line between participatory movements of the excluded and their interlocutors. Trade unions, student movements, women's movements, and religious movements, in particular, can be both; 'conscientizing' their own members and advancing their perceived interests from situations of relative disadvantage within national power structures, while trying to mobilize and guide the struggles of larger and worse-off sectors of the population.

Unavoidably, the interlocutors reinvent the latter sectors according to their own values and images of the Good Society. They cannot altogether immunize themselves against propensities to paternalism and manipulation. This applies even to the initiatives relying on principles of 'conscientization'. Their activists have themselves first been 'conscientized' into a set of expectations concerning the kind of consciousness the group will develop with their aid and the kinds of problems to which it will give priority. Moreover, the 'conscientizers', as well as organizers from political parties and bureaucratic agencies, are likely to have a bias toward discussion meetings as ends in themselves.[1]

The groups struggling to overcome exclusion, for their part, find it hard to interpret realistically the interlocutors' intentions and abilities, so they are likely to react with a mixture of suspicion and dependency. It would be futile, however, to scold the interlocutors for their shortcomings or write them off as necessarily sources of confusion and co-option. As the hitherto excluded become more diversely and contradictorily involved in a world in crisis, and as movements trying to grapple with different aspects of the crisis from different positions within it continue to proliferate, interactions are bound to become more intense.

Ideally, the different categories of interlocutors should become more critical of their own roles, less disposed to attribute their own values and aims to the groups with which they are trying to co-operate, more disposed to listen and interact as equals – without, however, falling into a sentimentalized abdication of their own class position and viewpoint, leading to the supposition that the dispossessed are always virtuous and wise. In practice, persistent ideological preconceptions, institutional constraints, and the present drying up of convincing socioeconomic policy alternatives offering hope to the excluded imply that interlocutors will find it as hard as ever to keep this ideal in view.

The interlocutors relevant to present purposes can be classified as 'individual' or 'collective', although there can be no clear dividing line; individuals who belong to religious congregations or bureaucratic institutions may function as interlocutors of popular groups and movements quite independently of the norms of the organizations.

Individual interlocutors

Intermediaries. Intermediaries can be functionaries of government agencies or voluntary organizations, schoolteachers, priests, lawyers, shopkeepers, innkeepers, returned military recruits, etc. Such local interlocutors, having some acquaintance with the wider society and some independence of the power of landlords, have throughout history been particularly important to peasant movements in their initial phases. Without the co-operation of literate individuals with some understanding of law and bureaucracy, peasant movements have commonly been unable to advance beyond quickly repressed flarings of violence against landlords and oppressive local authorities. In many cases, peasants have demanded that local teachers and priests take on the role of intermediaries.

In urban settlement movements also, individual intermediaries are important, and here the function is likely to become professionalized. The intermediary becomes a specialist who gains a living from organizing land occupations, obtaining services from authorities or protection from politicians. In both rural and urban settings, of course, the relationship readily becomes either a form of clientelism or a channel for party politicization. The intermediary obtains small favours for his clientèle and larger advantages for himself in exchange for mobilizing voters or demonstrators. Or the intermediary, if ideologically committed, builds on this function to enlist the local group in support of his own party. Schoolteachers are particularly likely to attempt this latter role.

Voices. 'Voices' can be social scientists and researchers in the universities, journalists, novelists, poets, musicians and artists. Significant organized efforts have generally been preceded or accompanied by intellectual and artistic presentations of situations of oppression, bringing them into the light before public opinion and legitimizing the struggles of previously invisible or despised groups. In many countries since the 1930s or earlier, novelists have done a great deal to change the ways in which educated urban sectors of the public have viewed their own societies – and possibly the ways in which some of the dispossessed have come to view themselves. Writers, musicians and artists have defended and disseminated popular culture against the monopoly of the 'official' European-dominated culture of the urban élites.

Collective interlocutors

Political parties. Throughout the world, national political organizations have been indispensable means of aggregating strength from local organized efforts so as to bring it to bear at the centre, and of conducting bargaining so as to derive more or less coherent national policies from the demands of conflicting classes and interest-groups. The parties have also notoriously subordinated organized efforts to the 'iron law of oligarchy', manipulating class and group interests to serve their own struggles for power. As was explained above, the conceptual effort to place 'social movements' ahead of parties was designed in part to find an alternative to the longstanding deficiencies of political representation-manipulation-sectarianism. A diametrically opposed solution has been the construction from above of one-party states, in which the single party is supposed to act as transmission belt between the state and a class in power or the 'people'. Up to the present, social movements have not been able to fulfil the more ambitious hopes of their proponents, and single-party systems have fallen into discredit. For all their shortcomings, competitive party systems seem to offer the hitherto excluded an indispensable means of making their interests heard and to some extent curbing the propensity of dominant groups to exploit them.

In a good many countries with multiparty systems, however, the better established parties have represented élite interests, and have not aspired to act as interlocutors of the hitherto excluded, as was described above in the case of peasants in Colombia, except in clientelistic transactions for votes.

The excluded, then, have faced unpromising political alternatives. They could rally behind populist movements, which tended to disintegrate their more autonomous organized efforts within mass mobilizations dominated by charismatic leaders, and whose eventual breakdown might leave them worse off than before. Or they could turn to the more radical ideologically committed factions that were competing to mobilize and guide them. Except in a few countries, these latter have been too weak and divided by sectarian quarrels to help the excluded to greater influence in national affairs. They have tended to commit the organizations of the latter to positions out of keeping with their perceived interests and their real strength, thus involving them in defeats, cutting them off from other possible allies, and eventually disheartening their members. A particularly clear instance of this process at work in the Colombian peasant movement is discussed below.

Religious movements. One of the most striking trends since the 1960s has been the effort by movements within the Catholic Church, particularly in Latin America, and by other religious bodies to act as interlocutors, exercising a 'preferential option for the poor'. This effort has succeeded in legitimizing organized struggles among strata previously too intimidated by the power structure and too preoccupied by survival to organize. It has also 'conscientized' important currents of opinion within the better-off classes, nationally and internationally, to the plight of the poor. Activists in these movements have been readier to share the living conditions of the squatter settlements and impoverished villages over the long term than most other interlocutors. The movements naturally have their own conceptions of the Good Society and the place in it of the hitherto excluded. These conceptions, as has been suggested in several contexts above, are often anti-political, communitarian, suspicious of capitalist or socialist modernization and centralization, valuing local reciprocity and austerity in consumption. Such values, in specific settings, are likely to clash with the real consumerist and individualistic traits of the excluded, their increasing geographical mobility, and their openness to combative political mobilization. At the same time, as is well known, some of the religious groupings find common ground, through liberation theology, with uncompromisingly revolutionary prescriptions for the excluded, and this, in turn, brings them into conflict with the higher authorities of their own congregations.

Academic social science institutions and researchers. For many years sociologists and other social scientists have studied and theorized about the different groups here identified as 'excluded'. During the period under review this activity grew and diversified extraordinarily and spread to additional countries. Social scientists increasingly identified themselves as 'committed' allies of the excluded. They acknowledged a duty to conduct research in co-operation with the subjects of the research and to make the findings accessible and useful to them. The UNRISD Participation Programme itself was inspired by this current in the social sciences, enlisted committed social scientists in debate and research, and tried to respond to perceived needs for information and analysis of organizations of workers and peasants.

For a time, particularly in Latin America, the efforts of social scientists to act as interlocutors of the exploited classes made the role of a good many indistinguishable from that of revolutionary ideologists. More recently, the dominant tone has changed again toward revaluation of pluralist democracy and scepticism concerning the possibility or desirability of organized efforts toward transformation of power structures. In Alain Touraine's words, the 'hyper-autonomy of the cultural actors' has become somewhat more restrained, and the 'professional critical tendency' has gained over the 'committed prophetic tendency'.[2] According to a similar but more disapproving evaluation, Latin American intellectuals have metamorphosed, through dependence on international foundation financing and academic jobs during the years of repression and exile, from 'organic intellectuals' identifying with popular revolutionary struggles into tame 'institutional intellectuals'.[3]

Trade unions. A contradiction can be expected within trade unions between ideological support of equality and aspirations to mobilize broad popular alliances, on the one hand, and aggressive defence of the acquired interests of union members, on the other. The traditional organizational structures of trade unionism are inapplicable to most categories of the excluded, and the urban poor are potential adversaries of the union members, working for sub-subsistence wages in small unregulated enterprises and discouraging strikes by their availability to replace strikers. At the same time, as earlier chapters of Part II have noted, many unionized workers live in squatter settlements, have family members in 'informal' occupations, and have ties to rural places of origin. Their organizations join in struggles over issues outside the work relationship: shelter, urban services, price controls on basic goods and services. The union leadership (generally tied to political parties) has to do its best to draw in the larger contingents of unemployed, self-employed and others in the 'informal sector' to strengthen mass protests against 'structural adjustment' programmes.

Urban organizations based on region or community of origin. Such associations, frequently multiclass and including well-off professionals, not only form nuclei for mutual aid and self-defence in the cities, but also act as intermediaries for the communities of origin of migrants, using their proximity to the central authorities to carry on negotiations over public services and protests against abusive or corrupt local agents of the state, sending material aid, and providing information or enlisting support for the political movements current in the cities. Thus, the high geographical mobility of people between national centre and periphery has probably done as much to strengthen regional or community self-assertion against the centre as to disintegrate community ties.

Student movements. In a good many countries, these have long been politicized, with the kind of politicization and capacity to mobilize the mass of students shifting continually. The student movements have reflected and sometimes exaggerated the sectarian conflicts of the left political organizations. They have also been highly motivated to providing services and proselytizing among the hitherto excluded sectors.

At the same time, as enrolment in the public universities has risen and student pressure has led to the abolition of fees and entrance examinations, youth from relatively impoverished origins have become the majority in some countries. As the state's shrinking ability to finance higher education or provide public jobs increasingly frustrates their expectations, the older impulse of 'going to the people' by students mainly of middle-class origin mingles with an involuntary movement back into the ranks of the excluded by youths who had hoped to use education to escape from poverty – making them a particularly volatile and unpredictable set of interlocutors. Among the directions their efforts to cope may take, the following seem important for present purposes:

• Employment as local-level workers in governmental or NGO programmes aimed at participatory organization and self-help. Here their desperate need for livelihood may produce a conformist assimilation of the rhetoric of the programme and a distortion of its content into protection of job security.
• Activism in confrontational movements trying to mobilize the excluded. The Maoist groupings of Colombia, India and Peru, discussed below, originated among university students.
• Non-ideological performance of traditional leadership and intermediary roles for local groups; legal and medical education are particularly relevant to this function.
• Informal or illicit entrepreneurship, including black market activities.

Women's movements. Here the interlocutors are organizations of middle-class urban women, striving to achieve for themselves a closer approach to equality in law, work opportunities, family relationships and societal attitudes, while at the same time entering into the incipient organized efforts of the doubly excluded women of the low-income settlements and of peasant communities.

National voluntary organizations. This category partially overlaps with a number of those mentioned above, but also includes increasingly numerous and diverse groupings, mainly originating in the educated middle classes, inspired by values of social justice and human rights to become allies of the disadvantaged.

International NGOs. These have become increasingly prominent in mobilizing international public opinion against oppressive governments and situations of exploitation, and against the acts of commission and omission through which their home governments and dominant economic interests support such situations. They have brought to the fore issues of human rights, environmental degradation and gender inequality, and have supported countless local projects with participatory intentions, including self-support projects among refugees and political exiles.

They face several contradictions that can be kept under control but not eliminated:

First, between maintaining good relations with governments and assuming militantly the role of spokesmen for the hitherto excluded. The former course may lead them into co-operating with programmes that they know to be misconceived and corrupt, and thus discredit them in the eyes of the people they want to help. The latter course may mean their expulsion. Or, if a given régime seems to share their participatory ideals, they may become unduly credulous concerning its claims for the programmes supposed to embody the ideals.

Secondly, a contradiction lies between their own democratic-humanitarian-nonviolent-environmentalist values and the real cultures and tactics of the excluded or the nationalist-religious-Marxist mobilizers of the excluded. The fact that they can provide material aid and international status desperately needed by local movements unavoidably fosters relationships of combined dependency and resentment and makes them potential scapegoats in local factional struggles.

Thirdly, there is a contradiction between their globalization of standards and interpretation of needs, and the extreme diversity of local situations.

The problem of relationships between interlocutors and the excluded recurs throughout the present survey, and indeed was crucial to the organization of the UNRISD Programme, although only one of the national researches, that in India, focused primarily on this dimension. The following pages will summarize a few examples that may help to clarify the generalizations made above and possibly suggest pitfalls that might be avoided.

Pobladores in Chile

The history of popular struggles in the low-income settlements in Santiago during the military régime has been summarized above. These struggles were shaped by encounters between the people of the settlements, who desperately needed external allies, material aid, and some means of making sense of their plight, and interlocutors from political, intellectual and religious circles that had long been trying to interact with the *pobladores* and conducting polemics over their place in strategies for social change. These circles were struggling to survive under the dictatorship and find means of organizing resistance. Elements among them came to look to the *pobladores* as the most likely protagonists of revolutionary struggle, because of the extremity of their poverty and insecurity and the direct confrontation of their interests with the régime's policies.

The relatively long history of popular organization and of ideologically committed social science research and polemics in Chile had much to do with the capacity of the interlocutors to insert their own conceptions into the survival-oriented struggles of the *pobladores*. The researcher's conclusion, however, has a wider application to other settings in which interlocutors are tempted to assign roles to their intended clientèles:

> more than in the case of other social actors, their processes of self-definition, of identification with the social situation in which they live, and of identification of the relations between their purposes and those of other social actors, are strongly marked by the formulations they receive from external agents. Perhaps this occurs precisely because of the weak specificity that the social action of the *pobladores* normally shows over the long term, action which at the same time faces an ample supply of organizing rationalizations. It seems, then, that the less a social aggregate is constituted as a stable social category or stratum, the more difficulties it has in producing by itself precise elements of self-identification, definition of its social situation, and of its relations with other social interlocutors.[4]

Thus, among the *pobladores*, it was common for ideologically-inspired leaders to create their own social base rather than *vice versa*. External formulations emphasizing the ideas of 'community' could produce community social action, and external formulations emphasizing 'social rupture' and exclusion could produce confrontational or revolutionary action.

Peasants in Colombia

The Colombian peasant organization, ANUC, discussed in Chapter 3, manifested particularly complex and ultimately frustrating interactions between a grassroots movement and a series of interlocutors with conflicting ideologies and purposes. While peasant struggles and party manipulation of these struggles had a long history in Colombia, ANUC took shape (during 1966-1970) as the initiative of a reformist government. At this stage, the interlocutors were functionaries of a governmental 'Division of Peasant Organization'. Some of them were sociologists or agricultural specialists with international experience. The majority were trained in local courses emphasizing peasant empowerment and participation in agrarian reform. By 1971, as the peasant movement became increasingly vigorous, autonomous and concentrated on land seizure tactics, government support dwindled and then reversed itself, and the interlocutors who had co-operated with the land seizures were purged from government agencies.

The organized peasants needed allies in their struggle against the counterattack of the organized landlords, now backed by the state and the armed forces. The two major political parties (including the party responsible for the creation of ANUC) were controlled by economic élites, and were not disposed to offer effective representation of peasant interests in exchange for peasant votes. The urban trade unions were weak and divided. Thus the interlocutors that offered themselves were Marxist factions, recruited largely from university students, purporting to represent the 'proletariat' but with little influence in the working-class organizations.

These factions, with first Trotskyists and later Maoists having the upper hand, viewed peasant tactics entirely in terms of their own revolutionary doctrines and the destined roles of peasants as derived from the Russian and Chinese revolutions. They managed to radicalize the greater part of the peasant leadership (particularly its component of rural schoolteachers) but the resulting 'revolutionary' tactics incurred mainly defeats and repression, and sectarian quarrels disillusioned the rank and file.

> All differences were turned into unconditional questions, promoting sectarianism and leaving almost no room for democratic debates and compromises. In the work at the grassroots level this resulted in incessant conflicts between doctrinaire activists who showed little concern about the dangers of political division within the peasant movement. ... In addition, the endless accusations of corruption and political duplicity aroused deep suspicions among the rank-and-file about the motives of their leaders, which blocked reorganizational attempts and cast doubt on the ideological legitimation that had previously stimulated the radicalism of the peasants.[5]

After a disastrous ANUC Congress in 1974 brought peasant delegates face to face with the extent of sectarian conflict, membership drained away, and eventually the remnant of ANUC retreated to modest aims and a dependent relationship with interlocutors in the public agencies and the major political parties.

The activist social scientists and agrarian reform specialists who had shaped the early stages of peasant mobilization remained to some extent alternative interlocutors. After 1971 they had little influence on the national political scene, and they could not offer revolutionary utopias as ambitious as those of the Marxist factions. However, they did have relatively coherent ideas on peasant tactics and they offered a bridge to international sources of funding for ANUC – charitable foundations, religious organizations, farmers' unions, etc., mainly in Europe. With the funding they introduced prescriptions for action.

The most influential of these prescriptions was that of the sociologist Orlando Fals Borda. It called for concentration on local 'strongholds of peasant self-reliance' practising collective cultivation. These were to serve as focal points for a gradual extension of non-capitalist relations of production in the countryside. This idea, which called for efforts to increase peasant production and incomes, came under attack from the Maoists, who also promoted peasant self-sufficiency, but with the proviso that 'production had to be reduced to a bare minimum so that the peasants would live at a subsistence level and their revolutionary potential would be preserved'.[6] In the Maoist attack on the policy of promoting strongholds, Fals Borda's access to foreign funds became a key feature of accusations against him. In any case, the advocates of 'strongholds' seem to have overestimated the capacity of the peasants to understand and act on the idea, and underestimated the propensity of local leaders to misappropriate funds distributed without adequate safeguards. None of the strongholds proved a success, and before long Fals Borda's group and then the Maoists themselves were ejected from ANUC in the course of the endless factional struggles.

Popular organizations in Peru

In Peru, as in Colombia, one finds a stage during the late 1960s and early 1970s in which interlocutors from social science backgrounds, acting from influential positions in the state apparatus, tried to indoctrinate the masses in their own schemes for local participatory organization, eventually lost their governmental backing, and were pushed aside by confrontational popular mobilizations that were guided and then disrupted by sectarian struggles for control by Marxist factions. In Peru, however, as was demonstrated in Chapters 6 and 7, the struggles were broader and more complex, as was the historical background of polemics over the role of different classes and the correct strategies for reform or revolution. In Peru, the peasants were not isolated in their militant mobilization, but became a secondary factor in the struggle for power. Both the state-promoted organizations and the later popular movements embraced the urban settlements of the poor and the unionized workers as well as the peasants and rural wage workers.

In Peru, the very rapid growth of the public universities and the mass entry of young people from the dispossessed sectors have been particularly important. The educated activists entering into contact with rural and urban communities have come from their own youth to a greater extent than in most other countries. The consequences for the communities have been ambiguous. Young people in the universities have been exposed to competitive proselytizing to such an extent that their period as students has been labelled 'compulsory revolutionary service'. Later on, their struggle for livelihood and the shrinking ability of the public sector to absorb them have probably contributed to the proliferation of rival political factions striving to act as interlocutors.

Among some of these would-be interlocutors, the tactics of persuading or forcing peasant communities to limit their production, cut their contacts with markets and state services, and accept austere living conditions for the sake of weakening the urban 'national' economy and strengthening their revolutionary spirit have been more aggressive than in Colombia, and equally remote from aspirations for a better life.

In Peru also, before and since the state-supported participatory schemes of the early 1970s, social-science-oriented groups promoting localized projects and communitarian ideals have been active and influential. As in Colombia, their ability to tap funds from abroad has made them vulnerable to attacks from the political factions.

Social action groups and non-party political formations in India

In India, the roles of interlocutors, as well as the range of categories of the excluded and the forms of exclusion, have been particularly complex and somewhat different from those in other countries in which the UNRISD Programme sponsored research. By the mid-1960s a welfare-oriented state-capitalist strategy of developing rural infrastructure and public-sector industries had slowed down. This period saw the first major famine since independence; official planning had to be suspended. The Indian state weathered the crisis through a combination of co-optive and repressive measures, but India never quite regained the stability and confidence that marked its transition process during the 1950s and early 1960s.

Since then, every institution – traditional or modern – has been in tension, undergoing re-evaluation, questioning and attacks. While important parts of the population during this period gained and improved their life opportunities, larger parts lost, in relative terms if not absolutely. Social cohesion became more precarious, and violent encounters pitting group against group became more ominous. While the credibility of the state as promoter of the general welfare and impartial arbiter of conflicts diminished, political parties and interest-group organizations did not gain in ability to channel the discontent and present convincing alternatives.

Under these conditions a wide range of initiatives originating in the educated middle classes and inspired by ideologies of social change took shape and tried to link themselves with the equally diverse survival strategies and organized protests of the different categories of excluded – landless labourers, poor peasants and other petty producers, urban workers and slum dwellers, tribal groups, 'scheduled castes' and women. These initiatives acted on the conviction that the development efforts of the state, whatever their original pretensions, had come to neglect or discriminate against the poor and powerless. Their proponents also reasoned that the macro-organizations claiming to represent the poor – political parties and their mass fronts – had become too bureaucratized or sectarian to carry out this function effectively.

The new initiatives took three main forms: (1) localized 'social' efforts to bring minimum services to the poor and help them improve their community life and livelihood through co-operation; (2) non-party political formations (NPPFs) aspiring to help the excluded groups to organize and defend their interests against exploiters and the manipulating state; (3) Maoist movements (the 'Naxalites') striving to mobilize the excluded for violent confrontation with dominant classes and the state.

The first initiatives were very loosely organized above the local level; they corresponded to the 'conscientization' efforts and 'base communities' in Latin America. The second initiatives had more in common with the Latin American hopes for multiclass 'social movements'. The third, originating among radicalized students but able to mobilize peasants in some parts of India, were soon eradicated by the state from most of these areas, although the insurgent movements have persisted and more recently regained some ground. Some of the survivors of the repression retreated to initiatives of the first or second type.

The UNRISD Programme sponsored two research projects in India. The first one focused on the localized social-action groups, and was conducted mainly through extended discussions between researchers, activists and villagers attending meetings, and among activists. The key objectives were to help the groups reflect on their own history, share their experiences with other groups, and thus come to understand the factors that hinder them from coming together in spite of similar concerns and methods. The discussions did not come to clear conclusions on this but did highlight two issues bearing on the prevalent disunity and similar to those brought out by studies in other countries.[7]

First, each action group included middle-class activists as well as activists from among the dispossessed. Rarely, however, did the groups take into account or even become aware of the differences between them in perceptions and work styles. The middle-class initiators of the local actions were motivated by an intellectual commitment to a certain vision of social change, and this led them to try to accelerate the pace of such change, dominate the other activists, and raise issues of little concern to them or their communities. This inevitably led to an escalation of intra-group tension. Time and energy then had to be spent on preserving internal unity, rather than on achievement of broader unity with other groups.

Secondly, the groups were functioning in settings in which the state and various political parties were seeking to intervene and monopolize 'local space'. The social action groups had to fend off efforts from several directions to co-opt them for purposes rejected by their members. Very often the people they were trying to mobilize viewed the state as well as the parties as forces making for exploitation and divisiveness. Thus, the activists clung to localized efforts they could understand and control, which did not risk conflict in the community. Their preconceptions and experiences inhibited them from negotiating with the state for whatever services it might provide, or from trying to enlist broad public backing through political channels.

The other research project consisted of a broad survey of the non-party political formations and their apparent impact.[8]

The NPPFs had emerged from an encounter between increasingly alienated and radicalized sectors of the middle classes seeking new forms of political action, on the one side, and various groups among the excluded seeking allies and new ways to articulate their discontent. The activists of the NPPFs generally looked down on the efforts of the social action groups as futile or conducive to popular demobilization, but also rejected the Maoist tactics of violent revolutionary confrontation.

The survey concluded that most of the NPPFs remained weak, hesitant and transient, unable to realize their original aspirations toward a new kind of politics, prone to vacillate between replication of the political party type of organization and localized social action. While they have had some successes in consciousness-raising and organization at the local level, their short life-spans and inability to achieve concrete gains might, in many cases, bring about a further demobilization of the groups they aspired to mobilize. They have been most successful in dealing with the most impoverished and excluded sectors of the population, such as the tribal groups, and in organizing campaigns around specific issues such as opposition to ecologically damaging 'development' projects. They have been much less effective in their contacts with sectors more directly linked to the market and the capitalist economic system, such as the industrial workers and peasants producing for the market. Here the traditional parties and unions, whatever their shortcomings, have left little or no space for alternative forms of organization.

The deep social crisis and the inadequacies of the mass popular organizations, together with the continual increases in the numbers of educated youth unable to find a satisfying role in the society, ensure that initiatives along these lines will continue to emerge, together with more anomic or sectarian protests. It seems unlikely, however, that the NPPFs can evolve into the main vehicles for social transformation. The survey concludes that the anti-participatory structures retain enough vitality to co-opt or crush such initiatives as they struggle with realities too contradictory to submit to their principles for action.

*

To sum up, groups and movements of the hitherto excluded cannot do without interlocutors and usually face a quite limited range of choice among the interlocutors that offer themselves. These interlocutors are likely to hold preconceptions and ideological commitments that correspond only in small part to the perceived interests of the group,[9] and they may or may not be able to offer the group significant resources, reliable information on the wider power structure, or access to allies with national influence. If the group's organized efforts persist, it should at the same time evolve its own leadership and assess realistically what the interlocutors have to offer. If the interlocutors then cling to a tutelary role, conflicts between the two kinds of leadership are likely. In some cases, external leadership, retaining static images of the exploited classes and their historic role, may push the local cadres beyond their natural preoccupation with immediate practical gains into a premature confrontation with élites and the state. In other cases of explosive discontent, the external leadership may be a voice for caution and realism, whether effectively or not. To the extent that both groups of actors gain ability to put themselves in the place of the other, their relationships will be more fruitful.

Notes

1. 'A plethora of meetings to exchange ideas may negatively affect their implementation. ... Projects provided for so many hours of meetings that to any neutral observer it was obvious that something was not working. The projects' objectives were social and economic development of the communities, not sitting down and talking about development.' Angulo, Alejandro, *An Experiment in Participatory Development*, UNICEF Innocenti Global Seminar on Participatory Development, Florence, May 1990.

2. Touraine, Alain, *Actores Sociales y Sistemas Políticos en América Latina*, PREALC, Santiago, 1987.

3. Petras, James and Morley, Morris, *US Hegemony under Siege: Class, Politics and Development in Latin America*, Verso, London and New York, 1990.

4. This and the following quotations are from Campero, Guillermo, *Entre la Sobrevivencia y la Acción Política: Las Organizaciones de Pobladores en Santiago*, Ediciones ILET, Santiago, 1987, pp. 244-7.

5. Zamosc, León, *The Agrarian Question and the Peasant Movement in Colombia: Struggles of the National Peasant Association, 1967-81*, UNRISD and Cambridge University Press, Geneva and Cambridge, 1986, p. 120.

6. Ibid., p. 169.

7. These discussion meetings were carried out under the auspices of the People's Institute for Development and Training (PIDT), New Delhi. The results and findings from this participatory research process are contained in a document that represents a collective endeavour of scientists, activists and villagers that had attended the various seminars and meetings. See PIDT, *Understanding Social Reality*, unpublished manuscript, PIDT/UNRISD, New Delhi, 1984.

8. The findings of this project are contained in Sethi, Harsh and Kothari, Smitu, eds., *The Non-Party Political Process in India: Uncertain Alternatives*, unpublished manuscript, UNRISD, Geneva, 1985. Parts of this work have been published in revised form in *Economic and Political Weekly*, Bombay, and in *Lokayan Bulletin*, New Delhi. India has continued to present a contradictory juxtaposition of numerous and varied social action groups and movements promoting 'positive' participation, and an alarming rise in both communal violence and anomic criminal violence. The activist-researchers publishing the *Lokayan Bulletin*, some of whom were formerly linked to the UNRISD Programme, have continued to try to stimulate dialogue among activists and concerned citizens on the manifestations of these contradictions.

9. The initial ideological position of interlocutors does not necessarily predetermine their long-term roles. According to a recent study in Durango, Mexico, a 'Comité de Defensa Popular', started in the early 1970s by student Maoists ideologically similar to those of Colombia, India and Peru, has evolved into a politically flexible and effective organizer of community self-help and struggle against environmental menaces. See Moguel, Julio and Velázquez, Enrique, *Organización Social y Lucha Ecológica en una Region del Norte de México*, UNRISD Discussion Paper No. 20, Geneva, April 1991.

Part III

The Future of Participation

9

The New World Context

The confounding of expectations

The 1960s and 1970s saw rising perplexity over contradictions in 'development', but also a persistent confidence that radically different policies could be devised and agents found to apply them, so as to make the dynamic processes of economic growth and societal transformation more equitable and more sustainable over the long term. During the 1980s, in countries differing widely in policies and experiences of 'development', including most of those of Africa and Latin America, economic growth stagnated or turned negative, contradictions multiplied, the livelihood of the majority deteriorated, and confidence in national capacity to find a way out of this impasse waned. Elsewhere, particularly in South and East Asia, in spite of satisfactory economic growth rates and rising consumption levels for the greater part of the population, insecurity concerning the future and political impasses blocking responses to urgent questions were evident. In general, neither governments nor popular movements seemed able to reverse widening inequalities and persistent poverty.

The inter-governmental and non-governmental schemes that had flourished during the 1970s, for a 'New International Economic Order' or 'Another Development', lost plausibility, although international forums continued to repeat and adapt their propositions. In most countries, policy makers and their advisers lowered their sights to 'adjustment' within a narrow range of options left by the national and international conjunctures, and were far from assurance that they could 'adjust' sufficiently to ward off breakdown. The ability of existing nation states to perform their traditional functions declined, while public confidence in this ability declined even more. A paradoxical combination of economic and political 'globalization' and internal segmentation of interests and demands challenged governments. International organizations became increasingly preoccupied by problems of governability or 'governance; in other words, whether they could find valid interlocutors for their advice.

In the early years of the 1990s changes throughout the world have accelerated and confounded conventional wisdom even more than before, most strikingly in the disintegration of the 'real socialist' model of political and economic organization. We cannot evade an attempt to sum up the main trends that bear on the 'organized efforts' that are our central concern. However, the trends are too diverse and precarious, and information on some of them lags too far behind the realities, for us to do this with

confidence. For present purposes, the quantifiable changes are less important than their reflections in the minds of millions of individuals and in the
behaviour of groups trying to relate their struggles to the future of the
societies to which they belong. Here generalizations can be little more than
guesswork coloured by the values of the observer.

One authoritative international survey, prepared by the World Bank in
1990, looks to a better future through sound government policies, with
popular participation a desideratum as long as it can harmonize with
existing power relationships. This survey emphasizes the 'enormous economic progress' made in the 'developing world' during the past three
decades, and envisages 'rapid and politically sustainable progress on
poverty' through a two-part strategy. Such a strategy would 'promote the
productive use of the poor's most abundant asset – labour' and would
'provide basic services to the poor'. This strategy would be 'more likely
to be adopted in countries where the poor have a say in political and
economic decision-making'. However, 'policies that help the poor but
impose costs on the non-poor will encounter resistance ... . Since political
power tends to reflect economic power, it is important to design poverty-
reducing policies that will be supported, or at least not actively resisted,
by the non-poor.' For most countries at present this rules out land redistribution, although 'a relatively egalitarian distribution of land increases
the effectiveness of other policies aimed at reducing poverty'.[1] The Bank's
1991 Report, while maintaining the stance of qualified affirmation that
'rapid and sustained development ... is an achievable reality', recognizes
that previous Bank forecasts of economic growth in Africa and Latin
America for the 1980s were exceedingly over-optimistic. It presents a
formidable array of incognita and mainly political difficulties in the way
of achievement of the development-assuring mix of policies.[2]

Another recent policy-oriented report, less optimistic and more radical
in its proposals, asserts:

> the state is best able to perform its demanding functions when there is a
> national consensus on the goals and purposes of development, and on the
> apportionment of the costs as well as the benefits of development. Demo-
> cratic institutions, which allow full participation and through which such
> a consensus can be reached, are therefore not only an objective of people-
> centred development, but its very means as well. Participation in the
> political process means much more than the opportunity to exercise the
> vote. It means as well having a political climate that not merely tolerates
> dissent but welcomes it. Dissent is at the heart of participation, for
> participation must imply the right to say to the establishment in all spheres
> – 'yes' or 'no' or 'but'.[3]

What can the groups and movements with which we are concerned
make of principles such as these at present? They might well be sceptical

of the possibility of mutually advantageous pacts with the 'non-poor'. They have tangible reasons to dissent from the structural adjustment policies the governments are applying but, even if the governments welcome such dissent, convincing alternatives are lacking. In many cases, the 'resources and regulative institutions' they might hope to control are disintegrating, subject to or involved in ideological attacks against the welfare state, undergoing 'privatization', losing relevance to their perceived needs. When they gain the democratic right to choose between representatives and policies they are told that it will be irresponsible and self-defeating for them to use this right to insist on secure livelihood and social equity.

The first democratically elected mayor of Moscow has delivered with particular bluntness a message that the hitherto excluded in most of the world have been hearing from their elected governments: 'There will be contradictions between the policies leading to denationalization, privatization, and inequality on the one hand and, on the other, the populist character of the forces that were set in motion in order to achieve those aims. The masses long for fairness and economic equality. And the further the process of transformation goes, the more acute and the more glaring will be the gap between those aspirations and economic realities.' Efforts to participate, in the sense of the definition we have been using, will amount to 'a renaissance of leftwing populism'. He concludes ominously that the achievement of democracy must 'seek new mechanisms and institutions of political power that will depend less on populism'.[4]

The terms of thinking about these questions (or evading them) continue to depend on the conceptions summarized in Chapter 2. Their relative plausibility has shifted and some of them are in eclipse but, with more terminological than substantive innovations, all of them persist among the heterogeneous currents of opinion trying to understand, guide or manipulate the equally heterogeneous groupings of the disadvantaged. Some of them offer more hope than others, from the standpoint of the values behind the present inquiry, but none as yet can claim more than localized and precarious successes toward the empowerment of the excluded.

Let us look first at the different dimensions of the world setting at the beginning of the 1990s and then return to the conceptions.

The economic setting

All countries at present are deeply and visibly involved in a world economic system that seems to dictate national responses, leaving governments some room for dexterity in crisis management and correctives, but no room for the more ambitious alternatives that were current a decade or two ago. 'Delinking' from the world economy has ceased to be a plausible strategy, in part because of the internationalization of production and of consumer aspirations, in part because innovations in financial institutions and communications have ruled out national control over monetary flows.

Within the world system, countries encounter periodic shocks and sometimes windfall opportunities, as in the case of fluctuating oil availability and prices, but in recent years the system has not offered the majority of the world's peoples the continually expanding markets and investment funds needed to support earlier expectations of 'development'. In some regions the main inhibiting factor is the burden of publicly-guaranteed debt, in others the imperatives of technological modernization and labour cost controls to preserve competitive advantages in the world market. Still others face the imperative of reforming and dynamizing bureaucratized welfare states, or of shifting from bankrupt command economies to market economies. A good many of the poorest countries seem to be even more excluded than previously from any viable insertion in the world economy, without achieving any compensatory capacity for self-sufficiency, even at a subsistence level, through their peoples' traditional means of livelihood.

An UNRISD research programme on Adjustment, Livelihood and Power, has focused on the impact of economic crisis on two groups of countries:[5]

First, 'the heavily indebted countries, mainly middle-income, with substantial industrialization achieved through import substitution and with good access to borrowing during the 1970s (heavily weighted towards Latin America ...)'. These countries during the 1970s 'opened' their economies to varying degrees, dismantling protectionism and controls over financial flows, with resulting changes in the structures of industrial and agricultural production, increasing dependence on imports and on exports to pay for them, and speculative financial booms financed by borrowing. Signs of impending difficulties were abundant, but economic growth continued, in some cases quite vigorously, until crisis struck suddenly in the early 1980s, when the flow of funds from abroad ceased, interest rates on the debt rose, and per capita incomes dropped by 10 per cent or more. Since then, the economies have been floundering, with some partial recoveries in the mid-1980s wiped out by renewed stagnation and rising inflation from 1987 onwards. In 1990, the gross domestic product for Latin America declined for the third year running. Consumer prices for the three years increased at the extraordinary rates of 779, 1,161 and 1,833 per cent. The total external debt continued to rise, from US $384 billion in 1985 to US $423 billion in 1990, and more countries fell into arrears on interest payments. In 1991, economic growth barely matched population growth for the region as a whole, and some countries made substantial gains, in a context of 'income inequalities even wider than those of the past, greater precariousness of employment, greater fiscal tightness, and a narrower field of manoeuvre for economic policy. All this implies a lesser capacity to effect transfers between economic sectors or social strata, but also inspires greater confidence in the persistence of the rules that orient public policy.'[6]

Secondly, 'low-income countries which are, at the most, at very early stages of the industrialization process (mainly Sub-Saharan Africa)'. Here, economic deterioration, mainly in the form of stagnant or declining revenues from raw material exports, and government inability to maintain previous levels of public services and investments, was evident from the 1970s or earlier, and accelerated during the 1980s. Urban-biased policies based on dictated peasant production of export crops and state appropriation of the proceeds ran into impasses of increasing resistance, decreasing marketable production and collapsing state capacity to collect and market what was still being produced. Debt, while a major burden, was less prominent than in the first group, since low-income countries were unable to borrow as freely and their creditors were more disposed to forgive uncollectable debts, but declining ability of the state to function and provide services has been more acute. According to the *World Development Report 1990*, while GDP per capita fell by 0.6 per cent annually in Latin America and the Caribbean in 1980-1989, in Sub-Saharan Africa it fell by 2.2 per cent annually during the same period. While this report forecasts a modest renewal of per capita growth for Latin America during the 1990s, it expects no such growth in Sub-Saharan Africa before 1995, and very slow growth for the rest of the decade – if the region 'perseveres with adjustment and continues to receive debt relief and financial aid'.[7]

Several other groups of Third World countries that have been less or differently affected by world economic turmoil can be distinguished. The four 'newly industrializing countries' (South Korea, Hong Kong, Singapore, Taiwan) that are usually grouped together have continued to flourish economically despite various forms of political insecurity. The larger countries of South-East Asia have experienced some of the difficulties seen in Latin America, but have not, with the exception of the Philippines, fallen into comparable crises; their dominant problems are still those of unbalanced, inequitable and environmentally destructive growth. In countries such as Burma, Pakistan and Sri Lanka political upheavals or impasses with international repercussions have overshadowed economic difficulties, while Vietnam continues to contend with the aftermath of an exceptionally destructive war and with the imperative of reforming an ineffective 'real socialist' model of economic and political organization.

In the countries of North Africa and South-West Asia, while falling oil prices dealt some of them serious shocks during the 1980s, international political struggles have been more to the fore. Most recently the aftermath of the Iraqi seizure of Kuwait has had economic repercussions from South-East Asia to Egypt, not only by reversing the downward trends in oil prices, but also by throwing the regional market for migrant labour into chaos, depriving governments and families in countries from Yemen and Jordan to the Philippines of revenues from their migrants in the Gulf area and confronting them with hundreds of thousands of returnees intensifying their burden of unemployment and underemployment.

Two very large countries, China and India, present particularly complex patterns of change in economic policies and realities, advancing some internal regions and productive sectors while marginalizing others. These shifts have been only secondarily affected by economic changes outside the national boundaries. Both countries, however, within their very different political contexts, are increasingly exposed to the competitive pressures and temptations of the global economy and consumer society, and both are experiencing wider internal inequalities in the course of their partial curtailment of systems of elaborate controls over economic activities. The *World Development Report 1990* credits these two countries with growth rates and growth prospects well above those of most others: for China an annual increase in GDP per capita of 8.7 for 1980-1989, with an annual rate of 5.4 forecast for the 1990s. For India, the respective rates are 3.5 and 3.4.[8]

Lastly, the former 'real socialist' economies, which until recently were generally considered to be relatively stable and insulated from shocks in spite of visible strains and signs of stagnation, have entered with surprising rapidity into multi-faceted crises of productivity, distribution, employment, investment, and in some cases unmanageable external debt, that resemble those of the Third World. These crises, which are discussed in various contexts in other parts of this book, have been particularly important in discrediting the main alternative model of economic organization, as well as depriving former client states of a source of aid, making national adaptation to the dictates of the world system and its financial institutions seem even more unavoidable.

An attempt to generalize for the Third World as a whole on the relations between recent economic changes and the prospects for popular participation would be obviously absurd. The following unavoidably oversimplified summary applies mainly to the first group of countries listed above, in which most of the Participation Programme's field researches were carried out. Some of the trends – toward declining state intervention through choice or necessity, toward informalization, etc. – undoubtedly apply more widely but manifest themselves differently in Africa and Asia.

Employment. Urban employment opportunities in the so-called 'formal' sector of industries and services have fallen sharply, and the public sector has lost most of its capacity to absorb educated new entrants to the labour force. In both private and public sectors, incomes of the still employed have fallen, in some cases by as much as half, as wages have lagged behind inflation. Pressures to emigrate in search of work have risen, but opportunities to do so have fallen or stagnated, not only closing a safety valve of considerable importance in some countries, but also curtailing major sources of foreign exchange, remittances from workers abroad. Many governments have embarked on policies of privatization of productive enterprises formerly in the public sector, bringing an end to subsidized wage levels and job security. Unions have lost much of their ability to protect workers' interests through collective bargaining and pressure on the government, although the frustration of their members may leave them no alternative to frequent strikes and attempted mobilizations against the consequences of adjustment policies.

Open unemployment has risen to some extent, but more generally the informal sector has continued to absorb most of the surplus labour, and the income advantages of 'formal' over 'informal' occupations have become less pronounced. At the same time, declining capacity of male breadwinners to support the family, or migration of the former breadwinner in search of work, has stimulated increasing participation by other family members, including women and children, in gainful activities such as home piece-work, artisanal production, street vending, gardening and animal raising. Thus, the distinction between wage workers as a class and other low-income groups has become less distinct. The increasing participation of women means, on the one side, their super-exploitation as a practically unorganized group burdened by housework and forced to take whatever income-earning activities they can find. On the other, it confronts them with new challenges to organized efforts, with consequences that can only be guessed at.

Public services and subsidies. From 1965 to 1980, 'general government expenditures' in the countries now heavily indebted rose at an annual rate of 6.9 per cent. In 1980-1985, the rate of increase dropped to 1.6 per cent, as the inflow of loan funds that supported it turned into a net outflow. The change in Sub-Saharan Africa was even more abrupt – from 8 per cent to 0.7 per cent. Domestic sources of revenue shrank with the economic downturn, and governments could obtain more only at very high costs in terms of inflation, capital flight and discouragement of the export activities desperately needed as sources of foreign exchange.[9]

The rate of increase of 'government consumption' was now well below the rate of population increase, and the share allocated to the social needs of the population had to be shrinking further, since high proportions of the funds had to be allocated to debt servicing and to expenditures protected by powerful domestic interests, in particular the military. While the previous share of government consumption for social purposes had been biased toward urban middle- and working-class groups, by the beginning of the 1980s the share reaching the poor was significant and a source of hope for rising future benefits. Now, government support for schools, health services and infrastructure for rural villages and urban low-income settlements fell. Even social projects financed mainly by international agencies such as UNICEF found it harder to get governments to meet their share of recurrent costs; many of them had to initiate controversial efforts to collect 'user fees' from the poor, enhancing their efficiency but presumably excluding the neediest among their clientèles.

The cuts also affected the middle strata through falling salaries and static or declining employment levels for public functionaries, including teachers. In some countries, governments withdrew from responsibility for what had been nationally financed and administered public services, turning them over to municipalities or private enterprises, making access depend on ability to pay and depriving functionaries of job security. The relative disadvantages of the poor became more pronounced, as the middle strata were in a better position to compete for scarce public services, and underpaid functionaries neglected their jobs or sought bribes for their services.

At the same time, governments became less able to subsidize food imports or use other means of keeping urban prices low, a serious blow to the consumption levels of the urban majority and to the parts of the rural population that did not produce food for sale or subsistence. Altogether, people accustomed to a high and rising level of government intervention and some capacity to obtain responses to their demands through 'organized efforts' found the state practically unable to respond, except through gestures such as decreed wage increases and price controls that soon proved illusory or self-defeating. As the crisis persisted, some governments, under the advice of the World Bank and other lending agencies, turned to 'targeting' policies intended to ensure that whatever social services they could afford or that the lending agencies might finance would reach only the neediest. Such policies could hardly expect support from the better-organized 'non-poor', who saw their own levels of consumption and access to services deteriorating, and as we have seen, the Bank's *World Development Report 1990* recommends instead distributions of benefits favouring coalitions of the poor and the non-poor.

Debt, austerity, adjustment. The opening of the economies during the 1970s, the discrediting of previous interventionist 'developmentalist' policies, and, once the crisis struck, continuing pressure from the international lending agencies for further opening, privatization and austerity in expenditure limited most governments in Africa and Latin America to adjustment and hope for salvation from a world economic upturn, with only sporadic efforts to control the manifestations of the crisis and reinvigorate the economies. A few bold 'heterodox' policies proved unable to control all the key factors and collapsed, as in Brazil and Peru. The need for foreign exchange to service the debt as well as pay for the imports that the previous style of 'development' had made indispensable enabled the lending agencies to dictate 'adjustment programmes' that generally intensified the fall in employment and incomes and the curtailment of social expenditures, while leaving the future burden of debt intact.

The highly visible negotiations with these external agents, the deferred hopes of debt reduction, and the frustration of most efforts to exert national policy autonomy, have undoubtedly contributed to a generalized sentiment that policy decisions have been removed to increasingly distant spheres, unresponsive to the needs of national governments and dominant classes, let alone those of the people. To some extent also, they have provided governments with an excuse for inability to cope with problems stemming largely from their own past errors, or those of their predecessors.

The patterns of distribution that took shape in Latin America during the decades of economic growth were notoriously more inequitable and wasteful than those of most Asian countries; they were not dictated by the world economic system. The *World Development Report 1990* emphasizes that 'nowhere in the developing world are the contrasts between poverty and national wealth more striking than in Latin America and the Caribbean' and argues that raising all the poor in the region (nearly one fifth of the population, according to the Bank's calculation) to just above the poverty line would cost only 0.7 per cent of the regional GDP – the approximate equivalent of a 2 per cent income tax on the wealthiest fifth of the population. The fact that the burden of adjustment has fallen almost exclusively on the poor and the middle strata has had more to do with the distribution of power and élite indifference to the welfare of the majority than with the constraints imposed by the lending agencies.

Transnationals. The crisis has had contradictory consequences for the penetration of national economies by transnational enterprises. The national subsidiaries of the transnationals can cope with changing conditions better than other enterprises, if this is to the advantage of the parent companies, and they become better able to drive hard bargains with the national authorities on taxes, repatriation of profits, etc., as well as with their workers on wages. Governmental resort to policies of privatization of public enterprises and debt/equity swaps opens new opportunities for transnational penetration of economies. At the same time, the transnationals presumably become more inclined to withdraw altogether from countries where a combination of extreme poverty of the majority, a labour force with rudimentary skills, inadequate infrastructure and state inability to improve it, and political instability make operations difficult and investment particularly risky. Transnational affiliates taking advantage of cheap labour and natural resources to produce for export to the rich countries naturally find the recent trends more advantageous than affiliates aiming mainly at domestic markets. This applies to agribusinesses, mining, forestry, fish- and prawn-farming enterprises as well as to consumer-goods manufacturing for export. For the present, at least, the possibility of expanding consumer demand for new products in the middle strata of the heavily indebted countries has shrunk, although upper income demand for luxury goods may still be strong. Once protection of domestic industries has been dismantled, however, the transnationals can supply this latter market through imports rather than domestic production.

Informalization. The visibility and the real importance of the 'informal' or 'underground' economy have increased together during the 1980s. Previously, while this ill-defined phenomenon had received some sympathetic attention from the International Labour Organisation and other institutions, economists and government policy-makers generally treated it as a residual and regrettable aspect of 'insufficient development'; depriving the government of tax revenues; competing unfairly with the formal sector; surviving by offsetting low efficiency and technological backwardness with miserable incomes; and evading the regulations needed for protection of the workers, the consumers and the environment. By the early 1980s, estimates were being made that it accounted for between 25 per cent and 45 per cent of the gross domestic product in the major Latin American countries, enough to deprive previous economic statistics of any validity as a basis for policy.[10] Its importance in many countries of Africa and Asia would probably be even higher.

It also became evident that the expansion of the informal sector was compensating for part of the slump in the formal economy, sufficiently, at least, to make the impact of the crisis less devastating than it otherwise would have been. A good deal of this expansion can be attributed to the need of the 'excluded' to find some means of subsistence rather than starve, but it also became evident that parts of the informal economy were relatively flourishing, able to provide goods and services cheaply enough to meet the needs of consumers no longer able to afford imports or the products of protected 'formal' domestic industries. It also accounted for the great majority of new dwelling units and for the provision of a good deal of urban infrastructure.

The phenomena lumped together as 'informal economy' are quite heterogeneous (they can include drug trafficking, for example) and support contradictory prognoses. The informal sector has generated aggressive organizations of street vendors, transport operators, even garbage pickers, although other components, in particular the mainly female home piece-workers and sweatshop workers, have been practically unable to organize. Clashes with societal interests in environmental and sanitary standards are important, as is the exploitation of self-defensive tactics by clientelistic and mafia-type networks. On balance, however, the ways of livelihood here considered contain some of the few positive factors for the organized efforts of the excluded in the rather bleak panorama of today. They are important to the efforts of various currents of opinion to revise their conceptions of participation and of options for future social orders.

These efforts, which naturally go beyond the economic sphere, will be discussed below in relation to the ideological setting.

The rural economy. A positive revaluation of peasant agriculture and associated forms of rural social organization has emerged in development discourse, although the prospect for effective incorporation in national policies and practices is far from clear. On the one side, it is evident that such agriculture has been able to survive under the most negative conditions of state policies that have exploited it through regressive taxes, dictation of crops to be planted, urban-biased price-setting and investment allocations, etc., and that have assumed its ultimate demise. On the other, 'modern' capitalist agriculture, after a period of very rapid growth and internationalization of markets, faces impasses in terms of erratic export prices, protectionism, rising costs of inputs and environmental aggression. Peasant agriculture, if supported by flexible state or private marketing services offering reasonable prices, transport, and supplies of consumer goods and farm inputs, could offer hope of meeting domestic demands for basic foods once shortages of foreign exchange hinder further reliance on imports. Furthermore, for most countries the expectation that industries, modern services and capitalist agriculture will eventually absorb the labour force released from peasant agriculture no longer seems plausible. Once channels for migration abroad are blocked and further urbanization seems unsustainable, the support of peasant agriculture, even through subsidies and exclusion of cheap food imports, may come to be the only visible alternative to the conversion of millions of families now subsisting precariously through combinations of farming and migratory wage labour into destitute and rootless unemployed.[11]

Such considerations have generated policy proposals, supported by several inter-governmental organizations, that include fairer pricing, freeing of choices as to crops and marketing, technical and community aid, and, in a very few cases, a renewed effort at land tenure reform. China, along with some of the other formerly 'real socialist' countries, has moved in a similar direction, away from centrally-managed collectivized agriculture and quotas for crop deliveries to peasant family responsibility for production decisions. In other countries, such as Thailand, in which government attention continues to focus on industrialization and large-scale export agriculture, the trend is toward a kind of benign neglect, leaving rural communities more leeway than previously in organizing and making their own decisions. Some of the new policies have recognized and accepted strong peasant resistance to state-sponsored co-operatives, collective farms, etc. that were formally participatory but in practice bureaucratically regimented.

To the extent that such initiatives advance beyond experts' recommendations and scattered pilot projects, a good many questions that have troubled past rural programmes will re-emerge. First, to what extent will benefits be monopolized by the better-off landholding peasants able to dominate community organization, employment and marketing? Secondly, to what extent can organizations restricted to the rural poor, which have been advocated and in a few cases created to offset this dominance, be viable without a degree of state intervention and encouragement of class conflict that are not to be expected in view of other state priorities and the nature of forces controlling the state? Thirdly, to what extent will bureaucracies continue to find means of control and exploitation in the name of aid and advice? Conversely, to what extent will the 'liberation' from state paternalism serve as a cover for abandonment of institutions and services that have become really important to rural people, however much their administration might be resented?

For the present, unfortunately, the predominant trend confronting peasant societies is toward further impoverishment and resort to heterogeneous survival strategies, as economic crisis shrinks local markets and destroys essential infrastructure for production and marketing, while adjustment policies continue to inhibit public responses mobilizing sufficient resources to make a difference.[12]

The political setting

The 1980s saw the following political developments:

Pluralist democratization. Pluralist democratic régimes replaced one-party or military-authoritarian régimes in very many countries, especially in Latin America, but also in parts of Africa and Asia and, most recently, in Central and Eastern Europe. This took place sometimes through semi-spontaneous popular uprisings, more often through negotiated withdrawal of régimes unable to cope with economic crisis or increasing conflict in their own ranks. A few authoritarian régimes overcame challenges through intensified repression, but with diminished legitimacy and a certainty that pressures for democratization will continue.

The trend has allowed a much wider scope for 'organized efforts' of many kinds and an arena for open political party competition, at a time when the capacity of governments to respond to popular demands is particularly precarious. In settings of lowered expectations and a partial convergence of major political factions on centrist or 'social democratic' positions, many governments have tried to achieve broad consensus on policies and the sharing of sacrifices through 'social pacts' endorsed after discussions by representatives of the major organized interest-groups. However, most of these pacts have broken down within a year or so after adoption, through the governments' inability to reconcile commitments and pressures deriving from the crisis, the lack or weakness of traditions of democratic consensus-seeking through debate, and the representatives' inability to commit their followings. Some countries have already drifted from a period of political euphoria to impasses threatening violent confrontations or a return to military tutelage.

For the most part, political parties have retained or recovered their roles as irreplaceable channels for intermediation between civil societies and the state. Broad and unstructured popular movements have been unable to displace them except during brief periods of multiclass mobilizations against dictatorships, as in Argentina, Chile and the Philippines. However, it is evident that political parties are encountering distrust and disillusionment in countries as different as Brazil, India, Italy, Peru and Poland. This affects the formerly one-party Marxist or nationalist states as well as states with long-established inter-party competition. The proliferation of social movements with militant pressure tactics and diverse agendas leaves the parties decreasingly able to reconcile or evade demands. The shrinkage of resources at the disposition of the state, and the rigidity of allocations of what remains leaves the parties impotent to comply with electoral promises or to offer convincing visions of a better future. The results include increasing fragmentation of parties and extremely unstable electoral behaviour as voters seek to punish the party in power or turn to candidates least identified with the past.

Bureaucratic insecurity. Public bureaucracies and technocracies, rising steadily in almost all Third World countries in terms of numbers, claims on public resources, and capacity to intervene in society, have faced a multiple crisis of budget cuts, instability of régimes and policies, and variously-motivated attacks from different sectors of public opinion. Declining salaries have intensified the chronic problems of corruption and multiple employment. Purges of the bureaucracy following changes of régime – whether toward democratization or away from it – and campaigns of 'deburcaucratization' have been recurrent. Influential groups have accused the bureaucracy of becoming a society within the state, concerned mainly to protect its own status and prepared to distort any government policy to this end. This criticism has combined with polemics directed against the desirability of government regulation of the economy, provision of social services and subsidies, management of industries and utilities, and planning in general. Parts of the bureaucracy, under such attacks, have felt a need to form alliances with clientèles of government services, including groups among the 'excluded', and thus have encouraged their demands for services the bureaucracy can provide if funded.

The *World Development Report 1990* argues that coalitions between service providers and recipients enhance political sustainability:

Pressures on governments to finance social services often come as much from the middle-income providers of services as from the beneficiaries. Teachers, medical personnel, social workers, and other middle- and upper-income services providers themselves benefit when the government devotes more resources to social services, and they often have voting power and organizational capacity to lobby successfully for greater investments in the development of human resources.[13]

The formation of such coalitions is certainly a legitimate expedient for the organized efforts of the disadvantaged. At present, however, its likely achievements depend on the very limited capacity of governments to respond other than by unsustainable inflationary financing. Moreover, the relevance of the level of resources to the needs of the recipients depends on their capacity to influence the content and prevent the bureaucracies from absorbing the lion's share of the benefits. The excluded might well suspect hidden motives both among their defenders within the public sector who argue for well-financed services and regulatory protection against exploitation, and the spokesmen within the private sector who argue for debureaucratization and 'empowerment' of the poor to provide their own services and their own defences against exploitation.

Democratization of local government. One accompaniment of political democratization in a number of countries has been the replacement of appointed by elected provincial and municipal authorities. Elected administrations for districts within cities have also been instituted, and ties between municipal governments and popular organizations have been formalized. These trends have responded to popular demands for local autonomy, but also to expedients by the central authorities, under the budgetary constraints discussed above, to transfer elsewhere responsibilities for social services and urban infrastructure. In fact, various authoritarian governments previously applied policies of administrative decentralization for the same reasons.

The probable consequences may be as contradictory as the motivations behind the changes. To the extent to which democratic local institutions take root and attract local participation they can indeed relieve the central authorities of detailed responsibilities for local affairs and permit greater flexibility in seeking solutions, but they can also become bogged down in conflicts with national agencies accustomed to control and backed by legal attributes. They can mobilize local resources and stimulate alliances of the excluded with the organized workers and parts of the middle classes, but such alliances are bound to focus on demands on the national government for a larger share of its resources, as have regional movements up to the present. New relationships between different levels of government will have to be worked out in settings in which the political forces dominant at different levels may be competitors for national power and the resources available at all levels will be insufficient to meet even the most urgent demands.[14]

In some of the major cities of Latin America, populist movements have received the main advantage from the new electoral opportunities. In others, Marxist parties or coalitions have come to the fore, as in Lima during the early 1980s and in São Paulo in 1988. The populist movements holding national office have been notorious for the contradictions between their promises of popular welfare and their economically unsustainable performances. The few Marxist régimes in Latin America have had comparable shortcomings, complicated by sectarianism and over-confidence in their ability to act as system-transforming vanguards. Hold-ing office at the municipal or provincial but not national level under present conditions confronts them with different challenges, in which extravagant promises will be quickly exposed, while national power-holders, including the military, will be considering the alternatives of co-opting them, toler-ating them as buffers for popular demands, or driving them out of office through economic sabotage or force. Their survival probably depends in part on maintenance of higher standards of administrative efficiency and honesty than their predecessors, and in part on ability to convince the urban majority that they are listening to demands and doing all that can be done to respond, but this will fall far short of the system-transforming rhetoric that has characterized their past political struggles.

Dilemmas for 'organized efforts'. Popular movements and organiza-tions have faced new difficulties in defining objectives that are realistic as well as inspiring for a mass following. Capacity to enforce demands on private employers or the state have been reduced, for reasons stated above. Socialist and populist alternatives have lost credibility and even in the countries not constrained by economic crisis and debt, governments have tried to keep popular demands within limits set by considerations of international competitiveness. Organized popular participation bearing on national policy has taken three main forms: negotiations over social pacts, reactive protests against intolerable conditions, and pursuit of group survival strategies. In relation to all of these forms, the economic context has made for greater segmentation of organizational initiatives and demands.

The techniques of the major traditional popular organizations, the trade unions and class-based parties, have proved more adaptable to the needs of the salaried middle strata facing impoverishment than to the needs of the informal sector. (Co-operatives and peasant associations are probably more relevant to the organizational needs of this sector.) For the most part, political activity in the informal sector – as distinguished from mutual aid and self-help – has continued to follow certain well-known paths not requiring permanent organization: clientelistic exchanges of material aid for votes and other services to political power-holders; and violent mass actions in protest against rising prices and deteriorating services. The increase in size of the urban 'excluded' population and the shocks to which it has been subjected do not seem thus far to have generated significant increases over earlier years in the incidence of spontaneous violent protests, which can have a high immediate cost to the participants. However, the possibility of this kind of 'representational violence' has assumed some importance in setting limits to adjustment policies, or in giving governments convincing arguments for resisting pressures to apply such policies.

Ethnic and related challenges to the nation state. The 1980s have seen throughout the world a sharp rise in the prominence and diversity of movements based on ethnic, cultural, linguistic, religious and related criteria for self-identification. These movements in many different ways challenge the legitimacy of the 'modern' secular state, demand autonomy or multicultural equality within state boundaries, form allegiances across state boundaries, or deny the right of minorities to belong to the 'national' family. While many of them are predominantly identified with one socio-economic stratum or another they reject class self-identification or subordinate it to other criteria. While movements of these kinds have a long and conflictive history their present vigour and the aggressiveness of their tactics have reversed trends toward nation-building, secularization and cultural homogenization that seemed to be dominant at least from the 1940s up to the 1970s. The reversal can be attributed in part to the increasing intrusiveness of the nation state itself and of the world economic system with its accompaniments of consumerism and mass communications; in part to the crises of the 1980s and the erosion of confidence in the nation state's capacity to plan development, provide services, reduce inequalities in distribution, or represent a common 'national interest'.

The diversity of movements, goals and national situations is too great to be discussed here.[15] However, their relevance to the present and future of organized efforts of the hitherto excluded is obvious. Some of the movements here considered have found common ground, at least temporarily, with class-oriented popular initiatives, but others violently reject the latter along with other manifestations of modernity, secularism and pluralism, as in Iran. Elsewhere, relatively spontaneous popular mobilizations that derived their solidarity from ethnic or religious self-identification, as in Northern Ireland, Sri Lanka or parts of India, have degenerated into interminable communal warfare, with escalating exchanges of atrocities and the diversion of scarce public resources to control or repression. The re-emergence of long-suppressed ethnic conflicts has been an ominous feature of the disintegration of 'real socialism' in the USSR and Yugoslavia, and has cast a shadow over recent progress toward democracy in South Africa.

The 'excluded' with whom the Participation Programme was concerned are probably not more prone to militancy in such movements than other social strata, and the activists and ideologists generally come from the middle strata, especially the educated youth, or from traditional religious figures. However, to the extent to which a historical memory of inter-group conflict pervades a population and combines with perceptions of discrimination and insecurity the potential for divisive mobilization is present, and the resulting conflicts may be harder fought than those directed solely toward better livelihood and a voice in public policy. The spokesmen for more secular and universal popular movements are naturally inclined to blame these movements on efforts by élites or the state to divide and mislead the people; this may be valid in some cases but not in others. Conflicts of interests between groups that are equally disadvantaged are real, and where the groups are ethnically distinct their aggression is likely to be directed against the most visible adversary. In any case, advocates of the kinds of popular participation envisaged so far in this book cannot take it for granted that real mobilizations of frustrated people will be directed toward universal goals of solidarity and equity.

The ethnic movements most relevant to the original conception of the UNRISD Programme are those of tribal and peasant peoples distinguished by language, culture, forms of livelihood, and sometimes physical traits, living in rural hinterlands, and forested, mountainous and arid or semi-arid regions. They are usually minorities within the national population, but sometimes constitute majorities among the rural poor. In such groups, ethnic identification has coincided closely with degree of exclusion from control over resources and institutions. They have experienced continual aggression from the state, in the name of assimilation and modernization, and from participants in the nationally dominant culture appropriating their land and other resources and exploiting their labour under systems equivalent to serfdom or debt peonage. New opportunities combined with intensified aggression are now transforming their previously localized defensive struggles.

On the one side, technological innovations and national urgency to increase exports have accelerated various kinds of large-scale encroachments on their land and livelihood, through exploitation of forests and minerals using heavy equipment, through construction of dams, and through land clearance for cattle raising and commercial agriculture. In some regions, competition between military forces and guerrillas to attract or intimidate them has had extremely disruptive, even genocidal consequences, or drug trafficking has brought new dangers along with new sources of livelihood. Meanwhile, population increase and impoverishment among the rural population belonging to the dominant ethnic groups generate continual encroachments by settlers and in some regions by mining prospectors.

On the other side, in a good many countries democratization and international concern for human rights have reduced the state's confidence in its right to use force to dominate or assimilate 'backward' minorities. The state may even take seriously a duty to protect these groups through dialogue rather than paternalism. The way is then open for them to organize and 'participate' along with the many other social forces contending for a share of control over resources and institutions. Or the state, overwhelmed by political and economic struggles and shrinking resources, may practically relinquish control over zones populated by minorities, leaving them to cope as best they can against encroachments, sometimes through their own armed forces.

The youth of the disadvantaged ethnic groups begin to migrate to the cities, bringing them into contact with national political currents, ideologies and techniques for organization, and also exposing them to new shocks of discrimination. Ethnically conscious educated élites begin to emerge and seek influence among their rural fellows, as seems to be happening among the Aymaras of Bolivia.

The communications revolution, at least in the form of radio, by now reaches even the most isolated groups, stimulating consciousness of identity and exploitation, facilitating ideological and organizational appeals, making possible links with counterparts and allies in other regions and countries. The emergence of a Native American movement throughout the western hemisphere is particularly striking; peoples of many languages, cultural patterns and sources of livelihood, previously practically unaware of one another's existence, are forming links based on a new common consciousness of exclusion from 'national' societies originating in conquest and expropriation. They could thus convert the 500th anniversary of the European 'discovery' of America into a focus for protest and solidarity.

Various kinds of allies and interlocutors with access to world public opinion are appearing. Environmental movements, in particular, identify themselves with the permanent viability of peasant and tribal societies. Aggression against a tiny Amazonian people can have repercussions that are transmitted back to the people themselves and enhance their confidence in the efficacy of organized efforts. In paradoxical ways, the shrinkage of the world and the narrowing possibilities for national political and economic autonomy are stimulating the reassertion and even invention of ethnic identities among some of the world's most disadvantaged peoples. Whether these positive new trends can prevail against the continuing phenomena of encroachment and violence remains to be seen.

Youth. In the countries hardest hit by the debt burden, economic downturn, and shrinkage of the state, a high proportion of young people, from the middle as well as the more disadvantaged strata, have found themselves excluded from any possibility of entering salaried employment. More broadly, the very high expectations aroused in youth of all classes by the widening access to education that has been one of the most striking social phenomena of recent decades have entered into contradiction with real opportunities. Participation in massified higher education, under typical conditions of precarious public financial support, deteriorating quality, and poorly prepared students, has been frustrating in itself.

Jobs, even when accessible, have corresponded poorly to status expectations and the content of education. Moreover, in many cases, political rigidities and forced conformism have generated in students and former students powerful resentments against the barriers in the way of their voicing their views on their own needs and those of their societies. These frustrations and exclusions coincide with unprecedented cultural currents influencing youth throughout the world to place many of them outside the control of conventional values and expectations. This has led in some cases to their incorporation in social or political movements radically or violently challenging the status quo, in others to cultural patterns and consumption norms seeking autonomy without pretensions to a definable role in societal change. Among the mainly unemployed youth of the urban poor, such cultural currents undoubtedly combine with rising levels of participation in drug consumption and traffic, and also with a greater propensity than other groups to engage in violent action, sometimes making them protagonists in mass protests against dictatorships, as in Chile in 1983-1984, sometimes involving them in xenophobic or neo-Nazi aggressions, as recently in parts of Europe.

In this area, it is particularly hard to distinguish between reality and fears of elders and authorities, and the temptation to over-generalizations is strong. State agencies and the better-off population, under democratic as well as authoritarian régimes, have reacted with a predisposition to use repressive violence freely, and to lump politically motivated youth movements with anomically violent protests. It is evident that trends among young people present many unknowns for the future of organized efforts by the excluded. In particular, the trends present problems for organizations trying to extend their following among youth, while sometimes also trying to cope with the intransigence of their own youth affiliates or the tactics of radicalized youth groups aimed at disrupting or capturing them.

The social setting

Recent international surveys agree, with varying emphasis, that living conditions for the majority of people in most Third World countries must have improved a great deal during the 1960s and 1970s, to judge from such indicators as infant mortality, life expectancy and coverage of basic social services. Income levels rose, although the meaning of this indicator for levels of welfare is problematic in view of difficulties of measurement, the rising importance for consumption of marketed goods vs. subsistence production, and the weight in the calculations of 'production' that compensates for environmental and other disbenefits of growth. Distribution of incomes and services became more equitable in some national settings and worsened in others. The percentages living in extreme poverty declined, although the numbers did not, in view of accelerating population increases in the poorer countries.

During the 1980s, measurable trends were more mixed and regionally diverse. For South and East Asia as a whole, previous trends of slow improvement for enormous numbers of very poor people seem not to have changed very much, and a continuation of this overall trend through the 1990s seems probable. This generalization, of course, is compatible with rapid gains in some groups and regions and further impoverishment in others, with both tendencies involving many millions of people. In Latin America as a whole, per capita incomes fell sharply during the early 1980s and have since stagnated. Educational and health services, which had achieved fairly wide coverage, deteriorated, in quality if not in quantity. In Sub-Saharan Africa the drop has been more extreme, long-standing, and from a lower level of basic consumption and services. In Latin America, the extent of the impact on levels of living is not entirely clear, since infant mortality rates and some other indicators have continued to improve in most countries. The incidence of malnutrition seems to have risen, as one might expect, and in Peru, one of the countries hardest hit by economic depression, the present cholera epidemic has been blamed in part on impoverishment, deteriorating health services, and worsening access to food and drinkable water for the urban poor. In Africa, malnutrition is definitely on the rise and several countries and regions have experienced periodic famines. In Eastern Europe and the former USSR, recent events have led to falling levels of consumption, deterioriating services and widening inequality in access to goods and services after a long period in which these factors seemed to be stable or slowly improving.

For present purposes, it would be pointless to enter into more detail on these questions, which are discussed exhaustively, and probably with a confidence in quantifications, composite indicators, international comparisons and specification of trends that the underlying statistical data hardly justify, in readily available sources.[16] The changes in incidence of poverty and the ways the recent surveys interpret them, however, are obviously important for the prospects of different forms of 'participation'.

The UNRISD Participation Programme was not, in practice, focused on the 'poorest of the poor' but on 'groups and movements' capable of making 'organized efforts', and mainly on a region, Latin America, where such groups and movements were relatively vigorous. Most of their members were poor but were self-defined by situations of exploitation or by presumably remediable lack of control over resources and institutions rather than by the degree of poverty. During the 1960s and 1970s, as we have seen, these groups had reason to expect that the national economic and political systems could reward their organized efforts, or possibly be replaced by different systems under their control. Quite apart from whatever material losses the 1980s have brought, these hopes have become more precarious than before. They hear from the economic and part of the intellectual élites insistent arguments that their organized efforts are likely to leave them worse off than before, and real national experiences seem to support such arguments. This applies particularly to organized efforts to obtain legal protection and redistributive measures from the state. They are told that increased insecurity will be good for them in the long term, as well as for the health of the national economy. In this respect, the conventional wisdom in the former 'real socialist' countries of Eastern Europe and even in some long-established capitalist welfare states has converged with the arguments current in Latin America.

Social policy discussions continue to feature equity and participation, but attention has shifted to groups defined by degree of poverty and vulnerability rather than relation to production and capacity for organized efforts. The aim then becomes protection of the vulnerable (particularly women and children) during a period of economic adjustment assumed to be unavoidable, and the enhancement of human resources for future development through basic health, education and nutritional services targeted to the groups in greatest need. This approach assumes that localized participation will be essential, since public resources are inadequate, major diversions to services for the 'non-poor' are politically unavoidable, and labour is 'the poor's most abundant asset', in the words of the *World Development Report 1990*.

This approach deals uneasily with the fact that impoverishment means different things to different strata of the population, and that the crisis has been particularly frustrating to the 'newly excluded' in the working class and the salaried middle strata. Their aspirations for 'modern' consumption, 'modern' services from the state, and upward mobility for the next generation have been abruptly blocked, and in many cases even basic consumption has been threatened. Moreover, the levels and forms of consumption assumed to be necessary for a decent participation in the social order have transformed themselves in recent years, particularly in the cities, but to some extent in rural areas in most of the world. The penetration of consumerist appeals through radio and television has narrowed the gap between the aspirations of different social strata. By the beginning of the 1980s, relatively poor families had entered the market for 'modern' goods, by buying on credit and skimping on food and other items of basic consumption. Some of them have really gained entry to the consumerist paradise through drug trafficking, and will not voluntarily be expelled. In assessing the potential contribution of popular participation to the distributive struggle, it is not enough to specify what the people ought to want within an equitable and sustainable style of development – satisfaction of basic needs, fair access to educational and health care, adequate housing, protection in old age and other contingencies. The world economic system and the revolution in communications are simultaneously stimulating and frustrating a world system of consumption aspirations. For the majority these can be satisfied only in very small part even by the most rapid imaginable economic growth, and if they could thus be satisfied the environmental consequences would be devastating. It would be presumptuous to offer prescriptions for this dimension of social change, but advocates of organized popular participation will be grappling with it for a long time to come.

The demographic setting

Population increase has continued during the 1980s, at slowly slackening rates except in the poorest and most crisis-ridden countries. According to the grouping of countries used by the World Bank the annual rates of increase in 1965-1980 were 2.7 per cent in Sub-Saharan Africa, 2.3 in East Asia, 2.4 in South Asia, and 2.5 in Latin America and the Caribbean. For 1988-2000, rates of 3.1, 1.4, 2.0 and 1.8 per cent are projected for the same regions.[17] The certainty of enormous increments in population and consequently in the need for additional sources of livelihood will loom over national efforts to achieve viable economic and political systems and over the survival strategies of the excluded during the foreseeable future.

However, controversies over the effectiveness and legitimacy of public campaigns to control population increase seem to have given way to more cautious hopes that spontaneous demographic transitions, with some help from public programmes, will eventually lead to stationary populations. It appears that even the most drastic policies to bring population increase to a halt, as in China and for a time in India, have their limits with regard to the motivations of families. It is not clear whether the economic and related crises of the 1980s will have any consistent impact on rates of increase. Infant mortality rates may be rising in some countries because of impoverishment and curtailment of public health services, but fertility rates in such settings may be rising also for the same reasons. During the 1960s and 1970s, publicly-supported contraceptive information and services became more widely available in many regions, even in the countryside. The promoters of family planning tried to introduce a participatory component in diffusion of the services through women's organizations. In general, however, family planning probably remained more a preoccupation of governments and NGOs than of the 'hitherto excluded'. The services have been vulnerable to the general deterioration of public funds and administrative capacity in Africa and Latin America, although presumably not in Asia.

Continuing urban concentration has produced agglomerations on a scale unprecedented in human history, and one might expect the crises to have a clearer impact on rates and patterns of urbanization than on population increase. The potential for a better livelihood through cityward migration is now much reduced, and in some parts of the world a reverse flow to the countryside may be under way. In general, however, the capacity of the countryside to offer subsistence to a larger population, without investments and agrarian reforms that most governments are in no position to undertake, is doubtful, and as long as rural rates of natural increase remain high, migrants will continue to seek alternatives. In several Asian countries, where populations are very large and the overwhelming majority still live in rural villages, the possibilities for urban concentration are on a scale hard to comprehend. In Latin America, the main wave has already taken place, producing several of the largest agglomerations in the world today, and future city growth will depend more on natural increase and inter-urban migrations than on rural contributions. In Africa, although the urban population is still a minority, the economic downturn seems to have brought cityward migration nearly to a halt.

Patterns of growth in the urban agglomerations, combining wasteful use of land, energy and automotive transport in the better-off zones with overcrowding and chaotic expansion in the irregular settlements, are generating such a complex of problems – air and water pollution, garbage accumulation, traffic strangulation, crime, deteriorating infrastructure and lack of shelter – that it is hard to see how they can continue. However, a few years ago it was hard to see how they could reach present dimensions without catastrophic breakdown. Even if policies and incentives to slow and decentralize urban growth become more effective than in the past, increasing numbers of agglomerations with tens of millions of people will continue to test resilience and social innovativeness.

The geographical mobility of people is continuing to increase and this has contradictory implications for their organized efforts, whether in mass movements or in localized reciprocity and self-help. One can find evidence to support a picture of enormous anomic floating populations with hardly any capacity for organization beyond the family, and with even nuclear family ties breaking down and leaving millions of children to fend for themselves. One can also find evidence to support a picture of increasingly complex and far-flung national and international networks linking migrants with communities of origin, providing the former with reference points and refuges in case of need, providing the latter with material resources, stimuli toward innovation and even opportunities for political mobilization. No doubt both pictures correspond to important realities, but their combination in the future will depend on the evolution of the world economic system and the political conflicts it is generating.[18]

International migration from 'poor' to 'rich' countries has become an increasingly important part of the picture, in spite of intensified efforts during the 1980s by governments of the 'rich' countries to limit entries. Since expectations for livelihood have become internationalized, the 'excluded' as well as highly educated professionals are familiar with labour markets in Europe, the United States, the Middle East, South Africa and the 'newly industrializing countries' of South-East Asia. Although some of these markets have also been affected by economic recession, pressures to enter them continue to mount as domestic prospects worsen. Many communities now depend more on remittances from workers abroad than on local sources of livelihood, and such remittances have become crucially important to the economies of the smaller countries of the Caribbean and Central America. In a sense, this phenomenon offsets the informalization and localization of survival strategies in the 1980s.

The sudden outpouring of millions of migrant workers from Kuwait and Iraq, the expulsion of others from Saudi Arabia with a politically-motivated shift in preferred sources of such workers, and the difficulties of re-absorption faced by their home countries, present the outstanding example up to the present of the size and vulnerability of the migrant labour force. Even within sub-regions such as West Africa, migrations of workers from the more impoverished countries to the somewhat more prosperous countries have been important, and have been followed by periodic large-scale expulsions.

Many of the migrants, of course, are rigidly excluded from organized efforts of any kind in the host countries and return home after a fixed-term work contract, possibly with savings to invest in land, a taxi or bus, a workshop or a store. (Often their own government expropriates a major part of their savings through obligatory official channels for remittances, or unofficial intermediaries take advantage of their difficulties in remitting savings to their families.) Other migrants become more or less permanently established in the host countries and set up families there, but remain in contact with their places of origin. Some of the migrants are political exiles or refugees and many more leave home for a combination of economic and political reasons. Thus they are predisposed to organize themselves abroad, try to influence public opinion and government policy in the host country, and support 'organized efforts' of many kinds back home. Efforts of this kind, of course, have been going on since the nineteenth century or earlier, and have been decisive in the historical evolution of some countries, but the scale and diversity of the 'diaspora' are unprecedented. The economically and politically relevant 'national community' can come to include groups abroad that represent 20 per cent or more of the size of the population remaining at home.

The rising tide of refugees introduces a note of desperation that cannot be separated from the broader problem of pressures to migrate from poor countries. Today the number who have fled from persecution or been violently expelled by ethnic cleansing is in the millions, and these acute cases merge into larger numbers who combine motives of danger, discrimination and impoverishment, or simply become refugees because this claim gives them better access to countries where they hope life will be easier. Governments of the host countries try ineffectively to draw the line between 'real' refugees trying to escape oppression and migrants trying to escape poverty. The UN High Commissioner for Refugees estimates the number passing the test at around 20 million. If one adds displaced persons within their countries of origin the number rises to an estimated 38 million. These figures are likely to double by the year 2000. While refugee status gives a claim to protection and subsistence, it often bars the refugees from employment and notoriously breeds xenophobia as their numbers increase.

The internationalization of the 'hitherto excluded', the 'newly excluded', and the better-off groups that feel insecure in their impoverished and conflict-torn homelands is bound to increase, encountering diverse forms of exploitation, discrimination and repression, and evolving new forms of solidarity to cope with these. Here too, trends are contradictory. The new ties of solidarity can be broader than the nation-state (pan-African, Caribbean, Latin American, Arab, Moslem, etc.) and can exert some influence toward regional co-operation over parochialism. Or they can be narrower, based on ethnic minorities, sects, political factions, classes, that are in conflict in their country of origin. They then continue the conflict in the new setting, seek allies there, and possibly exacerbate the conflicts back home.

The environmental setting

Trends in the 1980s have naturally intensified many of the threats to the environment that had become notorious by the 1970s. Governments desperate for foreign exchange tolerate uncontrolled exploitation of forests and mineral resources and ecologically dangerous practices of commercial agriculture. In any case, their ability to regulate, incipient in the 1970s, is being submerged by more 'urgent' concerns, by the general deterioration of public administration, and by ideological attacks against state activism. In many cases, private enterprises are able to disregard all regulations and override local protests through alliances with local functionaries or the military. Destructive land use by the rural poor is also on the increase, as their numbers grow, alternative sources of livelihood dwindle, road construction helps them to penetrate new areas, and the tenure reforms and agricultural services they need are not forthcoming. Finally, as noted above, the urban agglomerations present continually larger environmental deficiencies while public capacity to cope with these evils lags behind.

At the same time, struggles against sources of environmental degradation and accompanying loss of livelihood and physical as well as psychological well-being are becoming increasingly important rallying points for popular organization, in the countryside as well as the cities, in poor countries as well as rich. These struggles, as a consequence of the prominence of environmental menaces in global public opinion since the 1970s and of certain widely publicized man-made disasters such as Bhopal and Chernobyl, now mobilize multiclass and multinational alliances and are beginning to have some impact on the funding decisions of international lending and technical co-operation agencies. The construction of huge dams for irrigation and hydroelectric power, not long ago universally looked to as the most spectacular symbols of 'development', justifying enormous investments and disruptions of local livelihood, now encounters dwindling acceptance and militant resistance. Nuclear power installations have had a shorter span from popular acceptance to rejection.

One might also suspect that warnings of longer-term environmental menaces such as global warming, penetrating popular consciousness sometimes in distorted forms, are interacting with other sources of insecurity to foster mass fears and doomsday scenarios, and thus contributing to the fundamentalist reactions against modernization. The consequences for popular organization and aspirations remain to be seen.

Environmental constraints, like the economic constraints of the world system, might also justify lowered expectations for the organized efforts of the hitherto excluded, to the extent that these efforts are directed to higher levels of material consumption according to the standards that are being disseminated throughout the world from the 'rich' countries. The most obvious instance is that of the private automobile, which has already brought enormous disruption to the urban environment and to popular aspirations in countries where the majority cannot afford even cheap collective transport. As hopes for very rapid increases in production and more equitable distribution of incomes and consumption fade, environmental arguments can strengthen the case for shielding the majority from consumption aspirations that cannot be realized.

The most clear-cut instances of environmental concerns legitimized by world opinion as bases for organized efforts concern tribal minorities that are only marginally involved in 'development', as was discussed under ethnic movements above. Such minorities, in Brazil, India, the Philippines and elsewhere, are fighting the destruction of their forest habitat or the flooding of their land by large dams, sometimes successfully, more often defeated by military force, but increasingly achieving a voice in national and international 'development' decisions.

The next question is whether this kind of environmental awareness, leading to strategies for long-term defence of sources of livelihood and cultural identity, rather than short-term survival strategies requiring destructive land use, can penetrate the much larger numbers of peasant settlers in tropical forest areas, now engaged in losing struggles against the land monopolists and the land itself. The experiences of the organizations of rubber tappers and brazil nut collectors in the Amazon basin indicate that this can take place, even in the face of episodes such as the murder of the rubber tappers' leader Chico Mendes, if the state and external allies can help to redress the distribution of power and the scarcity of information.[19] Governments and inter-governmental organizations are now giving renewed prominence to environmental problems and policies, after relative neglect during the 1980s. In spite of the ritualism of many of the resulting conferences and declarations and the general reluctance to relate environmental menaces to questions of economic and political power, this trend promises to strengthen the legitimacy of popular self-defensive efforts, broaden their horizons and help them find effective allies. Up to the present, the general shrinkage of investment and the prohibitive costs – always larger than planned for – have done more to curtail environmentally destructive projects than organized resistance or a change of heart among the sponsors.

The ideological setting

Participatory initiatives always involve, *inter alia*, visions of the past and the future and attempts to make sense of social change. These attempts, as discussed in Chapter 2, are generally products of would-be allies, manipulators and adversaries of the groups trying to organize and act, although the 'excluded' may develop coherent and even utopian visions of their own. These are attempts to provide scripts for social actors or, in some cases, arguments that some would-be actors should be prevented from disrupting the important drama of development. It is no easier to assess recent changes in conceptions or scripts than changes in the real settings in which the dramas are enacted.

During the past decade the scripts previously current have remained on the world stage, along with their critics. Some arguments suggest that nothing has changed or that the prescriptions for action based on the scripts have hardened and become more dogmatic. The predominant impression, however, is the opposite. One finds greater scepticism concerning all comprehensive prescriptions, a more pronounced sense of limits and precariousness in human endeavours, a reluctant conclusion that experience has demonstrated that past hopes of rapid, uniformly positive, relatively plannable economic, social and political 'development' were illusory. This has affected some ideologies more than others, but probably fewer theorists and activists today are convinced that they know how the hitherto excluded and the newly excluded can emerge from their poverty and insecurity during the foreseeable future. One sees somewhat greater respect for the capacity of the excluded to make their own scripts, partly because of weaker confidence in the scripts that can be offered to them.

In the scripts underlying the action programmes of inter-governmental and non-governmental organizations, changes in terminology sometimes substitute for changes in conceptions. What presents itself as innovative, based on learning from experience and past errors, may in fact differ little from the reasoning behind programmes of thirty years ago. One might conclude that the constraints within which these organizations approach 'participation' bar them from radical innovations, while criticisms concerning the effectiveness of their past approaches continually push them toward efforts to present innovations.

The conceptions that now seem particularly important for their rising or declining impact on 'organized efforts' are as follows:

Neoliberalism. The rise or return to prominence of variants of a neoliberal, 'free market', anti-welfare-state, anti-planning ideology, originating in its explicit form in some of the leading industrialized powers, particularly the United Kingdom and the United States, was one of the most important factors during the late 1970s and the 1980s. This ideology legitimized only certain forms of participation: basically, those of the individual pursuing his or her own interests within certain legally codified rules of the game. It delegitimized most organized efforts by groups and movements to increase control over resources and institutions, as well as the mobilizing, regulating and welfare activities of the state, beyond the maintenance of public order and the financing of certain kinds of infrastructure. Its proponents have, in principle, favoured pluralist democratic procedures for legitimation of governments, but questioned the applicability of such procedures when they led to régimes that threatened the free market.

In practice, in parts of the Third World with populations already mobilized and accustomed to look to the state for many kinds of aid, or promises of aid, demobilizing military-authoritarian governments were needed to apply the prescription, and it became wedded to doctrines of national security with even stronger anti-participatory implications. Its proponents supposed that, particularly in poor countries, a high degree of income inequality and exclusion of a large part of the population were unavoidable for the foreseeable future. It followed that if the economic system were to achieve rapid growth it could not tolerate very much autonomous or party-directed participation by the excluded.

A good many governments in the Third World, of course, had long based their actions or inactions on views of this kind, and influential groups held the same views even in countries whose régimes were overtly for state intervention, planning and organized popular participation. The changes were in the increased explicitness of the ideology, imposition of its claims to scientific status and adoption in countries previously guided by quite different conceptions. The reasons lay partly in disillusionment with the results of developmentalist, state-interventionist policies and alarm at the consequences of populism; and partly in persuasiveness of arguments by influential economists of the industrialized countries. With the debt crisis, the dictates of the International Monetary Fund and the opening of national economies made variants of neoliberalism seem the only practicable bases for policy; the absence of plausible alternatives reduced the need for authoritarian enforcement. Most recently and unexpectedly neoliberalism has come to the fore, almost as a panacea, in the formerly 'real socialist' countries, in uneasy association with political democratization.

During the 1980s, variants of the neoliberal ideology emphasized a conception of 'empowerment' quite different from the conception of collective empowerment through organization envisaged by the UNRISD Participation Programme. 'Empowerment' becomes the removal of obstacles to individual choice and initiative presented by state regulations, state services and 'popular' organizations interacting with the state to control entry into labour markets, incomes, job security and working conditions. The excluded would thus be enabled to and spurred by necessity to participate without tutelage in the modern market-oriented society. This conception goes back to nineteenth-century attacks on guild regulations and communal landholdings that were said to stifle entrepreneurship and labour mobility. It has tapped a well-founded resentment of bureaucratized public services along with bureaucratized parties and unions. The post-crisis deterioration of state services and impotence of parties and unions have strengthened the resentment.

Modified neoliberal arguments for 'empowerment' in this sense come close in some respects to participationist ideologies that have nothing else in common with the support of capitalist economics. These arguments look to liberation and stimulation of popular initiative in the 'informal sector' more than to large modern enterprises and export-oriented production for overcoming economic stagnation. They attribute to the state wide responsibilities for making and enforcing 'good laws' supporting and harmonizing the strivings of individuals to better their lives and combine for freely chosen purposes. They also exhort the state to abandon the 'mercantilistic' tradition of trying to regulate everything and to cut down the jungle of 'bad laws' that drive striving individuals into illegality and give the bureaucracy opportunities for foot-dragging and extortion.[20]

The question remains whether the state can be expected to accomplish such an empowerment through enlightened leadership or only under pressure from the public, which can hardly be expected without strong political parties and other private-sector organizations. Thus the argument leads back to the unavoidability of tripartite tension and possibly creative conflict among three entities: the state, parties and other large organizations, and people pursuing local interests through many ties of co-operation and competition.

Developmentalism. The rise of neoliberal conceptions redefining and narrowing the legitimate functions of the state naturally paralleled a decline in the credibility of 'developmentalist' conceptions that had been under way since the 1960s. Developmentalism assumed a capacity on the part of governments to plan for the long term, invest intelligently, and promote and regulate a wide range of activities. While it gave overriding priority to rapid economic growth, mainly through industrialization, its proponents increasingly incorporated social objectives as supportive of such growth, particularly education and other forms of 'investment in human capital'. Its proponents also favoured state action directed toward full employment and more equitable distribution of incomes and consumption. While developmentalists did not disregard the importance of exports and international competitiveness to the extent that their critics later complained, they were more interested in stimulating modernized production for the domestic market and favoured controls over imports and external investments.

Developmentalism was associated with two of the conceptions of participation described in Chapter 2: participation as an aspect or consequence of 'modernization' and participation as a 'missing ingredient' in programmes expected to stimulate higher productivity and wider distribution of the fruits of growth.

Up to the 1970s or 1980s, economic growth and modernization did advance in most Third World countries, in some of them at unprecedentedly high rates, but the ability of governments to plan this growth and direct it toward unambiguous contributions to the general welfare came under question. Government interventions continued to be erratic and self-contradictory, depending on the changing influence of different groups of power holders, including different schools of technobureaucrats. Populist régimes borrowed what they saw fit from developmentalist doctrines, with unhappy results. At another extreme, military régimes in Brazil combined an economically effective developmentalist strategy with support of extreme income concentration and closure of most channels for popular participation.

Planning proved to be more a ritual or legitimizing device than a real influence on what was done in the name of development. The patterns of economic growth and cultural change wedded part of the population to consumption standards incompatible with adequate levels of saving and investment. Enormous miscalculations and disregard of environmental and other disbenefits in the more ambitious state programmes became evident. Even education, in quantitative terms the most successful of the state's activities, had results quite different from those expected by proponents of 'human resource development', particularly in the hypertrophy of low-quality higher education, with an output absorbable only through expansion of public employment, and in the failure of low-quality elementary education even to guarantee functional literacy or better access to the labour market.

The machinery of state intervention remained in place and became continually more complex through the contradictory demands on it and the growth of bureaucratic employment, but confidence in the capacity of the state to use it for coherent purposes shrank. During the 1970s, criticisms of developmentalism continued, from the opponents of state intervention on the one side and the proponents of different kinds of state intervention on the other, but, particularly in the middle-income countries, continued growth fuelled by borrowing permitted governments to avoid hard choices. With the crisis of the 1980s neither developmentalism nor the alternative prescriptions seemed very promising. The state could apply adjustment policies only at a high political cost and with no likelihood of revitalizing the economy as long as the debt burden remained and world demand for exports remained sluggish. For countries in which the greater part of the population is 'participating' to some degree there might be no politically practicable alternative to a return to some variant of developmentalism, backed by a good deal of comprehensively planned state intervention. However, governments are hindered from taking this path by the complexity and lethargy of the bureaucratic and regulatory apparatus already in place, the irreversible consequences of the previous opening of the economies, the intensified struggle over diminished public resources, the dictates of creditors and the loss of public confidence in the state's competence and in 'development' standing for a desirable and plannable future.[21]

'Another development', 'people-centred development', 'human development', 'sustainable development'. By the 1970s, as preceding pages have indicated in different contexts, developmentalism was under fire from a direction opposite to that of the neoliberals, through criticisms of the injustices and dangers of real processes of economic growth, rather than of the legitimacy and efficacy of state intervention. Some of the criticisms and policy proposals, without challenging the basic suppositions of modernization and industrialization, envisaged shifts in priorities toward income redistribution and elimination of extreme poverty, and insisted on the duty of the rich countries to transfer more resources with fewer strings to the 'developing' poor countries. Others were more radical, calling for a global transformation of values, power relationships and social organization without, however, adhering to the Marxist theoretical framework of the 'real socialist' alternatives that will be discussed below. At the same time, discussions in many international gatherings aiming at consensus produced 'plans of action' combining reformist and revolutionary prescriptions. The most prominent among the many declarations endorsed by governments were those setting objectives for the Second United Nations Development Decade and the New International Economic Order. The most prominent among the many non-official proposals was the 1975 Report of the Dag Hammarskjöld Foundation calling for 'another development', defined as 'geared to the satisfaction of needs', 'endogenous and self-reliant' and 'in harmony with the environment'. The quest for 'another development' was an important part of the intellectual climate that generated the UNRISD Popular Participation Research Programme, as well as a predecessor programme aiming at a 'unified approach to development policy and planning'.

During the 1970s the quest focused on the world as a whole and implied that nothing short of a global transformation could save the human race from disaster. This proposition has yet to be disproved, but its conversion into policy and practice demanded the conversion of most or all national governments and the power structures behind them, as well as the inter-governmental organizations. Since this did not occur, achievements at the national as well as international level were mainly rhetorical: an increasingly utopian content in the preambles to national development plans and in the declarations of international meetings. By the 1980s, 'another development' shared the partial eclipse of more conventional developmentalism. Although the crises bore out previous warnings, they led to lowered expectations and perplexity rather than to renewed conviction of the necessity of global transformation of values and policies.

Many of the proponents of another development retained their faith in popular participation but retreated from global prescriptions to modest and localized initiatives, sometimes trying to exert a 'participatory' influence within governmental and inter-governmental agencies, arguing for 'people-centred development', sometimes rejecting such ties and hoping that something not to be specified in advance would come of spontaneous social movements.

Ambitious efforts are now under way to reformulate the global challenge of 'another development' in terms more assimilable by governments and more compatible with the real potentialities and constraints deriving from recent history. One of these efforts, adopting the label 'human development', directs attention back to enhancement of human welfare as the main legitimate justification for development, and proposes goals, indicators and policies consonant with this justification.[22] The other effort attempts to integrate the environmental dimension with other imperatives in order to arrive at 'sustainable development'.[23] Both aim at comprehensiveness in prescriptions while recognizing the enormous diversity of real problems and of alternative means of coping with them. Both assume a very great enhancement at the level of states and of the international order in capacity to plan and administer complex policies – and a corresponding enhancement in public confidence in state ability to do these things. Both attribute great importance to popular participation but except for recommendations of relevant education have as yet little to say on the compatibility of such participation with global planning.

'Real socialism' and the 'socialist camp'. For more than seventy years, the direct and indirect influence of the main national models of 'real socialism' and the revolutions that brought them to power have inspired and complicated the evolution of popular movements throughout the world. These influences have been much too complex for adequate discussion here. They have included the ideological guidance and subsidization of parties that have tried to dominate popular organizations and movements. In more recent years they have also included military as well as economic advice and material assistance to régimes identifying themselves as Marxist-Leninist or simply nationalist and anti-imperialist. These efforts subordinated the immediate needs of the 'hitherto excluded' to the global strategy of the 'socialist camp' and to doctrines concerning the proper evolution of the class struggle and class alliances. Meanwhile, a good many régimes and development theorists not committed to the real socialist model assumed that the socialist states presented viable paths to development, that they had achieved through comprehensive planning and public ownership of the means of production a greater degree of efficiency and equity than the capitalist alternatives. The socialist countries subsidized the education in their own universities of generations of students seeking useful skills as well as political instruction, and most of these students returned convinced that the system functioned better than the systems of their own countries, if not always according to its pretensions.

States and political movements that were determined to prevent the spread of revolutionary socialism controlled by an adversary power combatted the claims of the socialist camp and the political movements and policy prescriptions stemming from it in an interminable Cold War. The contest in some settings helped popular movements to emerge and survive, but it also distorted their evolution and generated sectarian conflicts that became continually more complex with the split between the two main models of revolutionary socialism and the entry on the world stage of other socialist models (Albania, Algeria, Cuba, North Korea, Vietnam and Yugoslavia) that also aspired to influence parties and movements elsewhere. Struggles for national liberation or for the overthrow of oppressive régimes in Africa, Asia and Latin America evolved into wars by proxy that brought incalculable suffering, particularly to the poor and excluded.

The anti-socialist camp developed its own initiatives for popular participation to head off those of the adversary: community development, agrarian reform, support of trade unions and anti-poverty programmes. These sometimes helped the excluded toward autonomous organization, sometimes contributed to organizational rivalries and weakness. The upshot was frequently the violent suppression of the organized efforts of the excluded because of their real or imagined links with one or other of the contending camps, or because domestic anti-participatory forces found this a convenient excuse for crushing them. During the 1970s this reaction took on particularly virulent forms with the 'national security' and 'war against the internal enemy' doctrines of military régimes in Latin America and elsewhere, and the equally harsh repressions carried out by various 'socialist' régimes.

By the 1970s, the prestige of the real socialist camp was already in decline for many reasons, but a good many régimes and political movements in the so-called Third World continued to adhere to central planning along Marxist-Leninist lines as a viable prescription for development, and continued to rely on the socialist states as sources of expert advice and material aid. The other camp intensified its efforts to weaken or destroy régimes and movements adhering to these views.

In the late 1980s, the USSR and allied East European members of the socialist camp practically abandoned their claims to superior planning systems, encouraged searching self-criticism and entered into major reforms aimed at making their systems less regimented and better able to promote welfare, productivity and technological innovation. In the USSR, after a brief period of hope for socialist regeneration, these efforts were followed by accelerated economic deterioration, political impasses and the resurgence of competitive nationalisms. The other East and Central European countries rapidly left the socialist camp, and for the most part embarked on market-oriented policies within a political framework of pluralist democracy. The 'camp' then vanished altogether, as the USSR disintegrated and its component republics groped toward market economies. The realities of 'real socialism', suddenly exposed by its own former apologists, seemed remarkably similar to the problems of bureaucratization, corruption, squandering of investments and aggression against the environment with which most 'developing' countries (as well as the advanced capitalist countries) have been contending, but exaggerated by a greater capacity to conceal mistakes and suppress criticisms. The wealth of mass organizations in the socialist countries had not even been able to produce a shared illusion of popular participation in control over resources and institutions. Now, a wide range of hitherto excluded groups became visible and embarked on organized or individualistic survival strategies. The capacity of real socialism to serve as a convincing model, and the interest of the régimes in question in providing material aid and ideological guidance to other countries first declined sharply, then disappeared altogether.

The path of China, the USSR's main rival as a model for real socialism, has been quite different but not much more helpful to régimes and movements seeking such a model. The Chinese system continues to function well in economic terms, and has been much more successful than the Soviet in enlisting participation, particularly peasant participation, in productive reforms. Observers also give high marks to its achievements in extending basic social services in a population characterized by extreme poverty. By the 1980s, however, its leaders had abandoned the pretension to a unique egalitarian model for popular mobilization and social transformation, and renounced the effort to serve as guide to movements identifying themselves as 'Maoist'. The Tiananmen events of 1989 make long-term viability seem more questionable, by bringing into the open the difficulties of reconciling reforms with authoritarian controls, retaining the allegiances of the educated youth, and coping with the growth of a particularly excluded floating population expelled from the countryside by reforms in productive organization.

The consequences of the eclipse of real socialism for organized popular efforts in the rest of the world are only just beginning to be felt. For one thing, would-be mobilizers have lost a ready-made self-promoting utopia at a time when the prospects for any strategy that might promise the excluded 'increased control over resources and regulative institutions' seem unpromising. For another, the plausibility of arguments for disciplined mobilization and centralized planning under the control of enlightened élites has been shaken, as the leaders of régimes previously claiming to practise such policies have come to admit that they are no more exempt from misjudgements and self-inflicted crises than other régimes. The loss of credit of the real socialist utopia has combined with the limited appeal of the utopia represented by 'another development' to prevent the crisis of the 1980s from stimulating revolutionary hopes in the manner of earlier crises.

One response, evident in a few movements such as Peru's Sendero Luminoso, is a paranoid conviction of betrayal by the former socialist models, accompanied by intensified dogmatism and determination to mobilize the excluded for societal transformation at whatever cost to the excluded themselves as well as the rest of the society. For a short time, Albania emerged as the unlikely source of inspiration for this current, but soon fell from grace.

More generally, greater flexibility and autonomy can be seen among movements previously committed to one or other of the socialist camps, more attention to the immediate needs and potentialities of their followings and, above all, a slackening in the subjection of popular struggles to great power antagonisms. The doctrine of 'national security', according to which no popular movement could be tolerated if it risked coming under the control of the adversary global power centre, has lost plausibility along with the myth of the real existence of socialist utopias. One consequence has been government openness to the efforts of long-standing guerrilla movements, as in Colombia and El Salvador, to negotiate an entry into democratic political processes on condition of renouncing armed struggle. The changes, of course, also expose the former revolutionary socialist movements to the dilemmas with which social democratic movements have been struggling: what can they now offer the hitherto excluded in exchange for their support, under the constraints of insertion in the world economic system?

Finally, the self-discrediting of 'real socialism' has given weighty arguments to the proponents of a market-oriented world order, to the effect that all nationalist, populist and socialist resistance to this order is outmoded and irrational, that the only rational course is 'adjustment'. Or it may be argued that the burden of adjustment will be unbearable to the majorities in poor countries unless the rich countries make it easier by debt relief and openness to imports from these countries. The possibility that popular resistance to impoverishment may bring 'irrational' confrontations to the fore then becomes a useful bogeyman.

The myth of the proletariat. The declining plausibility of Marxism-Leninism as a guide to tactics, of the 'proletariat' as the destined revolutionary class, and of the necessity of an infallible proletarian vanguard party have involved ideological shifts related to but not identical with the eclipse of real socialism, shifts that were well advanced before this eclipse. This declining plausibility has affected activists and movements having no ties to either of the real socialist camps as well as the parties owing allegiance to one or other of them.

It has been evident for some time that the industrial working class, in the previously industrialized countries as well as most of the countries trying to industrialize, has been declining in relative importance in the labour force and diversifying in its organizational and occupational characteristics. For the most part, this class has shown no consistent predisposition to act as a revolutionary vanguard – something pointed out by such revolutionary strategists as Franz Fanon since the 1940s. Marxist-Leninist parties have been able to dominate many working-class organizations by providing disciplined leadership in struggles for the immediate demands of the members, but they have often lost these positions through unrealistic tactics or factional disputes, or been pushed aside by populist movements. Revolutionary movements in poor countries have found their leadership in parts of the educated middle classes, and their mass following more often among peasants than among workers. In their polemics, the term 'proletarian' has become hardly more than an assertion by one faction or another that it alone has the correct political line.

Even the versions of Marxism-Leninism that modified the exclusive reliance on the proletariat clung to reliance on the vanguard party and tended to place popular movements in a straitjacket by assigning fixed roles to the proletariat, the peasants, the sub-proletarian masses, the petty bourgeoisie, etc., and by deriving from past revolutions blueprints for the future. This did not prevent a few successful revolutions, but led to confusion or doctrinal sleight-of-hand when revolutions triumphed in countries in which the proletariat was small and weak, as in Nicaragua, or in which the 'revolution' really consisted of a coup or victory of an armed faction. It also contributed to defeats when the ideologically rigid leadership of genuine working-class movements could not accept peasants as allies on equal terms, as in Bolivia.

At present, most glaringly in the former real socialist countries but also in poor countries in which the state has striven to accelerate industrialization and in the countries long industrialized, much of the organized working class has been forced into rearguard defence of employment in large factories and mines that face declining demands for their products (particularly in the case of armaments) and are trapped by huge past investments in technologies that are outmoded and environmentally disastrous. The more militant these organized efforts, the harder it is for the 'proletariat' to find ideological partisans or common interests with the broader popular movements.

Only a very few movements capable of important mobilizations and a very few governing élites that are really dependent on military more than popular backing continue to cling to the myths of vanguard classes and parties. The more general trend is probably toward greater flexibility and recognition of indeterminacy in assigning roles to classes in social transformations. Hopes have turned toward movements that are multiclass and rely in part on sources of solidarity cutting across class: ethnic, gender or local self-identifications. Such approaches, of course, have their own temptations to over-generalization and over-optimism. One might expect also a greater awareness, based on experiences over nearly a century, that revolutions imposed by armed vanguards in the name of the proletariat will have unhappy outcomes -- overthrow by internal or external enemies or distortion into brutal and economically ruinous autocracies.

'Movementism' and 'spontaneism'. These ungainly labels apply to the resurgence of arguments for the spontaneous and diversified evolution of social movements negating the economic and political trends that now seem dominant. Some of these arguments go beyond the previous advocacy of localized conscientization, which invariably saw a role for outsiders as catalysts, and are wary toward the more structured views of social and political movements as means toward the taking of power. One version looks optimistically to the emergence of a 'new majority', freed by the present crisis from the illusions of development, modernization and Westernization, able to evolve its own systems of livelihood and reciprocity, turning its back on the state and the world system.[24] A similar formulation looks to 'another private' (the informal economy and personal relationships) and 'another public' (the ties of reciprocity and community organization) taking shape outside the control of the formal economic system and the state.[25] Still another formulation envisages social movements of many kinds, in the industrialized countries as well as elsewhere, acting on their own conceptions of justice, defending themselves against the aggressions or the neglect of various bankrupt economic and political orders, creating their own tactics in the course of struggle, rising and falling cyclically, but conceivably able to shape a new participatory social order (not to be defined in advance nor subjected to ideological prescriptions).[26] This last formulation denies the ability of any external agents to offer aid or guidance that would not become manipulative or counterproductive but leaves open the question of what can be external or internal to such an inclusive conception of social movements. Implicit in some of these arguments are catastrophist expectations that only the disintegration of the existing order will open the way to different and preferable human relationships. Conceptions of this kind claim to represent the real if unconscious aspirations of the excluded and alienated, but probably have raised some of the many contradictory trends now visible to undue prominence.

Fundamentalism, tribalism, xenophobia, irrationalism. As was indicated in relation to ethnic movements above, the 1980s and early 1990s have seen the resurgence of movements that have transformed the character of some previously secular 'modernizing' states and have threatened or brought about the disintegration of some multi-faith or multi-ethnic countries. The communal violence of the 1980s has struck countries that seemed to have achieved reasonably democratic and stable political orders, such as India, Lebanon and Sri Lanka, and also formerly 'real socialist' countries, such as the former Yugoslavia and many of the Republics of the former USSR, whose political élites prided themselves on having achieved enlightened solutions to ethnic and religious tensions. It has become only too evident that 'participation', channelled by popular historical memories and in-group solidarity, can have outcomes remote from the rationality of the would-be intellectual-ideological guides and allies who have taken part in the debates over participation.

These phenomena constitute the dark side of trends that otherwise seem grounds for hope: the decline in prestige of infallible prescriptions for development or revolution and the relaxation of ideological and organizational constraints on the spontaneity and diversity of social movements trying to cope with an indeterminate future, drawing strength from their cultures and the historical roots of group solidarity. In settings in which inter-ethnic and inter-faith conflicts are resulting in thousands of dead and millions of refugees it might seem fatuous to advocate participatory initiatives among the survivors, although it is evident that such initiatives do re-emerge and help them to rebuild their lives and their communities.

For the would-be allies of popular 'organized efforts' and still more for agencies of the state as well as the established political parties, the result might well be a dread of militantly autonomous initiatives, a fear that the decline of state capabilities and hegemony, together with the decline of modern mobilizing ideologies, points to an anomic 'war of all against all'. Two phenomena seemingly unrelated to fundamentalist and xenophobic excesses might well strengthen such a distrust of real or manipulated spontaneity: first, the realities of the Great Proletarian Cultural Revolution in China, which have gradually become general knowledge and confounded many who previously looked on this episode with hope; secondly, the rise or increasing visibility of anomic violence and criminality in urban and rural settings throughout the world. Advocates of spontaneous popular participation cannot satisfactorily answer questions such as these by drawing a line between 'good' participation and 'bad' pseudo-participation, the latter undoubtedly manipulated by anti-participatory forces. Human efforts to cope with change will continue to have outcomes that are sometimes inspiring, sometimes horrifying.

Notes

1. World Bank, *Poverty: World Development Report 1990*, Oxford University Press, New York, 1990, pp. 1-3 and 52-3.

2. World Bank, *The Challenge of Development: World Development Report 1991*, Oxford University Press, 1991, pp. 1 and 28.

3. South Commission, *The Challenge to the South: The Report of the South Commission*, Oxford University Press, New York, 1990, p. 116.

4. Popov, Gavriil, 'Dangers of Democracy', *New York Review of Books*, 16 August 1990.

5. Ghai, Dharam, ed., *The IMF and the South: The Social Impact of Crisis and Adjustment*, Zed Books, London, 1991.

6. UN Economic Commission for Latin America and the Caribbean (ECLAC), *Preliminary Overview of the Economy of Latin America and the Caribbean 1990*, Santiago, December 1990; and ECLAC, *Panorama Económico de América Latina 1991*, Santiago, September 1991.

7. World Bank, op. cit. in n. 1, pp. 11-17.

8. Ibid., p. 16.

9. Ghai, Dharam, ed., op. cit. in n. 5.

10. Vera Ferrer, Oscar H., *La Política Económica y el Sector Informal en el Contexto de la Crisis Latinoamericana: La Experiencia Mexicana*, paper presented at XVI Congreso Interamericano de Planificación, San Juan, Puerto Rico, 22-25 August 1988. It has been pointed out that widely differing definitions, descriptions and estimates of the size of the informal sector depend on the uses advocates of different policy prescriptions wish to make of them. Guerguil, Martine, 'Some Thoughts on the Definition of the Informal Sector', *CEPAL Review*, no. 35, August 1988.

11. Hewitt de Alcántara, Cynthia, Introduction to *Reestructuración Económica y Subsistencia Rural: el Maíz y la Crisis de los Ochenta*, El Colegio de México, Mexico City, 1992.

12. Hewitt de Alcántara, Cynthia, ed., *Real Markets: Social and Political Issues of Food Policy Reform*, Frank Cass, London, 1992.

13. World Bank, op. cit. in n. 1, p. 52.

14. 'The ground rules for this partnership remain to be worked out. They will involve the allocation of new resources, the definition of new roles for provincial and municipal governments (the local state), the democratization of the local state,

the representative organization of the local community, and the opening up of a new political terrain in the regional and local spaces. This is a large agenda that will take many years to accomplish. But without it, the problem of urban poverty remains without solution.' Friedmann, John, 'Collective Self-empowerment and Social Change', *IFDA Dossier 69*, January/February 1989.

15. An UNRISD research programme on Ethnic Conflict and Development has been exploring this diversity through numerous national studies. One of the conceptual papers prepared for this programme warns against a facile identification of ethnic conflict with traditionalism and reaction against the modernizing state. Rather, violence may stem from intensifying competition for the prizes offered by modernization. In India, over the past twenty years, instances of communal violence have risen by 700 per cent, almost entirely within the more urban and modernizing areas: 'Exactly those parts of the country which have done better in development have done better in turning against the minorities.' In the mass culture generated by modernization, 'ethnic differences are by themselves seen as dangerous and homogeneity is seen as congruent with modern nationalism and secular statecraft'. Justifications for new kinds of violence that originate in 'middle-class formations identified with various religious revivalist movements which are often themselves a byproduct of Westernization ... make perfect sense to the lumpen proletarian elements which provide the muscle power for participation in the actual acts of violence in urban South Asia. Both the middle-class consciousness and the new legitimacy created for violence, in turn, are sustained by a state apparatus which fears cultural plurality and the reaffirmation of local cultural identities as threats to national security.' Nandy, Ashis, *Note on a Study of Ethnic Violence*, mimeo, Delhi, February 1990.

16. See United Nations Development Programme, *Human Development Report 1990 and 1991*; The World Bank, *World Development Report 1990 and 1991*; South Commission, *The Challenge to the South: The Report of the South Commission*, 1990; UNICEF, *Adjustment with a Human Face: Protecting the Vulnerable and Promoting Growth*, 1987 (all published by Oxford University Press).

17. World Bank, op. cit. in n. 1, Table 26.

18. The following quotation shows the dimensions and suggests the unpredictability of the consequences of population mobility in China, a country in which the greater part of the rural population, according to statistical indicators, has been gaining in income levels in recent years: 'Internal migrations of part-time workers and disaffected or unemployed rural and urban populations were also reported to be uncontrollable. Tentative government figures suggested 8 million Chinese a year were moving to urban areas. ... the "floating population" of unemployed or laid-off workers was said to be 1.8 million in Shanghai and over 1.1 million in both Peking and Canton. Such huge migrations were only part of a larger problem, since changes in rural land use and production methods ... had made 180 million farm workers "redundant"; 250 million more were expected to be in the same plight over the next decade'. Spence, Jonathan D., *The Search for Modern China*, W.W. Norton & Company, New York, 1990, p. 736.

19. UNRISD's research programme on the Social Dynamics of Deforestation in Developing Countries is now exploring these issues. See, in particular, Diegues, Antonio Carlos, *The Social Dynamics of Deforestation in the Brazilian Amazon: An Overview*, UNRISD Discussion Paper No. 36, Geneva, July 1992; and Utting,

Peter, *The Social Origins and Impact of Deforestation in Central America*, UNRISD Discussion Paper No. 24, Geneva, May 1991.

20. A presentation of these arguments that has received wide attention in Latin America can be found in De Soto, Hernando, *The Other Path: The Invisible Revolution in the Third World*, Harper & Row, New York, 1989.

21. Many of the country papers presented at the UNRISD/ISER conference on 'Economic Crisis and Third World Countries: Impact and Response' (Kingston, Jamaica, April 1989) confront policy dilemmas of this kind. See Ghai, Dharam, ed., op. cit. in n. 5.

22. United Nations Development Programme, 1990 and 1991, op. cit. in n. 16. 'The main objective of human development is to enlarge the range of people's choices to make development more democratic and participatory.'

23. See for example ECLAC, *El Desarrollo Sostenible: Transformación Productiva, Equidad y Medio Ambiente*, CEPAL, Santiago, 1991.

24. Esteva, Gustavo, *El Proyecto Político de los Márgenes*, paper presented at the XVI Congreso Interamericano de Planificación, 22-26 August 1988, San Juan, Puerto Rico.

25. Quijano, Anibal, 'New Light on the Concepts of "Private" and "Public" ', *CEPAL Review*, no. 35, August 1988; and Quijano, Anibal, *Estado y Sociedad en América Latina (Notas de Investigación)*, draft manuscript, 1988.

26. Gunder Frank, André and Fuentes, Marta, 'Nine Theses on Social Movements', *IFDA Dossier*, no. 63, January/February 1988.

10

Participation in the 1990s

We are now in the early 1990s. Political contenders throughout the world are promising 'empowerment' and 'participatory democracy'. Voluntary organizations aspiring to act as allies of the excluded are flourishing, multiplying, and claiming new responsibilities. International funding agencies are insisting that development programmes incorporate active participation of the beneficiaries.

To what extent do these new affirmations of the importance of participation represent serious commitments to confront the problems discussed in the preceding chapter, in particular the forces making for exclusion and alienation of much of the world's population, and the desperate, violent reactions that are emerging? To what extent do they incorporate a better understanding of the real diversity of the excluded and of their survival strategies, the real constraints of evolving political and economic systems, the real capacities of activists and bureaucracies? To what extent is the renewed currency of participation as a bannerword a cyclical phenomenon, fuelled by the need of politicians and experts to offer something apparently new, marked by the same evasions and ambiguities as in the 1960s and 1970s?

This chapter represents frankly an unresolved tension between the authors' hope that something really new and important is happening, that authentic participation of the hitherto excluded is becoming more practicable as well as more self-evidently necessary for the human future; and their exasperation at the recurrence of pseudo-participatory rhetoric, reluctance to confront the full implications of empowerment of the excluded, sluggishness in the study and drawing of operational conclusions from the now abundant material on participatory experiences and anti-participatory structures; and, finally, at the shortcomings of their own efforts to do better.

Participation at the grassroots

A recent popular book reflects a widely held view when it states that 'throughout the world, from Western to Eastern democracies, from developing to Communist countries, there is a groundswell of popular movements, [a phenomenon that] will become increasingly important, though controversial, throughout the 1990's'.[1] Another publication speaks of the 'silent revolution arising from the grassroots ... which is increasingly influencing organizations and policies at other levels of power'.[2] Yet others glorify grassroots participatory organizations as the very foundations of democratic society and predict a 'fundamental restructuring of the institutional field of development (as a result of the extension of) processes of self-development' in the Third World.[3]

Such conclusions about the impending advent of true participatory democracy seem somewhat over-optimistic. Reality is more complex and, for the hitherto and newly excluded, much grimmer. While it is true that in a majority of countries new and unexpected institutional and political spaces have opened for the kind of 'organized efforts' that we have been discussing in this book, it is also true that ever larger and more heterogeneous groups of excluded find it increasingly difficult to defend their livelihood through such participatory initiatives.

The limits of democratization, and the search for new identities. One of the most striking developments of recent years is, no doubt, the rapidly spreading wave of democratization processes that started in Latin America in the 1980s, extended to Central and Eastern Europe, encountered tragic setbacks in part of Asia along with a few victories, and is now under way in Africa. This has led, in many countries, to the downfall or disintegration of authoritarian régimes and the establishment of new formally democratic structures of government. Though the historical roots, the form, scope and intensity of these processes differ from region to region, they are sufficiently similar to be considered part of a global trend. In most cases one of the most visible forces behind democratization was a newly emerging, semi-spontaneous, nation-wide popular movement, a collection of 'organized efforts' of many kinds, whose vitality and success took by surprise even the activists who had worked towards this end. Inability of governments to cope with the world economic crisis, popular frustration about increasing hardship, and decreasing ability of states to provide essential services have been major reasons for the events, but often a single catalytic event has produced the decisive mobilization. Earlier decades have of course seen waves of such popular uprisings; what is new today is the great number of such events, the speed with which the process has spread and the level of international support it has enjoyed.

While these events open significant new institutional and political spaces for popular action, and thereby provide much wider scope for organized efforts of many kinds, other simultaneous trends and developments seem to restrict severely the extent to which the excluded are actually able to make use of such new opportunities.

First, democratization processes have in many countries been linked to, and in part resulted from, economic crisis followed by the implementation of structural adjustment policies. These policies have not only advocated deregulation, privatization and a restriction of the public sector but have also curtailed the welfare state, severely cutting state budgets for basic social services and for many administrative functions serving the general public. As a result, levels of health, education, transport and communications tend to stagnate, or even deteriorate. The effects of such policies are by now harshly felt by the 'hitherto excluded' and by a wide range of 'newly excluded', particularly since traditional social 'safety nets' had earlier been destroyed or weakened by modernization policies, and modern social security systems, closely associated with the state, are now gradually breaking down. Inequalities between rich and poor, between men and women, between urban and rural regions and between areas of growth and marginalized regions are thus increasing, even in countries that are formally democratic and reasonably successful in the economic consequences of adjustment.

What is important for our discussion is that beyond an increase in poverty, marginalization and exclusion, these trends seem to lead gradually to a fundamental change in the people's perception of and attitude towards the state. The excluded do not normally share the generalized hostility against the state and its bureaucratic institutions that some of their middle-class allies manifest. They may distrust the state and its agents, avoid it, respect it; they do not fundamentally question it, however, and they expect it to perform a minimum of functions centred around the provision of physical security and basic social and economic services. Today, in the eyes of many, the state is no longer able to perform such basic functions. As a result, its legitimacy and authority are increasingly questioned. The upsurge of sub-national, ethnic and religious movements, which in many cases threatens the very integrity of existing states, is both a consequence of this declining legitimacy and a cause of its further decline. While the state's authority is thus threatened from below, it is simultaneously eroded from above as key decisions are increasingly taken by international and transnational actors or influenced by international trends which leave to the state only a narrow range of available options.

The decline of state legitimacy, apparent in many countries, leads naturally to a questioning of that of other, intermediate, political structures and institutions which traditionally derived their authority from the state, related to the state through regulations and subsidies, and expected to influence state policies on behalf of their members: parties, trade unions, co-operatives, structures of local government, former social and economic arrangements for marketing, credit or distribution. For the excluded, who have been fighting for better terms of incorporation into dominant economic and social systems, the very object of their struggle becomes questionable as these systems and their institutions are now disintegrating and their resources disappearing before their eyes. The ensuing loss of institutional terms of reference for participatory struggles has particularly dramatic consequences in those countries where institutional forms of association and group action were formerly monopolized by the state or a single party and its sub-organizations.

This gradually deepening crisis of institutions and of politics, felt by all social actors at local, national and international levels, reinforces at the level of the individual and of collectivities an already present or latent crisis of identity which has its sources in increasing economic insecurity, the destruction of traditional sources of livelihood, physical uprooting, the decreasing efficiency and reliability of collective and public mechanisms of social security and the disintegration or decreasing relevance of former institutional forms of co-operation and solidarity. The search for new individual and collective identities, taking place in a context of democratic affirmation of the rights of people, naturally tends to take nationalistic or religious-sectarian forms. The national or ethnic myth and the myths of communities of faiths are natural corollaries of the call for participation and democracy. They entail the search for collective historical conscious-ness and memory. In a context of institutional instability and of economic and social crisis, and in the absence of alternative and credible collective identities, participation and democracy thus easily turn into extreme new forms of collective intolerance and exclusion.

Secondly, the fall of authoritarian régimes and the establishment of formal democratic institutions, even if accompanied by impressive popu-lar upsurges and mobilization, does not necessarily lead to wider and more effective 'organized efforts' by the excluded in terms defined by the UNRISD Programme. This for two main reasons:

(1) In most countries where democratization has taken place, democ-racy remains essentially limited to changes in formal structures. It has not usually brought about a fundamental change in the balance of power in favour of the excluded and their allies who have not been the dominant social force behind the changes. They have rather played the role of 'foot-soldiers' in mobilizations led by the national bourgeoisie, the urban intelligentsia, by dismissed and frustrated members of the bureaucracy, and by unemployed educated youth of the urban middle classes. It is these latter groups that form new parties and newly recognized political move-ments; the participation of the excluded tends to find expression through religious fundamentalist movements, through sub-national ethnic move-ments, to some extent through established trade unions and peasant organizations, and through localized, generally short-lived informal asso-ciations.

(2) Formal institutional changes, such as the introduction of multi-party systems, parliamentary structures and mechanisms of representative de-mocracy, are not sufficient to bring about a functioning democratic system. A functioning participatory democracy requires a relatively strong and articulate civil society, a network of participatory institutions at all levels through which social groups can defend their interests, and vertical mecha-

nisms of consultation which allow the local level to defend its interests at higher levels. Much of this is lacking, or present only at an embryonic stage, in a good many of the countries that have suddenly achieved formal democracy. This may be due to history, the absence of a democratic tradition, but reflects also the continued social polarization and the political weakness of participatory efforts and movements of the excluded.

Processes of legal and institutional reform by themselves probably have little chance to sustain a democratic process and prevent new authoritarian structures from emerging. It is only the organized efforts of the people, of the excluded majorities, which could ultimately sustain the democratic process and make it a viable proposition. It remains to be seen to what extent the latter – with the help of their allies and profiting from the newly acquired legitimacy of their struggles – can make use of new institutional and political spaces that have opened, to make their interests heard and respected by powerholders and governments, to what extent they will be able successfully to defend and improve their security of livelihood before new structures of anti-participation consolidate to protect emerging monopolies of power and wealth, and to what extent they can avoid the temptations of the more extreme and intolerant deviations of participatory democracy.

New forms of exclusion and participation. The visibility of participatory struggles and grassroots movements has considerably increased in recent years, as probably have their number and vigour, and their actions now extend to new and diverse areas and concerns. Whatever the teleological or ideological interpretations that are made of these initiatives, they remain first and foremost expressions of struggles to survive and cope with shocks to previous expectations for livelihood and social ties.

Several factors explain why popular responses to crisis and change take increasingly heterogeneous forms today.

First, the 'hitherto excluded' have been joined by an increasing army of 'newly excluded': victims of the adjustment policies of the 1980s such as laid-off workers and public sector employees, young educated unemployed and lower-middle-class groups who have joined the informal sector; victims of the environmental destruction of their resource base such as fishermen, tribal groups or small farmers; and countless refugees and migrants, victims of man-made and natural disasters and of wars. The increasing heterogeneity of the excluded naturally leads to increasingly diverse forms and expressions of their struggles, and probably to increasingly complex linkages of support and opposition with other social groups and actors.

Secondly, the events in formerly 'real socialist' countries, and new revelations about the reality of regimented participation in countries such as China, have discredited national institutionalized forms of participation and prompted the search for alternative solutions that would be more responsive to real popular aspirations and local realities.

Thirdly, the limited adaptability to new challenges of traditional structures and channels of participation, such as trade unions, co-operatives, farmers' associations, local government structures or parties, and the decline of their legitimacy, has led to a weakening of organizational forms and frames of reference for collective 'organized efforts' of the excluded and has encouraged the emergence of more localized, often innovative, forms of participatory activities and efforts.

In Latin America, the proliferation of such recent organized grassroots activities, with their ideological biases towards local democracy and idealized visions of community, their distrust of large-scale formal bureaucracies and formal apparatuses of the modern state – their distrust of size as such – has been called *basismo*.[4] The purpose of these movements or activities seems not to be seizure of state power but rather the effective defence of a variety of local popular claims. They aim to force the state to become more responsive to the needs and interests of the excluded, to force it into public accountability. Whether *basismo* will contribute to render liberal democratic institutions more sustainable by creating new channels for pressure groups and allowing the excluded to by-pass traditional parties and politicians, or whether it will contribute to weaken the institutional basis of democracy and give new impetus to clientelism, depends, on the one hand, on its capacity to transcend inadequate institutionalization at the grassroots. On the other hand, and primarily, it depends on a positive response of the state, on the state's capacity to reform and to envisage co-operation with a rapidly growing and strengthened popular sector.[5]

In Africa, the harshness of the economic environment and, in many countries, the advancing disintegration of the state, of its administration and of the social fabric itself, has prompted many of the excluded and their allies to invent new forms of association, co-operation and organization based on fresh interpretations of traditional communitarian values. Such traditions of collective organized efforts have shown unexpected strength and vigour and have naturally led in recent years to the emergence of countless grassroots initiatives among pastoralists, small farmers and in poor urban neighbourhoods. Some of these efforts have received wide publicity as ideal examples of 'true' participatory grassroots movements. This is the case of the Naam groups in Western Africa, for example. These are traditional bodies of mutual co-operation and community work which have evolved into development-oriented popular organizations and have, through the Six-S Movement, extended over several countries of the region.[6] Like many other, similar but less well known organizations and popular initiatives, they engage in collective work, in the pooling of labour and other resources, and in collective credit schemes. From what is known about some of them, they have proven to be extremely vigorous, adapting in a flexible way to new realities and constraints and constitute certainly a formidable asset for the poor majorities in Africa.

It remains to be seen to what extent this new generation of vigorous grassroots activities in Africa will be able to replace former public programmes and services in social, educational and health fields, fill the void left by a retreating state, and to what extent they can resist co-option by the state and manipulation by the many new NGOs and other intermediaries that emerge with the professed intention to organize them, co-ordinate them, channel funds to them or to study them.

Grassroots efforts throughout the world have probably shown most vigour and innovativeness in recent years, and have acquired most visibility, in the informal sector, in struggles over local environmental issues and for consumer concerns, and in the defence of tribal or ethnic minority rights. Popular struggles of this sort will be discussed only briefly here, as they have already been examined in Chapter 9.

In the informal sector, organized efforts concentrate commonly on mutual aid or self-help activities. Beyond these are the more political organized efforts which range from clientelistic exchanges to violent mass actions and which resist any temptation to classify them or explain them in terms of a rational pattern of collective interests, loyalties and alliances. The pragmatic adaptation to changing conditions and opportunities, on which survival in the informal sector is based, seems to express itself also in an extremely complex and opportunist political behaviour.[7]

Popular struggles against sources of environmental degradation and for the safeguard of livelihood supporting natural resources have become increasingly important in recent years, in rural areas as well as in the cities. The scope of such struggles is likely to increase as objective environmental conditions continue to deteriorate and as the international and sometimes national legitimacy of such action increases. Recent studies, sponsored by UNRISD, on the dynamics of struggles waged by marginalized groups for control and preservation of natural resources that are threatened by outsiders show that such grassroots action can have a significant impact even against powerful entrenched interests, and this particularly when such environmental struggles are able to mobilize multi-class or even multinational alliances.[8]

Towards a democracy of diminished expectations. What chances are there for the hitherto and newly excluded to increase their control over resources and regulative institutions as a result of such localized struggles, and what relevance does this goal have when conventional resources disappear and institutions become visibly impotent or parasitic? It is natural, in such a context, that popular struggles increasingly focus on local level self-help and co-operation that not only offer hope of immediate material gains, but also of modifying in the longer term social relations between the excluded and the élites. Grassroots activists and their allies seem thus to attach increasing importance to the 'quality', the 'purity' and the self-reliant and autonomous character of the participatory efforts rather then to their size and their quantitative achievements.

Scholars sympathetic to participatory development have recently introduced a distinction between 'participatory development' and 'people's self-development' in an attempt to stress the qualitative characteristics and differences between different kinds of participatory struggles. While 'participatory development' is used to describe people's participation in development activities that have been designed for them by the state or other external agents, 'people's self-development' describes a liberating process of awareness-raising and creative collective action which ideally leads to self-reliant development and confers on the group or organization the necessary clout to negotiate on new terms with powerholders, parties and the state.[9]

Recent studies have given much publicity to examples of such 'people's self-development', presented and glorified as living examples of the best of grassroots politics. Evidence is too scant to draw conclusions as to the wider relevance and viability of such examples. Many crucial questions remain open. Experience shows that the financing of such participatory self-development raises delicate issues and often results in new relations of dependence on national or international NGOs or other temporary allies. Also, such participatory efforts are often unduly dependent on an exceptional leader and the support of committed social activists. This raises questions as to their continuity and capacity to survive change in leadership and alliances. Furthermore, the very emphasis on the participatory quality of these efforts limits them usually to small-scale, localized activities and raises questions as to their replicability and their capacity to influence supra-local, macro-level politics. Attempts to co-ordinate such successful participatory micro-actions into larger, more powerful movements have raised new problems and contradictions. Successful examples, such as the Western African Six-S Movement referred to above, are so far exceptional and too short-lived to support any clear conclusions.

A basic question regarding all participatory grassroots action is the relationship between the 'genuineness' of the participatory efforts (i.e. the participatory, autonomous and self-reliant character of the organization) their relative size and rate of expansion, and their real effectiveness over time (i.e. their capacity to negotiate their claims with powerholders, parties, unions and the state). Past experiences, confirmed by the findings of the UNRISD Programme reported in Part II, tend to reject claims that small can be both beautiful and effective in the long run. To what extent 'scaling up' through co-ordination and 'networking' of grassroots organizations and local participatory efforts can overcome the inevitable contradictions between smallness and effectiveness and between largeness and participatory authenticity is a question which in the present political post-democratization context is of burning interest.

The UNRISD studies, as reported in Part II, have shown that the real effectiveness of organized efforts of the excluded depends to a large extent on the nature of their alliances with other social groups and, of course, on their relations with the state and its agents at the local and national level. These conclusions are still valid today. We have seen earlier that the increasingly diverse forms and expressions of participatory struggles seem to have led to increasingly complex relations of support and opposition between the excluded and other social groups and political actors. We will discuss below the critical but ambiguous role that NGOs play in this respect, and the way in which states and their agents tend to view participatory efforts in the present context.

The declining authority of the state, its progressive withdrawal from areas of economic and social development, and the idealized vision of a reinvigorated and organized civil society that would 'stand up to the state' and 'fill the void', should not make us forget that the state and its agents at local and national levels remain key actors in the 'game of participation'. The 'excluded' are well aware of this and do not usually share, or even understand, their intellectual allies' vision and goal of an 'anarchist utopia from which the state is absent and where only "community" remains'.[10] The goal of grassroots organizations is thus not to conquer or vanquish the state but to forge selective alliances with parts of the state and its bureaucracy while avoiding new clientelistic constraints. Such successful political action would gradually lead to what the excluded would view as a 'better' state, one where their claims and interests are taken more seriously and where authorities may be willing to tip the balance of power in their favour.

The Inter-American Foundation, which grappled with this problem through a variety of studies of local initiatives in Latin America, concludes in one of its reports:

> Those of us who, by instinct and experience, do not like governments or central authority may wish for a purer (that is, a stateless) development scenario. In our mind's eye, we can imagine tens of thousands of diverse, independent, autonomous nongovernmental organizations that challenge or replace the functions of the state. We see a vast, decentralized profusion of independent organizations – as if development were a rich spread of wildflowers rather than a cultivated field. It may well be that wildflowers do grow by themselves. But grassroots organizations do not. They are cultivated, in large measure, by just policies and competent government agencies that do their job.[11]

As another observer of the Latin American scene states, the claim that *basismo* 'can achieve development or democracy, or that it can meet basic needs, without requiring the co-operation of the state is as unsustainable as the claim that the state can make progress in those aims without the parallel deepening and strengthening of popular organizations'.[12] In the last analysis, there may be no alternative to the joint efforts of a reformist state and a reinvigorated and organized civil society in which the excluded can make their voices heard.

NGOs: between the grassroots and the state

Non-governmental organizations have rapidly gained in importance and numbers throughout the developing world and are becoming respectable partners in the eyes of governments, international organizations and development assistance agencies. In some regions, such as Africa, they have gained a reputation as leading practitioners of rural development and as efficient delivery mechanisms for relief and for social services in difficult areas. They are thus increasingly used by international donors as channels for development aid and are burdened with unprecedented responsibilities. It has been calculated that 'Northern' NGOs collectively now transfer to the 'South' more than the World Bank group does.[13] For the 'excluded', NGOs have become important actors, and usually partners and allies though at times new patrons, in the never-ending development drama.

Problems of definition. The term NGO today embraces a wide range of organizations and movements of diverse size, origin, purpose and character. It is at times even used for governmental pseudo-NGOs that have been set up to control the local NGO scene or as convenient channels for development aid. Theorists and practitioners of development have repeatedly attempted to impose some conceptual rigour by classifying these organizations into different groups and by inventing new, supposedly less ambiguous terms. Distinctions have thus been made between international, national and local or community-based NGOs, between membership and service organizations, and of course between Northern and Southern NGOs. New terms and acronyms have been proposed such as 'private voluntary organizations' (PVOs) or just 'voluntary organizations', 'self-reliance promoting organizations' (SRPOs), non-governmental development organizations (NGDOs), or 'grassroots support organizations' (GSOs). It has also been proposed to group them into 'first, second and third generation NGOs', referring thereby to the historical evolution of NGOs from relief organizations to the local development-oriented organizations of the 1970s and finally to the self-development promoting organizations that have emerged in recent years.[14]

The UNRISD Participation Programme has not attempted to resolve these terminological and conceptual complexities, but in practice restricts the use of the term NGO to those organizations that have been discussed in Chapter 8, i.e. to those organizations that support, assist, promote, help, study, co-ordinate or manipulate the organizations of the excluded, and not to the latter themselves. This admittedly imprecise and possibly over-simple expedient has served its purpose and is also used in this chapter.

Reasons for increasing NGO presence and strength. The increasing importance of NGOs as actors in the development game is of course related to the progressive weakening of state power and state presence in many countries. Particularly on the African continent, the emergence of count-less NGOs has followed closely the progressive abandonment by governments of ambitious attempts to direct development and promote general welfare from above. The African famines of 1974 and 1984 and subsequent plans of action brought to light not only the helplessness and inefficiency of many government administrations, but also the relative vitality and efficiency of NGOs in relief and development work and as conduits for international assistance. Practical evidence suggests that NGOs have generally performed better than government agencies, particu-larly in providing such services as primary health care, water and sanitation facilities, small-scale credit programmes or low-cost housing schemes. They are usually less encumbered by bureaucratic rules and thus more flexible, have a low-cost management style, their staff works often on a voluntary basis and is more motivated than lower-level government staff, and they are more open to participatory development approaches.

Increasingly inter-governmental agencies and governments have thus been tempted to use NGOs as 'delivery mechanisms' for projects expected to benefit the poor. Greatly increased financial support from the North has led in some areas of Africa or Asia to a real explosion in the number of newly formed NGOs. In some countries NGOs become a new career avenue for the educated middle-class youth who formerly would have joined government services but are now facing unemployment due to the curtailment of such services.

NGOs profit today from an unusual conjunction of ideas in which development theorists of many ideological persuasions seem to agree on the ineffectiveness of the state and the need for institutional alternatives. Many see NGOs as an at least partial solution to the problem. For some, NGOs are ideal vehicles and agents for participatory development and key actors in strategies to empower the poor and excluded. Others value NGOs as instruments to reduce state intervention and promote the privatization of development action, particularly in regions such as Africa where the private sector is still little developed, where organizations such as trade unions, co-operatives or professional associations are often co-opted by the state, and where the non-profit voluntary sector constitutes *de facto* the only alternative to the public sector.[15] It is thus hardly surprising that even the World Bank has begun systematically to increase NGO involvement in the operations it supports, particularly in projects where 'beneficiary participation' and grassroots organizations are considered important factors to ensure efficiency and sustainability of operations.

Ambiguous but on the whole positive impact on organized struggles of the excluded. How does this new strength and presence of NGOs influence the kind of 'organized efforts of the excluded' that have been at the centre of the UNRISD Programme? Research carried out under the UNRISD programme and elsewhere suggests that organized collective action by the excluded usually requires, at least in the initial stages, the action of an external agent as catalyst, animator or facilitator. It is out of this encounter between the external agent and the group of excluded that participatory action is usually born.[16] This catalytic role can be played by a sympathetic or interested individual – an urban middle-class activist, a teacher, a priest, a political party activist, a trade unionist or a local government official. In a great many cases, however, NGOs have done so. The wider presence of NGOs, their increased influence, legitimacy and access to resources, and the emergence of relatively radical NGOs that advocate conscientization and animation work among the excluded, are thus undoubtedly contributing to the blossoming of new grassroots movements and activities.

Besides acting as animator or catalyst, NGOs also provide other supportive services to participatory projects and groups: they facilitate access to technical knowledge and information and to funds and material support; they serve as mechanisms for the delivery of credit and social services; they help establish horizontal lines of communication between different movements and organizations that allow for the exchange of experiences and the co-ordination of supra-local action; and they establish contacts between the grassroots action and sympathetic and influential individuals, groups and institutions at national level. More generally, NGOs can provide the 'organized efforts' with tactical allies at various levels that are able to get a hearing in the centres of power and thus help defend the excluded against local exploiters and agents of the state. In some cases tactical NGO support to local causes can reach international levels of publicity and support through the action of international NGOs, particularly when local struggles concern specific policy areas such as environmental protection, human rights, health, nutrition, education or consumer concerns.

The overall importance of NGOs to participatory struggles and initiatives is thus beyond doubt, but so is the fact that NGO action and alliances with 'organized efforts of the excluded' easily lead to manipulation and may create new bonds of clientelistic dependency. All the ambivalences in relations between participatory movements and their allies and interlocutors that we discussed in Chapter 8 remain valid here.

Even in the best of cases, where NGOs do not set out to manipulate the poor nor to profit themselves from easily available funds, in cases where

NGOs are committed to people's self-reliant development and pledge to transfer control and initiatives to group members and then to withdraw, such a policy is often difficult to implement. A recent study, evaluating the impact of NGO action on rural poverty alleviation in Bangladesh, states: 'The second finding is simply this: the members do not want NGOs to withdraw. The push towards "member control" comes from national and international development theorizing, not from the clients themselves.' And the study continues:

> While on the one hand NGOs state their aim as fostering self-reliant development among the poor, on the other they build themselves up as institutions that look set on staying. With one voice they go to the poor with something to offer; with another they say that the poor should stand on their own feet. Whatever the rhetoric, the institutional logic of NGOs does not favour their continual divestment of hard won *samitis*.[17]

Behind such differences of views between NGOs and members of participatory groups about the desirability of NGO withdrawal lie fundamental differences in their perception of reality. For the poor and excluded NGOs can offer above all protection, and some insurance for the future. They represent new patrons to whom the poor can look for support, for protection from repression, exactions and exploitation and for support in times of economic hardship. In a context of extreme poverty and gross power inequalities, concepts like 'self-reliance', 'autonomy' and 'self-development' are likely to sound in the ears of the poor like exhortations that they should continue to face alone insurmountable odds.

A similar ambivalence characterizes relations between donors and international NGOs on the one hand, and national and local NGOs on the other. Donors extol the virtues of self-reliance, but their offer of generous funds encourages national and local NGOs to evolve into oversized institutions which will be unable to keep going on self-generated resources. In countries where NGOs are still young and have little practical or political experience, as is the case in many countries in Africa, this can take extreme forms when international donors encourage the institutionalization of local NGOs merely as local counterpart through which they can channel aid, ignoring the fact that many of these hastily formed NGOs have no popular base, no links to the grassroots, no activities except the receiving and channelling of foreign aid. But even genuine local NGOs are liable to lose their authenticity as a result of overgenerous foreign aid: as they receive ever larger funding from donor agencies, and spend more and more time servicing donor requirements, they tend to become increasingly bureaucratized, inefficient and distant from the grassroots. There is an inherent and perverse contradiction in the very proposition to support self-reliant development with material means.

Finally, the rapid growth of the NGO sector, particularly in Africa and some countries of Asia and Latin America, contributes in a more general sense to increase the opportunities for the excluded to make their voices heard. NGOs help to pluralize the institutional environment by providing new structures of association and thus offer alternatives to the monopolies of the state and its co-opted mass organizations. To the extent that they develop internal mechanisms for holding leaders accountable they contribute to an emerging democratic political culture which probably is an important precondition for the actual functioning of a democratic political system. The mere channelling of services to the grassroots through NGOs, on the other hand, is not likely to promote local creativity and self-reliance and may actually be detrimental to it.

NGOs and the state. Relations between states and NGOs tend to be as ambivalent as those between the NGOs and the excluded, ranging from distrust, hostility and open conflict to rather rare instances of genuine co-operation. Governments recognize the usefulness of the voluntary sector, they value NGOs because of the funds that they can attract and tend to bow to international pressure to confer legitimacy on them. They will, however, inevitably seek to control them through a variety of legal, political and administrative measures, confine them to certain sectors, co-ordinate them, monitor them, co-opt them, dissolve them or try to set up their own pseudo-NGOs. Rather than regarding them as potential allies in the development game they tend to perceive them as potential political challenges, or worse, as trouble-makers liable to stir up discontent and mobilize the people against the legal authority. Most NGOs show an equally innate hostility to the state and its bureaucracy. To the extent that NGOs consciously move into vacant political space they do of course represent a political challenge to the state's authority.[18]

In Latin America, relations between the voluntary sector and governments have been particularly tense as NGOs have for many years fought in alliance with opposition forces against military régimes and for the restoration of civil society. To a greater extent than in other regions, international NGOs have interacted with vigorous popular organizations trying to mobilize the excluded against repression as well as adjustment policies. The resulting mutual distrust, which is only gradually waning, remains a significant barrier to what would seem a natural collaboration between NGOs and new democratic régimes.

In South Asia, on the contrary, relations between governments and NGOs have been traditionally more positive. Relatively democratic governments have given priority to poverty alleviation programmes and attempted to transfer responsibility for some activities to NGOs, or have included NGOs in the implementation of government-sponsored projects. In practice, however, tensions between the public and the voluntary sector are also common here. NGO support of ethnic minorities and of protests against threats to local livelihood from such 'development' activities as dam construction and exploitation of forests have become recurrent sources of conflict. Also, some Asian NGOs increasingly resent their role as substitutes for state services and providers of superficial relief to the victims of adjustment programmes. As one prominent Indian NGO recently wrote,

> voluntary development organizations and other non-governmental organizations have been 'seduced' to participate in a massive initiative for providing a Human Face to the consequences of structural adjustment programmes in many countries. As the state is forced to withdraw its social welfare and service providing functions (in issues such as health, education, skill-building, re-training, etc), resources are induced into voluntary development organizations and NGOs to take over these functions. Similarly, NGOs may be induced to support informalization of Indian economy in the face of growing privatization.

And the same source proceeds to warn against the ideological role that NGOs are being made to fulfil against their will:

> It is in this context that voluntary organizations working all over the country in different ways and at different levels need to begin thinking about the implications of these programmes in India. It is in this context that we need to guard against the possibilities of becoming unwitting allies to the globalization of capitalism and homogenization of our cultural heritage. We need to reflect upon our roles and contributions in evolving creative alternatives to the contemporary 'myth' of a singular model of development.[19]

The African situation is still rapidly evolving. As one scholar explains,

> African institutions are themselves embryonic [and] relations among institutions are necessarily fluid and incipient. In Africa, both centralized states and developmental NGOs are relatively new structures and the limits of their popular support and managerial capacity have yet to be fully tested. We can expect relations to swing back and forth as each side probes to discover a workable set of inter-institutional arrangements that suits African conditions.[20]

In the longer term it seems inevitable that more stable forms and terms of NGO-government collaboration be found and eventually institutionalized. Both sides can only win from the process: NGOs can gain access to public resources for purposes of programme replication and will be able to tackle increasingly large-scale and complex operations. State bureaucracies will probably improve their performance under pressure from below. NGOs may finally provide the state with the indispensable link to the grassroots and help it to recover some of its authority and legitimacy. In general, the increasing importance of NGOs suggests that their real or imagined political roles will continue to complicate the choices open to the excluded, and that NGOs will need a high degree of political insight and restraint to avoid the pitfalls.

The state: control or participation?

The state has probably never encountered such diverse ideological attacks and threats to its functioning since the genesis of modern nation-states two centuries ago. Radical proponents of participatory development and empowerment theories tend to see in it a main cause of continued poverty and inequality, and pursue, consciously or not, an anarchist utopia from which the state would be absent and where only the 'people' or the 'community' remains. Their opponents from the right join them in this almost visceral anti-state attitude. They advocate further dismantling of the welfare state, deregulation and privatization, and argue for the inherent curative and productive virtues of the free market and of individual initiative. Historical evidence suggests that both assumptions about the role of the state may be wrong and that a healthily functioning state is probably indispensable both for the development of a free-market economy and for the functioning of a participatory democratic system.

From the standpoint of this inquiry into participation, whatever the recent upheavals and confusions, the state and its agents remain key actors in the development game at the national and sub-national levels. And key questions relevant to the 'organized efforts of the excluded' remain the extent to which the state can become willing and able to promote or tolerate such efforts, and the conditions under which state agents can help the excluded achieve more control over their own livelihoods and an authentic voice in shaping their and the country's future.

The call for an 'enabling environment'. Previous chapters have shown how states have periodically attempted to promote or institutionalize popular participation in some form or another, and how they have attempted to reconcile conflicting objectives of central control and decentralized participation while responding to equally conflicting pressures from below and from above. Pressures for states to promote participatory development, and practical reasons for doing so, have probably never been as strong and manifold as today. Divestment of state authority, downward transfer of state responsibilities and decentralization of administration – all policies that implicitly call for a re-definition of the relative roles and responsibilities of the state, the market and the private sector – have been part of the package of adjustment policies imposed by the international lending institutions on many governments. Mounting social and political tensions stemming from these impositions have led to the present 'generation' of policies calling for 'adjustment with a human face',[21] good governance, the strengthening of civil society and the search for a new national consensus to support the application of the policies. The promotion of popular participation is an integral part of such an approach, both as a component of the liberal democratic ideology, and as a practical tool to enable people to support themselves through self-help in areas in which the state is deficient. The role of the state becomes logically one of creating an 'enabling environment', first for market forces and private initiatives and now for popular participation and the development of self-help initiatives at the grassroots level.[22]

The prime force behind this new approach is clearly the international development and donor community – international organizations, the international lending institutions, major donor countries and development co-operation agencies – which increasingly make assistance conditional on a poor- and participation-orientation of government policies. Most Third World states have probably not much choice but to go along with this, both to please donors and to counter the rising ungovernability and anomy of their societies.

Inherent contradictions between control and autonomous participation. Any government attempt to translate principles of participation into practice brings to the light inherent contradictions. On the one hand, governments face pressure from international forces to apply more participatory and democratic policies. They are also tempted by the opportunity to transfer responsibilities and costs downwards and by the possibility of mobilizing and harnessing new local resources through participatory approaches. On the other hand, governments understandably shy away from the power implications of participation and its inherent potential for social conflict. Governments are not neutral administrative bodies but political expressions of dominant social forces, and the poor and excluded are not part of these ruling forces and alliances unless, briefly, in revolutionary political conjunctures. Quite naturally, governments tend thus to resist any policy that entails dilution of power and above all participatory approaches that aim to empower the hitherto excluded.

This natural tendency of power to concentrate and remain at the top has in many Third World countries been reinforced by the historical circumstances of the immediate post-independence period. In order to consolidate the young states in the presence of numerous divisive and hostile forces, governments centralized administrative and political control and gradually acquired a distinctively authoritarian and interventionist character. Large state bureaucracies were put in place whose very function was to regulate and organize in order to control and which, by definition, distrusted autonomous initiatives from below.

Even when states feel obliged, or tempted, to open spaces and encourage wider popular participation – because problems have become unmanageable, because governments' capacity to plan and implement coherent policies has been eroded or because international pressure grows – they will normally attempt to control such participation and channel it into well defined areas and forms. Even then, states and their agents are likely to retain control over basic decisions and resources and confine participation to the implementation and running of programmes and projects that have been defined without the people who are supposed to be the ultimate beneficiaries.

All this is not new, and accounts of UNRISD research in Part II provide ample evidence of the ambiguities of state-sponsored participation and of the authoritarian pitfalls into which it tends to fall. It seems nevertheless useful to recall today, when democracy and participation have again become widely used bannerwords, that governments have a persistent and inevitable tendency to translate participation into exercises of mobilization, and that political and bureaucratic constraints make the pursuit of a coherent participatory policy by governments virtually impossible.[23]

Decentralization policies and the promotion of participation in specific social sectors. Governments are most likely actively to seek, or to tolerate, active popular participation through 'organized efforts' in fields that do not seem directly threatening to local élites and state agents, such as public health, in areas where active co-operation from the people is vital to the success of policy, such as in the field of population control or environmental conservation, or in activities that are costly, difficult to administer and politically unattractive.

Public health and primary health care have offered one of the more attractive entry points for local participatory organization. Since the late 1970s the shortcomings of previous ambitious but bureaucratized and top-down curative health strategies had been recognized, and in 1977 WHO adopted the 'Alma Ata Declaration on Health for All by the Year 2000'. An important component of this new strategy was the active involvement of the people themselves, both in the support and functioning of health services and in the determining of health priorities and the allocation of scarce health resources.

Since the 1980s the concept of Community Involvement in Health Development (CIH) has come to stand for such a new participatory approach. However, the translation of this concept into practice until very recently has not gone very far, often because of a lack of political commitment, of bureaucratic resistance to decentralization and of inadequate attention to the participatory nature of the approach.

Recent developments now make such participatory approaches to health development more attractive. Severe cut-backs in public health budgets have made access by the rural and urban poor to health services more difficult, and in some regions health conditions have started to deteriorate. Governments and international agencies such as UNICEF and

WHO have fallen back on participatory primary health care schemes that can be staffed and managed by local communities – after some training – and supported by local resources with only modest external aid.

The 'Bamako Initiative' is an example. The initiative was launched in a meeting of African Ministers of Health in 1987 as a means of revitalizing primary health services on the continent and has been supported by various international organizations such as WHO and UNICEF. The initiative aims at decentralizing primary health care schemes and developing community financing mechanisms by introducing payment for basic drugs and other 'user charges'. The underlying idea is that local groups would manage and decide themselves about their local health schemes and support them materially in a participatory way. Experience so far is inconclusive. Reports from the field, however, show that government agencies tend to empty the initiative of its basic participatory elements and to apply the plan in a rigid, centralized and bureaucratic way which reduces local participation to the payment of user charges.

The very concept of 'user charges', which is becoming fashionable with governments and international organizations, is of course eminently ambiguous. While some advocate it as a practical and operational expression of participatory development and self-reliance, others see in it a convenient way to transfer costs for basic services from the state to the people, irrespective of the negative consequences that such an approach can have on the poorer groups who may not be able to afford such charges.

There is only inconclusive evidence of the extent to which the intended beneficiaries of participatory health schemes really welcome this approach and the extent to which it serves as an entry point for broader and more contentious 'organized efforts'. One drawback, of which the people are likely to be quite conscious, is that it can lead to a permanent dual system of health care, in which the excluded would be expected to support services that would not be accepted by groups better able to demand state-subsidized modern medicine. Resistance to the perpetuation of a dual system seems to have decided the Chinese authorities to replace their famous system of 'barefoot doctors'. Also, the supposedly non-controversial character of primary health care has not consistently protected 'conscientizing' movements and NGOs involved in such activities from harassment as subversives.

Environmental issues have paradoxically become one of the most conflictive areas for spontaneous participatory action of the excluded, as we have seen in Chapter 9, and a promising focal point for state-local co-operation. In many cases local élites and agents of the state have initially reacted by repressing such popular struggles, particularly when private profit or internationally funded 'development' projects were at stake. But the increasing magnitude and seriousness of environmental problems, the continued and growing inability of governments to act on them, and increasing international advocacy of sustainable development approaches have made governments more open to participatory initiatives in this field. NGOs have also increasingly taken up environmental issues as convenient entry-points for participatory action which do not seem overtly threatening to the state. While all the actors involved – the state, the NGOs and the people concerned – have their own agenda and objectives, they now occasionally join forces in support of local participatory struggles by the excluded for environmental conservation.

This is not surprising, as it is in this field, perhaps more than in any other, that the necessary complementarity of state action from the top and organized popular action from below imposes itself. Environmental management, in the framework of a sustainable development approach, requires a long-term, coherent, comprehensive policy approach which governments are rarely able to pursue. As in other policy fields, they have to deal with and respond to a great many conflicting interests and forces from various sides and levels, and they must cope with an array of public entities and established programmes that have built up their own interests and inertia, with legislative provisions that can be changed only slowly, and with organized resistance from different sectors of the bureaucracy and from social forces and classes. State action in this field is only likely to be effective if it is supported by the people concerned, who, organized in groups to defend and manage their livelihood-supporting resource base, can support the state's conservation programmes and control the local implementation of environmental legislation.[24]

Here and there specialized government agencies have been able to enter into genuinely participatory relationships with their clientèles, shaping projects through discussion and respect for local views, insulating their work over relatively long periods from negative national political and bureaucratic environments, and eventually making a significant difference to organizational capacity as well as incomes. One experience that has been studied with sufficient detail and objectivity to demonstrate the requisites for success is that of the Philippine National Irrigation Administration between 1976 and 1986.[25]

NGOs and proponents of participatory development have recently raised the question whether local staff of central government agencies, or local government officers, could not use participatory animation techniques that have been developed by NGOs. The idea of combining the quality, flexibility and participatory nature of the NGO approach with the nationwide coverage and leverage that governmental programmes can provide is tempting. Some governments see in such an approach a way to remedy the chronic inefficiency of public extension services and to bring extension workers closer to the grassroots. NGOs hope that local government agents could perform the catalytic role of animators on a much larger scale than they are themselves able to do.

One example where such an approach has been experienced somewhat systematically and over a period of more than five years is the 'Planning for Rural Development at the Village Level' (PRDVL) project in Tanzania. The project faced initial suspicion from central government and party offices but initial successes made them aware that participatory animation may be a more effective way of mobilizing people than traditional extension work. Evidence of the success of this experience, and of its interest for the government, the NGOs and the excluded, is as yet inconclusive. Despite support from the government, the party, the international NGO community and international organizations the project has so far not been able to expand beyond the stage of a pilot project. The fact that animators remain public servants, are paid by district councils and thus accountable to public entities rather than to the people, introduces potential contradictions and can lead to serious conflicts of interest when priorities and perceptions of the popular groups clash with those of the government. It is also likely that state agents will attempt to use animation work as just another technique for popular mobilization rather than participation.

The project has received some publicity as a revolutionary, unique and innovative experience. Impressions gathered in the field seem to indicate, however, that people's participation in the project is much less genuine and widespread than one would imagine from project reports. Present plans to expand the coverage of the project from a few selected villages to a whole district and to train all ward extension officers as animators may give better indications of feasibility.

Finally, a note about administrative decentralization. Dwindling central resources, rising demands for regional and local autonomy and international pressures have prompted more governments to carry out administrative reforms in order to decentralize development planning and transfer central government responsibilities to regional or district levels, and sometimes even to NGOs and neighbourhood associations. It is not realistic to assume that such reforms will necessarily lead to increased participation of the excluded in public affairs, even if these reforms take place in a newly democratic context. Often decentralization does not involve deconcentration of power but simply strengthens the technical authority of government field officers over the local process of resource allocation. When set in a traditional, top-down development context, such reforms serve to channel administrative instructions and information more efficiently down to the grassroots and to mobilize people better in support of them. If such reforms do lead to an actual transfer of power from the centre, this usually benefits local élites rather than the excluded.

Even when governments genuinely intend to reinforce new democratically elected local bodies and to grant wider authority for local development issues to neighbourhood associations, contradictions are likely to persist. Central governments primarily want to hand over responsibilities and costs while keeping control over what is done locally. Local bodies will want and need subsidies from the state, while the state will be reluctant even to transfer control over local sources of tax revenue. Contradictions such as these are inevitable and persist even in the countries with firm traditions of pluralist democracy and well functioning systems of public administration, with continually shifting balances between centralization and local autonomy, subsidies and forced self-reliance, centrally enforced standards and local resistance to such standards.[26]

The 'project approach' and the technobureaucratic bias. In practice state-initiated participation usually boils down to what is called 'beneficiary participation' within development projects or activities. As we have seen, past experience of this kind of participation is not encouraging. There is unfortunately no reason to expect future initiatives of this kind to be more successful, as the contradictions, inherent in this approach, will continue to frustrate the hopes and expectations of committed bureaucrats and people alike. An effort to understand the motivations and constraints of the different actors better can possibly render these contradictions more manageable but cannot altogether eliminate them.

First, there are basic contradictions between the requirements of people's participation as defined in the UNRISD approach and the 'project approach to development' which continues to determine government action. Agents of the state and their advisers tend to see development as a series of precise and sequential, usually sectoral, outside interventions called 'projects', which are to function within clearly defined budgetary and time frameworks and are supposed to achieve well defined and thus quantitatively measurable physical and financial goals. The intended beneficiaries of such projects are not, as a rule, consulted about their perceptions and ideas of problems and priorities and about the kind of development action that should be initiated, nor do they participate in project planning or design which is considered the domain of technicians, bureaucrats and consultants. People's participation is often restricted to the execution phase of the projects and takes the form of 'voluntary' labour or contribution of resources.

Participation in terms of organized and collective efforts by the excluded in defence of livelihood obviously does not fit well into such a conceptual project approach. The emergence of functioning participatory organizations at the grassroots supposes rather a long-term process during which social relations are gradually modified: collective self-confidence is built up among the excluded that is stronger than their individual propensity to risk-aversion, alliances are explored and tested with other social groups, relations of trust emerge possibly with some agents of the state, common interests and objectives are defined, and terms of co-operation are negotiated between the excluded, the state and other social actors in the pursuit of common goals. This process, which usually requires much time, obviously cannot be replaced by a simplified organizational model to be imposed by decree at the beginning of a project or a government programme. The process may evolve in unforeseen directions and may not show quantifiable or measurable results or impacts in the short term. Just as democracy at the national level, participation thus introduces a fundamental principle of uncertainty which politicians, planners and national and international technobureaucracies find hard to accept. Along with the obvious power implications of participation, this uncertainty factor constitutes probably the major reason why agents of the state usually shy away from such participation.

Secondly, there is an inherent contradiction between the very nature and characteristic of a participatory process and the nature and functioning of public administrations and technobureaucracies. Administrative systems, on which governments necessarily rely to execute programmes, are hierarchical and bureaucratic, favour paperwork and written communication rather than oral debate – which often would be better suited to local traditions – and blur lines of accountability. As one long-standing observer and participant of African development efforts noted: 'The administration administers; it does not delegate, it does not negotiate, it does not consider groups of peasants or town-dwellers as partners. When it asks for their participation, its aim is the execution of predetermined tasks at the lowest possible cost, or else the alleviation of its own obligations'.[27] Government bureaucrats are not used to or willing to put up with pressures from below.

From the point of view of the individual bureaucrat, particularly at the field level, this behaviour is of course understandable and rational. He has usually no motivation or incentive to encourage participatory activities, even within government projects, as such activities are by definition time-consuming, introduce elements of uncertainty and are not likely to show positive results quickly. Moreover, if popular participation leads to strong grassroots movements, existing patron-client relations may be threatened. The prevalent bureaucratic reward mechanisms are such that local bureaucrats will not experiment with participatory activities and projects which are complex, risky and may be considered politically suspicious. Even if the government of the moment, or one of its agencies, is vigorously promoting participation, the local functionary has good reasons to suspect that enthusiastic identification with the policy will leave him or her vulnerable to reprisals once the policy or the régime itself changes. The local group has equally good reasons to withhold full support from a project on which it was not consulted and which the régime might abandon or modify at will.

Tensions between bureaucracy and participation are thus inevitable in any society. The state, in order to function with a minimum of efficiency and co-ordination, needs a body of civil servants to apply a set of rules, laws and regulations which by definition are not tailored to local needs but are made to assure uniform standards in the implementation of government policy. Interpretation of these rules depends on local bureaucrats for whom regulations tend to become ends in themselves and who are faced with the temptation of exercising discretionary power in a partial and sometimes corrupt way. Ordinary people who face bureaucracy often either have no choice but to resist the restrictions on their initiatives imposed by bureaucratic rules or are lost in a labyrinth of contradictory rules and regulations.

As was pointed out in one of the global sub-debates organized under the UNRISD Programme, the technocracy (or technobureaucracy) poses somewhat different problems for participation:

> While the traditional bureaucrat relies on norms and precedents to stifle participation in red tape, the technocrat may be highly innovative but also more manipulative or coercive. The main tension between technocracy and participation lies in the confidence of the technocrat that his professional tools qualify him to find the One Right Answer to development problems. Thus legitimate participation by other forces in the society must consist in learning the implications of the Answer and acting accordingly.[28]

The situation in the early 1990s is likely to exacerbate rather than reduce such inherent tensions between technobureaucracies and participation, but make at the same time the search for new arrangements more imperative. State bureaucracies face today unprecedented responsibilities for 'steering the boat' in a period of rapid change, of increasing scarcity of resources, and of conflictive democratization of societies while being deprived of their previous confidence in development theories and of their previous job security. Their interests and objectives, and those of organized movements of the excluded who attempt to use new legitimate political space to make their voices heard and respected, are obviously in conflict. Ideally the state should develop mechanisms of response to the grassroots which are transparent and non-clientelistic. Solutions to the present crisis ultimately require joint efforts at re-defining roles and responsibilities for development among different collective social actors, i.e. the excluded and their organizations, NGOs, traditional interest groups and the state's own agencies and agents.

In fact, such a new definition of tasks and of authority, in ways in which 'official and unofficial provisions can be flexibly combined so as to exploit the virtues and circumvent the vices of the various organizational forms available',[29] is already being actively sought at many levels, and new 'social pacts' have been negotiated in concrete situations. To what extent can states, NGOs and grassroots movements learn from such examples and build at all levels strong new institutions, representing a new consensus about governance and a basis for participatory and democratic forms of government?

International organizations and agencies:
the gap between rhetoric and reality

The official development discourse prevailing today in international organizations has taken up much of the progressive language that characterized the alternative development approach of the 1970s. Slogans such
as participation, democracy and self-reliance are prominent in official
statements and resolutions of all international organizations and agencies,
including the World Bank, and plans of action call for the involvement of
NGOs and grassroots organizations. Participation has never enjoyed as
much official legitimacy as today.

What should the 'organized efforts of the excluded' and their intellectual and political allies make of this rhetoric? To what extent is the
international development community willing and able to translate professed intentions about participation into reality? To what extent is this
likely to increase the opportunities and chances for the hitherto and newly
excluded to make their voices heard?

New advocacy and old ambiguities. International organizations, technical co-operation agencies, and above all international lending
institutions such as the World Bank, regional development banks or the
International Fund for Agricultural Development, at times exert a decisive
influence on national policy. Directly or indirectly they can legitimize and
approve some approaches and condemn others, and they provide aid and
assistance accordingly. Protests against the conditionality of aid as a new
form of imperialism may be justified but do not change reality. Present
economic conditions and trends, with many countries near bankruptcy and
private capital generally scarce – particularly in Africa – are likely further
to increase such dependency.

This is not to say that present processes of democratization have been
masterminded and controlled by international organizations; they are
rather the outcome of increasing economic and political contradictions and
of the emergence of new social forces within the countries concerned. But
the vigour of these processes and the legitimacy they enjoy obviously has
much to do with the ideological (and material) support that they receive
from the international development community.

The fact that participation, self-reliance and democracy today occupy
a privileged place in the official development discourse, that the importance of NGOs, and to a lesser extent of grassroots groups, as responsible
collective actors is generally recognized, and that the United Nations now
actively advocate 'human development', defined as an 'enlargement of
people's choices',[30] creates a new legitimacy for participatory action in
many countries. It contributes to the opening of unexpected political and
legal space for organized activities and participatory struggles. Whether,

and to what extent, 'it actually influences and in practice changes the development activities of international organizations and agencies is another issue that will be discussed below. First we will attempt to identify the reasons behind this renewed advocacy of participation.

In a very general sense the revival of participation reflects the dismal failure of past development efforts to solve basic problems of poverty and human survival and reflects new hopes that more participatory approaches may provide a way out of otherwise insoluble crises of human relationships and livelihood. The official development discourse calls for people's participation both as an instrument and as an objective, as a means and as an end goal. It is however less for ethical or moral reasons, but essentially for functional and practical ones, that the international development community attempts today to promote popular participation in development.

First, internal and commissioned studies, carried out since the early 1980s by some international organizations on the correlation between project success, sustainability, local institution building and 'beneficiary' or 'target group' participation, have lent increasing empirical evidence to earlier arguments by individual scholars and by institutions such as UNRISD that failure of past development projects, and of official development aid, was linked to the absence of participation. They have also argued that participatory projects, in spite of initial delays and confusion, ultimately often function more efficiently and effectively, lead to better local resource mobilization and capacity building, and may be more sustainable. The World Bank identifies 'inadequate participation' as one of five main reasons why aid projects have been ineffective. It concludes:

> Donors and recipients ... have not been sufficiently aware of the important role that the poor themselves can play in initiatives designed to assist them. Evidence supports the view that involving the poor in the design, implementation, and evaluation of projects in a range of sectors would make aid more effective ... . Participation of local community organizations has improved performance in many urban poverty projects; organizations of beneficiaries in aid-supported irrigation schemes have made important contributions to the maintenance and operation of project works; and involvement of organized groups of low-income borrowers has facilitated repayment of loans in small-scale credit programmes.[31]

Such functional arguments for increased popular participation are not new; the fact that international organizations and agencies have since the late 1980s chosen to pay more attention to them had to do with the increasing questioning in industrialized countries of the purpose and effectiveness of official development aid, and with publicized comparisons with aid channelled through the NGO sector which appeared more effective in its impact and more efficiently handled.[32]

Secondly, the neo-liberal arguments for a reduction in the activity and involvement of the state, and the objective deterioration of social and economic conditions in many areas as a consequence of crisis and adjustment policies, led to concrete calls for a downward transfer of former state responsibilities to the people themselves. Something had to be done to make adjustment socially, and thus politically, supportable, to give it a 'human face'. Since the states did not have the means to do it, the people had to be helped and encouraged to do it themselves. With its well-known advocacy for 'adjustment with a human face', UNICEF writes:

> Community participation is an essential ingredient of adjustment with a human face. On the one hand it can help generating the political support needed to overcome short-term political and bureaucratic opposition. On the other, it is essential for the planning, implementing, and success of the approaches devised, as well as for keeping the cost of the programmes down by means of community contributions.[33]

Such arguments were reinforced by the rising international concern about global environmental issues, manifest in the organization of the UN Conference on Environment and Development in June 1992, and by the greater attention given to the sustainability of development efforts and to the responsible management of the finite natural resource base.

Thirdly, the promotion of a more participatory and democratic society fits well into a new international strategy advocated by the World Bank, known as the 'governance approach', which intends to counter the rising ungovernability of many countries and create conditions favourable to the development of a flourishing free-market economy. The Bank's interest in governance, like its interest in participation, arises from its concern with the effectiveness of the development efforts it supports. What is sought is 'good governance' seen as requisite to sound economic policies. Main components of 'good governance' are the accountability of public officials, the presence of a legal framework that makes rules and regulations predictable, the availability of information and the transparency of decision-making processes. People's participation and the strengthening of the 'citizen's sector' were initially spelled out as further components of good governance, but in later bank documents popular participation has been subsumed under the call for public accountability of officials and transparency of decision-making processes.[34]

In view of the condemnation by a good many progressive development analysts of the human consequences of adjustment policies associated with the World Bank, it is ironical that in contrast with the superficial, half-hearted and often hypocritical nature of most other organizations' efforts in this field, the World Bank seems to have embarked on a relatively systematic effort to come to grips with an interpretation of popular participation and to realize it in its field projects. Since 1988 the Bank has started to involve NGOs more systematically in its operations,[35] and in mid-1991 a three-year internal learning programme on participation was initiated. The aims of the programme are to monitor participatory components of Bank projects, to draw lessons from a current study of twenty selected Bank projects that involve popular participation, to sensitize operational staff to aspects of participation and to identify how the Bank's operational policies may have to be modified in order to encourage popular participation more widely in its projects.

Such generally growing consensus among international organizations about the need for more participation owes much to continued ambiguities in definition. Many interpretations current today have little to do with the way in which UNRISD defined participation and are probably of limited relevance to the 'organized efforts of the excluded'. Lack of conceptual clarity about the meaning of participation manifests itself in the imprecise use of seemingly interchangeable words such as 'participation', 'mobilization', 'animation', 'self-reliant development', 'dialogue', etc. It is difficult to avoid the impression that vagueness and ambiguity in the use of such terms are not accidental, and that conceptual confusion serves a purpose: it allows international organizations and their agents to limit themselves when convenient to general proclamations and advocacy of participation without having to spell out the practical implications, the political aspects, and thus the power consequences of participation.

This evasion of political and fundamental paradigmatic questions by international organizations appears not only in the imprecise usage of the term 'participation' but more generally of the term 'development'. Even today development is often regarded and treated as a technical engineering exercise and little attention is paid to historical, cultural, social and political realities. Lack of historical consciousness applies not only to the object of action, the field, where 'development' takes place, but to the subject, i.e. the international organizations themselves. Most international bureaucracies appear to have a very short 'historical memory' and seem pathetically unaware of the numerous times that, over the last half century, they have re-invented similar hopes and rhetoric.

There are a few exceptions, however, and some recent attempts by international organizations to suggest new directions for development policy have openly confronted the political and power implications of participation. In particular, the Economic Commission for Latin America and the Caribbean, dealing with a region in which organized efforts have long been vigorous and varied, states in its most recent report to member governments:

Since the type of economic and social policy which encourages the simultaneous development of competitiveness and social equity is aimed at fostering greater popular participation in institutional reform, resource management, access to services and programme execution, a political complement is needed, namely the representation of the demands of these sectors in political party discourse, in public debate and in taking the decisions which affect policy design and the allocation of government spending.

The same report emphasizes the potential of new telecommunications and information technologies (telematics) to make the organized efforts of the excluded more effective, and gives some examples in which this is already happening:

> These isolated examples illustrate the synergetic potential of the dissemination of telematics in providing linkages between social agents, so as to increase their representation and ability to exert pressure on government decision-making bodies. This synergetic potential is self-evident in view of the wide range of opportunities which are opening up: access to information (on services, rights and common demands), influence on public opinion (through radio broadcasts, access to computerized networks or publicizing documentary tapes), aggregation of demand (through the use of databanks and greater 'telematic connectedness'); and transcending the barriers of censorship (using horizontal networks for circulating information).[36]

The new accent on democratization and governance has introduced eminently political issues into the development debate. In principle, the international development community now recognizes the importance of setting development aid and technical co-operation within a workable political strategy. In practice, however, political factors continue to be acknowledged or ignored as seems convenient. When the objectives are to enforce democratic reforms or the liberalization of a country's economy, the interventions of international organizations are primarily political. Such action is then justified in terms of general, universally recognized objectives such as the guarantee of fundamental freedoms and the protection of human rights, or in terms of economic efficiency. The ambiguities and potential contradictions appear clearly in a recent statement by the present UN Secretary General who, after pleading for the duty of the United Nations vigorously to promote democracy and development, declared that 'United Nations activities to promote democracy must not become a means of intervention in the internal affairs of member States'.[37] The same ambiguity was expressed more crudely by the former President of the World Bank in a memorandum to Bank managers in which, after justifying the new governance approach and the need for the Bank to broaden the focus of its intervention from actual operations to the wider national context, he continues:

There remains some apprehension among our borrowing members that our staff might exceed the Bank's mandate in ways which could be interpreted as interfering in the political affairs of our borrowers. This concern, given the difficulty of drawing neat lines in this area, is understandable. I am confident that you will respect the sensitivities and concerns of borrowers while not shying away from issues relevant to development performance when these need to be raised.[38]

When it comes to practical operations and technical co-operation programmes in the field, however, the same organizations, and their consultants and agents in the field, generally choose to ignore political factors and realities and concentrate exclusively on economic and technical factors, assuming that good sense of governments and measured pressure of international financial institutions will ultimately lead countries in the desired direction. This avoidance of political factors is often responsible for over-ambitious and politically naive development plans and for an almost total absence of tactical and strategic analysis and planning when it comes to translate such plans into practice. We will discuss the practical implications of this political evasiveness below when examining the many difficulties that international organizations meet when attempting to introduce popular participation into their programmes and projects.

Similar contradictions between theory and practice and between different levels of intervention also prevail in the definition of development itself. While at a theoretical level development is now generally seen as a long-term historical process, in practice the activities of international organizations continue to be planned and executed within a traditional and a-historical 'project approach'. In its extreme form, the a-historical project approach continues the tradition of 'pilot projects' that postpone the problem of resources for large-scale replication, limit themselves to technical and service areas that do not lead to power confrontations, and give only perfunctory attention to the lessons of experience.

People's participation in practice: the gap between rhetoric and reality. It is in their practical interventions in the field that the international organizations' and agencies' professed commitment to participation must be examined and the real impact of this new rhetoric on 'organized efforts of the excluded' be judged.

Studies conducted recently in various international organizations, both at headquarters and in the field, show that instances of real participation as defined in this book continue to be rare exceptions. When it comes to the practical implementation of development policy, international organizations invariably tend to put aside the 'empowerment' rhetoric and revert to traditional 'beneficiary' or 'target group participation'. Even such limited forms of participation may provide a space for the excluded to defend their broader interests, particularly in today's climate of democratization, but it is hard to find evidence that this is really happening.

In fact, evidence from the field suggests that little has changed at that level: international organizations continue to have few direct contacts with the actual grassroots communities – the rural and urban poor who are supposed to benefit from their intervention – or with their organizations, or even with local NGOs. Their main partners remain government agencies at central, and possibly down to district levels, other international agencies, international NGOs, and consultants and technicians. Future beneficiaries of projects – the 'target group' – are as a rule still not consulted about the need for the project, they do not participate in project design and preparation, and their participation in implementation usually takes the form of 'free and voluntary' contribution of resources and labour.

The gap between rhetoric and reality is particularly pathetic in those organizations and agencies that like to maintain a progressive image: while the organizations' top management and their governing bodies call for extensive beneficiary participation in all projects, and while their policy departments translate and legitimize these calls within a flamboyant rhetoric, the agencies' staff at headquarters and in the field are confused or ambivalent, do not know how to translate participation into reality within concrete projects against often overwhelming practical and political obstacles, and finally put it aside as one of these new 'soft' elements that complicate development projects, introduce factors of risk and unpredictability and create difficulties in implementation. What remains is in most cases a traditional top-down and non-participatory approach which focuses on the achievement of physical and financial project targets, sanctified in appropriate statistics, albeit within a new rhetoric. Within this new rhetoric statements about 'reaching the grassroots' or 'social mobilization' do not therefore refer to participatory projects, but simply to the downward channelling of information and instructions, a top-to-bottom process of communication with usually no feedback from the 'target groups'.

The few projects in which people's participation has been successfully introduced and pursued are almost without exceptions 'accidents' which *a posteriori* become the organizations' widely publicized success stories. They are normally due to the special efforts of one or a few committed individuals in the organization or the 'target group', and are not the result of any planned guidance by the organization. They are often short-lived, because of their dependence on individuals who are likely at some point to be transferred or promoted, and because of their very rise to prominence and fame which brings unexpected attention and funds.

The conceptual confusion over the meaning of participation and the political ambiguities regarding its practical implications and its implementation that have been discussed above are in part responsible for this continued inability of international organizations to translate professed intentions into reality. A range of other reasons for this failure can be identified. Some of them stem from the external environment in which the organizations attempt to intervene, others are internal to the organizations themselves and represent 'in-built dysfunctionalities'.

External constraints to the implementation of participation in and through development projects have mainly to do with the real or imagined political power implications of such participation. Opposition to participation arises naturally from local and national élites and powerholders, particularly in societies where power and wealth are concentrated in the hands of a few. If beneficiary participation will increase the self-confidence and social clout of the poor and loosen clientelistic relations of dependency, then the local élite will quite naturally oppose it, unless it is perceived as a lesser evil to insurgency or revolution. If in the course of a project participatory groups of beneficiaries are nevertheless set up to receive and distribute some of the material benefits of the project, then local élites will attempt to co-opt and control these groups and potential project benefits.

In many cases the state itself, or the single party, will *de facto* oppose any form of popular organization that may emerge outside its control, even though they may publicly endorse policies of popular self-reliance. Several examples of this have been discussed in Chapter 6. Their attempt to monopolize all forms of collective action leaves little space for autonomous, creative and participatory expressions of popular aspirations and interests.

A fundamental constraint faced by international organizations stems from their obligation or compulsion to work only with and through governments. Development programmes and projects are almost exclusively worked out with governmental counterparts and executed through governmental structures and mechanisms. The implementation of such programmes and projects thus depends on the quality and the dominant value systems of public administration and of government staff. In most countries, as was emphasized above, government structures are centralized and oriented towards control, however little control they may be able to exercise in practice. At the lowest level – district and sub-district – where government functionaries should be closest to the people and most open to participation, they are usually poorly trained, poorly paid and poorly motivated. Their attitude to the poor is often contemptuous, authoritarian and at best paternalistic. On the whole they view participation of the excluded as a threat or at best a nuisance from which they have everything to lose and nothing to gain. It is through this lower-level government bureaucracy, however, that a large majority of internationally financed development projects are ultimately implemented in the field.

Technical personnel who have been brought to the field for the project are usually not much better disposed towards participatory initiatives. They are usually hired by the government and owe allegiance to it, not to the target group or even to the project. They are thus not likely to promote beneficiary participation if this creates conflict and endangers the smooth running of the project. Technical experts, consultants and assistance staff believe quite naturally in their superiority over the local people. They are there to give technical expertise which the target group has to follow. In fewer cases, some of which were described in Part II, part of the technical staff may be trying to advance its own ideas of popular empowerment, at odds with the central authorities as well as local power structures, but over-prone to impose its own ideological framework on the local group. Episodes of this kind can be dangerous to the technicians themselves as well as the excluded, by triggering abrupt repressive responses from power holders.

In projects where on the insistence of international organizations NGOs have been brought in to promote or facilitate the implementation of a participatory approach, such an approach is often endangered by the open or latent conflict between the responsible government services and their staff and the NGOs that have been asked to help with group formation and other 'soft' aspects of the project. The problem is often more psychological than political, with each side feeling the need to justify its role and assert its authority. The tensions created are however real enough to bring otherwise promising projects to a total standstill. At the origins of such conflicts is often the neglect to decide precisely and in advance the division of work and responsibilities between government, NGOs, the international agencies and their staff, and future beneficiaries' groups, or the inability to reach agreement on this issue.

It is precisely because international organizations and their field staff are aware of such political problems and constraints, or have experienced them in earlier projects, that they tend to avoid political issues and concentrate on technical and economic aspects of development. They are thus inhibited from defining clear strategic and tactical plans of operation. The unwillingness to face or even acknowledge political realities sometimes takes grotesque forms. In one case an international organization had been preparing for several years an ambitious integrated rural development project that was to involve local NGOs and to promote beneficiary participation at various levels. During all this time the organization's staff and its consultants chose to ignore the fact that a large part of the project area was controlled by insurgency groups, a fact that the government did not want officially to acknowledge. The organization also preferred to ignore the fact that some of the NGOs pre-selected for collaboration had in fact been set up by government officials or members of their families, because of government reluctance to get 'real' NGOs involved and for the purpose of receiving international funding through this future project. In another case, an international organization made ambitious plans for extending a community participation approach to health care and nutrition from a pilot area to the country as a whole but chose to ignore the presence of a single party which tried to maintain a strict monopoly over collective actions and popular organizations, on whose stand towards such a project its chances for success obviously depended.

The above is symptomatic of a general inability, or rather unwillingness, of international organizations to perceive and understand local reality in its full complexity. Their understanding of government, of the bureaucracy, of NGOs and of the people is generally limited and simplistic; they fail to understand the different survival strategies that determine different actors' behaviour, and their assumptions about how these actors will behave are thus necessarily faulty.

International development assistance is usually based on the implicit assumption that governments, the bureaucracy, private economic actors and the people basically lack accurate information, technical knowledge, insight and resources and that this explains why they do not take what international experts consider to be the right decisions. That they lack resources is usually true, but the rest of the assumption shows a considerable degree of political naivety. Governments rarely have much choice, particularly if they are in a situation where governing boils down to short-term crisis management. They are beset with an array of conflicting demands and requests, from political and social forces inside and outside the country, which far exceed their capacity to respond. The decisions that are taken represent more the need to strike a balance between these forces than an attempt to implement a coherent long-term strategy, and are of course crucially influenced by the decision-makers' own personal interests and survival strategies.

In the same way the intended beneficiaries of development projects, the rural and urban poor, have to follow carefully calculated survival strategies which follow a logic of risk minimization rather than output or profit optimalization – a logic difficult to understand for UN staff and technical experts. Any development project, and particularly one that proposes to introduce or support collective participatory action of the poor, will be scrutinized against these survival strategies in order to see whether potential benefits are worth taking the risks.

Finally, let us consider some of the internal factors, 'in-built dysfunctionalities' as we have called them, that make it difficult for international organizations to promote participatory projects.

(1) The lack of conceptual clarity about the meaning and implications of participation leads many staff members to consider participation as just another project, or another aspect to be attached to projects or programmes. The new focus on participation has usually been decided by top management or governing bodies and imposed on the staff without clear guidance

as to what it means in practice. Confused about its meaning, and failing to understand clearly the reasons that have prompted the organization to promote it, cynical also about the regular coming and going of new fads, the staff is likely to pay lip service to it, add a participatory component to project documents to get them approved, but disown the component once it starts creating difficulties in the field.

(2) International organizations and their staff lack the time and the patience necessary to promote participatory projects. For political purposes and in order to remain credible and worthy of continued financial support, international organizations set ambitious global and national goals that have to be achieved in relatively short periods of time. Results have to be visible and if possible expressed in statistics and percentage figures. The promotion of participatory development projects and processes takes time, however, and the evolution of such processes is often unpredictable and results are not necessarily visible or spectacular as they may to start with be limited to changes in social relationships and only later find concrete expression in collective action.

(3) The way in which projects are identified, designed and prepared, and later implemented and evaluated – the nature of the 'project cycle' as such – is not conducive to the introduction of popular participation, even in the limited sense of 'beneficiary participation'. Projects are typically identified and designed by international staff and consultants after one or several missions to the field during which they have usually no time or possibility actually to reach the 'target group' or even to identify it precisely. The supposed future beneficiaries of the project are normally not organized in identifiable groups that would correspond to the 'target' as defined in the project. International staff is usually accompanied by official government staff, and this makes direct contacts with the poor, when they do take place, difficult and artificial. It is hardly possible to establish relations of confidence in order to elicit the people's comments and opinions and to understand their perception of problems and possible solutions.

A substitute for direct contact with the target group, sometimes sought by consultants or international staff who are conscious of the superficiality of their knowledge of local realities and people's perception, may be to collaborate with local NGOs that have long-standing experience in working with the people concerned. But even the identification of such NGOs usually proves difficult for international missions and is not encouraged by government staff who, at best, may propose some large and 'reliable' NGO that is known to the government.

Not much attention is paid during project identification and preparation to analysis of the local socio-political and cultural reality, to identification of the different relevant social actors and forces and their respective survival strategies, in comparison with attention to administrative, financial, organizational and purely economic and technical issues. Lack of information and understanding of local realities leads to the artificial definition of target groups along primarily technical or geographical lines whose members may not share a common perception of collective problems and possible solutions. A major World Bank study of the organization's experience with rural development projects identifies 'inappropriate project design resulting from a lack of information on beneficiary populations' as the most frequent reason for small farmers' lack of interest and participation in projects, or outright rejection of them.[39]

While preparation and design of projects is thus often superficial and too hasty, actual implementation in the field is often too slow to start. Years can elapse between the first missions and actual implementation, and in cases where future project beneficiaries and local authorities have been involved to some extent in project design, or have simply been informed about the future projects, they are then left waiting, gradually losing any interest or enthusiasm that they may initially have shown.

(4) The inevitable contradictions between bureaucracy, technocracy and participation, discussed earlier, are also manifest here, in the implementation phase of supposedly participatory projects of international organizations. The bureaucratic bias is fundamentally a problem of insecurity, the technocratic bias one of arrogance and lack of humility. The extent to which both can influence and possibly kill any participatory initiative depends above all on the professional and human qualities of the local and international staff and their conditions of work. Most agency staff, however, have neither the necessary field and political experience nor the necessary sensitivity or appropriate professional training to be able to analyse and cope with the complex political, social and cultural processes triggered by participation. The same is true of consultants and experts who, as one experienced consultant comments, are 'irrelevant to the needs of the poor people who simply want to gain a little more control over their lives without at the same time increasing their risks'.[40]

The whole bureaucratic organization of development aid and the prevalent internal recruitment and reward mechanisms produce a fascination with bureaucratic processes rather than results achieved. What actually happens in the field becomes in extreme cases irrelevant. The official rhetoric helps to confuse reality and wishful thinking and leads, in extreme cases, to a perverse and narcissistic attitude of self-congratulation on imaginary achievements.

International financial lending institutions such as the World Bank, the International Fund for Agricultural Development or Regional Development Banks, face additional constraints that operate against participatory field projects. Their function is to lend money – the more the better as their power and influence increases with the size of their portfolio. There is thus an in-built pressure to increase the size of loans and to process them rapidly. Participatory development, however, cannot take place on an enormous scale. It is most likely to be successful in small, qualitatively good projects where relatively modest sums of outside assistance supplement locally generated resources. International lending institutions sometimes kill good participatory local initiatives when, after 'discovering' such initiatives that correspond to their own rhetoric, they turn them into 'pet projects' and flood them with excessive sums of money. Big money kills participatory initiatives, corrupts and perverts popular leaders, government staff and NGOs, and attracts to the projects people whose minds are not set on alleviating the conditions of the poor. The excessively large sums of money allocated by such institutions to supposedly participatory projects cannot possibly be spent within participatory approaches. By necessity the main thrust of the project will thus move elsewhere – where the money can be spent – and participatory activities and mechanisms will be relegated to a marginal role.

The meeting of idealism and efficiency: a chance for participation? In spite of the formidable alliance of anti-participatory forces, factors and biases exposed above, a handful of truly participatory projects and processes have been successfully initiated, promoted and supported by the staffs of some international organizations and agencies. This is the work of a few individuals and groups, committed advocates of participatory development approaches, that are to be found scattered throughout the international system. Most of them have earlier been supporters of the 'alternative development' approaches and have progressed from these within their respective institutions and agencies, profiting from temporary spaces that legitimized participatory initiatives, functioning at different levels and supporting each other as far as possible through an informal network of solidarity, friendship and communication. Such actions have always been marginal to their organizations' activities and temporary, disappearing when political or bureaucratic spaces closed and sometimes reappearing later within another department or organization. They have never had a significant quantitative impact, but as 'pockets' of progressive thought and action they have often played an important catalytic role within the international development community. UNRISD has at times played such a role, as have various programmes and offices in, for example, the ILO, UNICEF, IFAD or even FAO. They have at times been able to contribute to the redefinition of official development goals and approaches, particularly in periods of crisis when new paradigms and approaches were sought, and their language, concepts, approach and even projects have occasionally been co-opted by their organizations. They understandably tend to glorify and mystify successful participatory projects or experiences, which are then widely publicized, and they tend to overestimate the real long-term impact that their projects can have in the field. Their weakness and strength lies in their sometimes excessive and possibly naive idealism and in their conviction that ultimately their small actions throughout the system will add up to produce a cumulative effect.

In the present context their messages and experiences are likely to be taken more seriously as international organizations increasingly grapple with problems of popular participation, trying to increase the effectiveness of development aid and promote good governance. There is reason to hope that they may be able to give some substance to the present rhetoric about participation and democracy, that their experience may help part of the international bureaucracy to avoid some of the contradictions and pitfalls of participatory projects, that they may convince their colleagues in international organizations to adopt a more flexible and fostering attitude towards participatory initiatives and organized efforts of the excluded, and that they may be able to keep their distinctive participatory approach from being co-opted and domesticated by the system.

Notes

1. Clark, John, *Democratizing Development*, Earthscan Publications, London, 1991, p. 19.

2. Rau, Bill, *From Feast to Famine*, Zed Books, London, 1991.

3. Hong, Kwan Kai, ed., *Jeux et Enjeux de l'Auto-Promotion*, Presse Universitaire de France, Paris, 1991.

4. Lehmann, David, *Democracy and Development in Latin America*, Polity Press, Cambridge, 1990.

5. For a further discussion of *basismo* and its relations to the state and other social actors and forces in Latin America, see Lehmann, David, op. cit. in n. 4.

6. For a discussion of this and other similar grassroots organizations, see Rahman, Anisur, *Glimpses of the Other Africa*, WEP Working Paper, ILO, Geneva, 1988, and Ghai, Dharam, *Participatory Development: Some Perspectives from Grassroots Experiences*, UNRISD Discussion Paper No. 5, Geneva, 1988.

7. Bangura, Yusuf, Gibbon, Peter and Ofstad, Arve, eds., *Authoritarianism, Democracy and Adjustment*, UNRISD, Scandinavian Institute of African Studies and Christian Michelsen Institute, Uppsala, 1992.

8. For a collection of such studies see Ghai, Dharam and Vivian, Jessica M., eds., *Grassroots Environmental Action: People's Participation in Sustainable Development*, Routledge, London, 1992.

9. Hong, Kwan Kai, op. cit. in n. 3.

10. Friedmann, John and Haripriya, Rangan, eds., *In Defense of Livelihood: Comparative Studies in Environmental Action*, Kumarian Press, West Hartford, Connecticut, 1993.

11. Annis, Sheldon and Hakim, Peter, eds., *Direct to the Poor: Grassroots Development in Latin America*, Lynn Rienner, Boulder, Colorado, 1988, pp. 217-18. See also Hirschman, Albert O., *Getting Ahead Collectively: Grassroots Experiences in Latin America*, Pergamon Press, New York, 1984; and Carroll, Thomas, *Intermediary NGOs: The Supporting Link in Grassroots Development*, Kumarian Press, West Hartford, Connecticut, 1992. A Rural Development

Committee at Cornell University has also studied local initiatives and their relations with state institutions with critical sympathy. See Esman, Milton J. and Uphoff, Norman T., *Local Organizations and Rural Development: The State of the Art*, Cornell University Press, Ithaca, New York, 1982.

12. Lehmann, David, op. cit. in n. 4, p. 207.

13. Clark, John, op. cit. in n. 1.

14. There is by now a vast and still expanding literature on NGOs and their role in development. Among this we may suggest for further reading on these definitional issues the special supplement to *World Development* (vol. 15, 1987) that contains among others articles by Korten, David C., on 'The Third Generation NGO Strategies: a Key to People Centred Development', and by Gordon Drabek, Anne, on 'Development Alternatives: the Challenge for NGOs – an Overview of the Issues'. See also Clark, John, op. cit. in n. 1; Padron, Mario, *Development Cooperation and the Popular Movement: the Non-Governmental Development Organizations*, Westview Press, Boulder, Colorado, 1988; Lehmann, David, op. cit. in n. 4; and Bratton, Michael, 'The Politics of Government-NGO Relations in Africa', *World Development*, vol. 17, no. 4, 1989.

15. Bratton, Michael, op. cit. in n. 14.

16. See Part II of this volume; also Oakely, Peter et al., *Projects with People: The Practice of Participation in Rural Development*, ILO, Geneva, 1991.

17. White, Sarah C., *Evaluating the Impact of NGOs in Rural Poverty Alleviation, Bangladesh Country Study*, ODI, London, 1991. The Overseas Development Institute (ODI) has initiated a research project which aims to assess the impact of NGOs in poverty-alleviating projects in different geographical and institutional settings. Four country studies have so far been published, namely on Bangladesh, India, Uganda and Zimbabwe. *Samiti* is a Hindi term used to designate an organization or association, particularly one formed to achieve political objectives. In this context it refers more generally to collective action by the poor.

18. See for a discussion of these ambivalent NGO-state relations Bratton, Michael, op. cit. in n. 14, and also Bratton, Michael, *Enabling the Voluntary Sector in Africa: the Policy Context*, mimeo, 1991.

19. Society for Participatory Research in Asia, 'The Seduction of NGOs?', Newsletter, no. 37, January 1992.

20. Bratton, Michael, op. cit. in n. 14.

21. UNICEF was among the first organizations to draw attention to the negative social and economic impact of earlier adjustment policies and to call for such a new approach. See Cornia, G.A., Jolly, R. and Stewart, F., eds., *Adjustment with a Human Face*, 2 vols., Clarendon Press, Oxford, 1987 and 1988.

22. The concept of 'enabling environment' has been advocated by international organizations since the late 1980s, particularly in the African context. In 1989, the UN Economic Commission for Africa (ECA) wrote in its *Alternative Framework to Structural Adjustment Programme for Socio-Economic Recovery and Transformation* (ECA, Addis Ababa, 1989): 'The key role of the government ... will embrace the creation of an enabling environment and institution building and vigorous support for grassroots initiatives. On the other hand, democratization and popular participation will encourage the people to increase their development effort and to accept whatever sacrifices that may be implied by the programme, thereby consolidating and deepening the process for national self-reliance.' In

1990 the ECA organized a major international conference, regrouping all African states, in Arusha, Tanzania. The conference adopted an African Charter for Popular Participation in Development (E/ECA/CM.16/11) which contains probably the most comprehensive official call for widespread popular participation at all levels. For a discussion of the specific role of the state to be played in this context, see the paper prepared for this conference by Stiefel, Matthias and Racelis, Mary, *The Role and Responsibilities of Government and Development and Donor Agencies*, 1990.

23. Governments and international organizations consistently confuse 'participation' and 'mobilization' and use these terms, often consciously, in an imprecise and interchangeable way. For proponents of participatory development, and for scholars and analysts, it is important to distinguish clearly between the two terms on conceptual, policy and strategic levels and to be aware of the type of social relations that each one implies. Mobilization comes from Latin *mobilis*, something that is mobile, can be moved. Mobilization is the act of making something mobile; it presupposes an actor, a subject, that makes one or many objects mobile. The objects can be natural resources, or in this case people that are to be assembled, organized, made to perform certain functions – thus the use of mobilization in military terminology. Both participation and mobilization denote specific forms of social organization. Neither exists or is conceivable in an absolute form; they exist to various degrees and come in various shades, evolving over time as the quality and nature of relations between different social groups and the state and its agents evolve dynamically. Genuine popular participation can turn into mobilization when new monopolies of power and bureaucratic control emerge within popular movements or organizations, or when these are co-opted by the state. And mobilization may turn into participation, though more rarely, when people become conscious of their collective strength, when their perception of their own powerlessness against the state, its agents and the 'big' people decreases as a result of a first successful collective action, or when they enter into alliances with new interlocutors and social forces that lead to a temporary change in the balance of power. The dividing line between participation and mobilization is thus often very fine and is constantly moving in concrete situations.

24. For a further discussion of the inter-play between state and grassroots action in this field, see Ghai, Dharam and Vivian, Jessica M., op. cit. in n. 8; and Stiefel, Matthias, *Sustainable Development and People's Participation: Some Reflections*, paper prepared for the United Nations Conference on Environment and Development (UNCED), Geneva, 1991.

25. See Korten, Frances F. and Siy, Robert Y. Jr., *Transforming a Bureaucracy: The Experience of the Philippine National Irrigation Administration*, Kumarian Press, West Hartford, Connecticut, 1989. One observation that deserves particular attention in the present context is the following: 'The introduction of a new data source ... is seldom sufficient in itself to improve decision-making in a development organization. There must also be a capacity and an incentive to use the data. It is the sad reality that most development agencies have neither the capacity to use nor an interest in using field data – even if they have it. Such data may actually complicate the design and construction process because – just as with farmer participation – the data challenge the viability of standardized solutions and highlight the need for actions that may delay project completion and require changes in the budget. Responding to such data may result in reprimands from superiors who are not evaluated in terms of the performance of the resulting irrigation system, but rather in terms of budget expenditures, schedules and facilities constructed' (p. 131).

26. Wolfe, Marshall, 'Social Structures and Democracy in the 1990s', *CEPAL Review*, no. 40, April 1990.

27. Bugnicourt, Jacques, *Popular Participation in Development in Africa*, paper presented at the International Seminar on Popular Participation, organized by the United Nations Department of Technical Co-operation for Development in Ljubljana, 1981.

28. Wolfe, Marshall, *Participation: The View from Above*, UNRISD, Geneva, 1983.

29. David Lehmann, op. cit. in n. 40.

30. See UNDP's *Human Development Report* for 1990 and 1991, Oxford University Press, New York and Oxford, 1990 and 1991. The very existence of these reports, which should now appear annually, in some sense as a pendant to the World Bank's annual *World Development Report*, is symptomatic of a conceptual change in the dominant United Nations development thinking.

31. World Bank, *World Development Report 1990*, Oxford University Press, New York, 1990, p. 133.

32. See for example Hancock, Graham, *Lords of Poverty*, Macmillan, London, 1989.

33. Cornia, G.A., Jolly, R. and Stewart, F., eds., op. cit. in n. 21, p. 295.

34. See for example such World Bank documents as: Landell-Mills, Pierre and Serageldin, Ismail, *Governance and the External Factor*, World Bank Annual Conference on Development Economics 1991, Washington, D.C.; or *Managing Development: The Governance Dimension, A Discussion Paper*, World Bank, Washington D.C., 29 August 1991. For a further discussion and critique of the governance approach see also Stiefel, Matthias, *Democratization, Participation and the Search for a New Polity, A Discussion Paper*, ILO, Geneva, November 1991. The author here opposes 'governance' to 'polity', arguing that governance carries the values of a basically top-down approach to social organization and development.

35. See *Involving Nongovernmental Organizations in Bank-Supported Activities*, World Bank, Operational Directive 14.70., August 1989. The mere fact that international organizations and donor agencies channel more and more funds through NGOs does not necessarily indicate a change towards a more participatory development approach. In most cases it simply shows that the former consider NGOs to be a more efficient delivery mechanism for the implementation of their projects.

36. United Nations Economic Commission for Latin America and the Caribbean, *Social Equity and Changing Production Patterns: An Integrated Approach*, Santiago, 1992. The material on telematics is adapted from Ames, Sheldon, 'Giving Voice to the Poor', *Foreign Policy*, 84, 1991.

37. Statement by Boutros Boutros-Ghali, delivered before the United Nations General Assembly on his appointment as the new Secretary-General of the United Nations, January 1992.

38. *Managing Development: the Governance Dimension. A Discussion Paper*, World Bank, Washington, D.C., 29 August 1991.

39. *Rural Development: World Bank Experience 1965-86*, World Bank, Washington, D.C., 1988, p. 57.

40. Cross, D.W., quoted in Hancock, Graham, *Lords of Poverty*, Macmillan, London, 1989, p. 123.

11

What Next?

The subtitle of this book posed a question: 'Popular participation in development: utopia or necessity?' What, if anything, have the preceding pages contributed to an answer to this question? Unfortunately, our exploration suggests that there are as many answers as there are collective social actors and that the different interpretations of 'development' and 'participation' internalized by these actors perpetuate a dialogue of the deaf.

First, from the standpoint of the global establishment of political and economic leaders and theorists, popular participation as we have understood it is certainly an alien utopia in relation to the market-oriented style of development they have created or stumbled into. As sorcerer's apprentices, these actors are dazzled by the interacting economic, political and cultural transformations that are taking place and alarmed at the prospect that these processes may be losing their dynamism or running into impasses. They discuss continually, at summit meetings and elsewhere, prescriptions for more vigorous and harmonious growth. A good many of them are convinced that popular participation, in the sense of organized efforts by the excluded to achieve control over resources and institutions, is a dangerous utopia, a manifestation of discredited populism or socialism, that could cripple the ability of the style of development to realize its full potential and frustrate their own efforts to guide it. Others believe that political participation, in the sense of pluralist democracy and electoral competition, is a necessary though problematic complement to the market, a means of educating the people in the requisites of development and making them feel responsible for the decisions that have to be made as to how gains and sacrifices are to be distributed. Still others see participation, in the sense of local empowerment and decentralization, as a necessity in practical, anti-utopian terms, a means of helping governments function more smoothly by delegating responsibilities. Thus organized efforts by the excluded, with aid and guidance from state agencies and voluntary organizations, can alleviate poverty, introduce more productive means of livelihood, and through local control maintain services that the state can no longer afford or that it performs inefficiently.

Secondly, from the standpoint of the intellectual critics of the global market-oriented style of development – the advocates of 'another development', 'human development', or 'sustainable development' – participation continues to represent both an achievable utopia and a necessity in terms of their values and images of the Good Society. At present, however, many of thém are baffled by the discredit of the great prescriptions for socialism or for comprehensively and humanely state-planned development that in the past seemed capable of generating and incorporating participation. They are trying to make sense of the present reality of pluralist democracy, as a field for participation paradoxically legitimized and contradicted by the dominant style of development, implying permanent uncertainty and competition of ideas and interests, possibly enhancing human welfare and creativity over the long term, but fundamentally anti-utopian, alien to the ideal of a classless, egalitarian and permanently harmonious social order. Some of these intellectual actors are seeking to rehabilitate the democratic state as necessary protagonist in the permanent struggle to cope with the inequities and disbenefits of development. Others have turned to conceptions of participation that have little to do with 'development' under whatever definition: to a vision of 'new social movements' evolving spontaneously toward a future order for which it would be absurd to draw up blueprints. Still others look to utopias of strictly local participation in autonomous communities with simplified production and consumption patterns, and to a withering away of the state along with other large bureaucratized political and economic institutions.

Thirdly, the 'excluded' with which this book has been primarily concerned, through the style of development in some countries and the style of disintegration in others, have experienced continual shocks to previous expectations, imperatives to adapt or perish and, for a good many, challenges to take advantage of promising new opportunities. They have hardly had time to think of themselves as participating or not participating in an abstraction labelled 'development'. The numbers prepared to think in these terms are probably smaller today than 20 or 30 years ago, when the myths of planning development, national liberation or social revolution still retained mobilizing power. Their previous adversaries – capitalists, landlords, dictators – have become obscured by continually shifting impersonal processes. The main categories of the excluded are themselves changing in ways that blur their class identities and call for rethinking of their potential roles.

There are the hundreds of millions of peasants, still trying to follow risk-minimizing tactics of self-provisioning cultivation and accommodation-avoidance-struggle in their relations with village tyrants, landlords, moneylenders, commercial intermediaries and functionaries of the state. Many of them have been in contact with would-be allies who have introduced them to participatory ideals and techniques, sometimes successfully. Peasant unions and community self-help organizations continue to emerge and achieve some gains for their members. Both more traditional and recent peasant tactics confront continual threats to their viability. Shifts in markets and many other factors make gains permanently precarious. More and more peasants migrate in search of wage work or decline into landlessness and dependence on miserably paid casual labour. More and more peasants become exposed to competitive terrorization from military forces, guerrillas, drug traffickers and fellow peasants who speak a different language or practise a different religion, sometimes leading to depopulation of the countryside and accelerated flight to the cities. Recent democratization processes here and there have brought relief from such insecurity and have given some peasants a better chance to influence through their votes national policies bearing on their livelihood, but for the most part organized efforts by peasants represent self-defence against development more than participation in development.

There are the hundreds of millions of people in transition between rural and urban self-identification or established in 'informal' ways of urban livelihood, pursuing multifarious survival strategies that, on balance, contribute significantly to market-oriented development by their production of goods and services and by availability as a cheap labour reserve. They cope in many ways, including mass mobilizations and voting, that can affect the political viability of development or structural adjustment policies, but they participate mainly through neighbourhood mutual aid associations, localized occupational groupings and aggressive individualism. Among these heterogeneous groups organized initiatives by women are becoming particularly important, stemming from their own survival strategies as breadwinners and heads of families.

There are the tens of millions of workers in industry, mining, transport, communications and power generation, the better organized among whom could have been confident in the past that their rising numbers, indispensability to economic growth and status as a 'proletarian vanguard' guaranteed them participation in development. Now, except in South-East Asia, their numbers are static or declining. Their wages, job security, retirement benefits and other gains from many years of organized efforts are being eroded, and they are reduced to rearguard actions in self-defence against the creative-destructive logic of market-oriented development. Moreover, with the rise of highly skilled technological specializations, on the one side, and the increases in semi-skilled or unskilled mainly female labour producing consumer goods for export, on the other, wage labour has diversified so much that the idea of a working class with common interests concerning development loses plausibility.

There are the tens of millions of newly excluded, the permanently displaced former industrial workers, plus the middle strata that seemed to have achieved participation in development and preferential access to the political system through education, public and private white-collar employment, academic and professional careers. The public employees have been particularly hard-hit by curtailment of state activities, campaigns of debureaucratization and erosion of salaries through inflation. Critics of state-planned developmentalism have struck directly at their morale, accusing them, with some justice, of corruption, inefficiency and proce-duralism. Meanwhile, university-educated young people risk being excluded altogether from the main source of employment open to them at earlier stages of growth of the developmental state. The impact of these new forms of exclusion must be particularly devastating in the former 'real socialist' countries. The diverse groups that can be counted as newly excluded or threatened can now 'participate' in contradictory ways: through adaptation to new technological, managerial and other job oppor-tunities that the style of development does offer in considerable quantities; through organized resistance to threats to status; and through radical criticism of the style of development itself. For the present, the scarcity of plausible alternatives blocks the last choice.

There are the tens of millions of migrants across national frontiers, drawn from all the categories of excluded mentioned above, as well as from groups that were relatively privileged in their countries of origin. Migrants encounter many forms of insecurity and discrimination, but for the most part adapt to alien societies and new sources of livelihood, forging links between their old world and their new. Their remittances of funds have become vitally important not only to their families and communities but also to the economic survival of their countries of origin. A good many return to participate politically as well as economically in their home countries. A mounting flood of refugees is becoming nearly as important quantitatively as the economically-motivated migrants. A good many of the refugees manage to adapt in the same ways as other migrants, but millions are experiencing the most extreme exclusion; barred from em-ployment in the country of refuge, isolated in camps or shelters. In many cases, a second generation is now growing up in this kind of limbo.

In this book we have explored many kinds of participation. The pre-cariousness of successful organized efforts, the needs of groups and movements for continual innovative coping with new challenges, and the capacity of economic and political changes in wider spheres to obliterate even the most firmly established gains have become all too evident. Previously it could plausibly be expected that development would even-tually incorporate most of the hitherto excluded, so that attention could focus on the terms of incorporation. Now, in rich countries as well as poor, exclusion seems to be gaining over incorporation.

Previous sources of collective identity that served as frames of refer-ence for organized struggles over terms of incorporation have been disintegrating and a groping toward new – or very old – collective identities is evident. It is also evident that if the excluded cannot hope to participate in development as an accessible and intelligible process, many of them are prepared to change the subject, to indulge in the non-material satisfactions of millennialism, religious exclusivism and xenophobia. Whether the clashing efforts that are now visible will end in adjustment to the currently dominant style of development, whether they will help to transform this style into human development, or whether they will cause it to disintegrate through unmanageable conflict remains to be seen. The decade and a half since UNRISD decided to inquire into participation has brought astonishing transformations but has confirmed the dominance of a 'development' that seems very doubtfully compatible with the organized efforts of the excluded. The coming decade will bring its own surprises.

References

Angulo, Alejandro, *An Experiment in Participatory Development*, UNICEF Innocenti Global Seminar on Participatory Development, Florence, May 1990

Annis, Sheldon and Hakim, Peter, eds., *Direct to the Poor: Grassroots Development in Latin America*, Lynn Rienner, Boulder, Colorado, 1988

Annis, Sheldon, 'Giving Voice to the Poor', *Foreign Policy*, no. 84, 1991

Ballón, E. and Tovar, T., *The Development of Popular Movements in Peru, 1968-1982*, unpublished manuscript, UNRISD, Geneva, 1985

Ballón, Eduardo, ed., *Movimientos Sociales y Crisis: El Caso Peruano*, DESCO, Lima, 1986

Bangura, Yusuf, *Authoritarian Rule and Democracy in Africa: A Theoretical Discourse*, UNRISD Discussion Paper No. 18, Geneva, March 1991

Bangura, Yusuf, Gibbon, Peter and Ofstad, Arve, eds., *Authoritarianism, Democracy and Adjustment: The Politics of Economic Reform in Africa*, UNRISD, Scandinavian Institute of African Studies and Christian Michelsen Institute, Uppsala, 1992

Barraclough, Solon, *A Preliminary Analysis of the Nicaraguan Food System*, UNRISD, Geneva, 1982

Barraclough, Solon, *An End to Hunger? The Social Origins of Food Strategies*, UNRISD and Zed Books, London, 1991

Barrera, Manuel and Falabella, Gonzalo, eds., *Sindicatos bajo Regímenes Militares: Argentina, Brazil, Chile*, UNRISD and CES, Geneva and Santiago, 1990

Barrera, Manuel, Henríquez, Helia and Selamé, Teresita, *Trade Unions and the State in Present Day Chile: Collective Bargaining as an Instrument of Popular Participation*, UNRISD and CES, Geneva and Santiago, 1986

Bhatnagar, Bhuvan and Williams, Aubrey C., eds., *Participatory Development and the World Bank: Potential Directions for Change*, World Bank Discussion Papers, World Bank, Washington, D.C., 1992

Biro, Andras, *Apprenticeship in Participation. An Experience of Dialogical Research in a Mexican Village*, unpublished manuscript, UNRISD, 1981

Bratton, Michael, 'The Politics of Government-NGO Relations in Africa', *World Development*, vol. 17, no. 4, 1989

Bratton, Michael, *Enabling the Voluntary Sector in Africa: The Policy Context*, mimeo, 1991(?)

Breman, Jan, *Wage Hunters and Gatherers*, Oxford University Press, New Delhi, 1993

Bugnicourt, Jacques, *Popular Participation in Development in Africa*, paper presented at the International Seminar on Popular Participation, organized by the UN Department of Technical Cooperation for Development in Ljubljana, 1981

Calderon, Fernando and Dandler, Jorge, eds., *Bolivia: la Fuerza Historica del Campesinado*, UNRISD and CERES, Geneva and La Paz, 2nd revised edition 1986

Campero, Guillermo, *Entre la Sobrevivencia y la Acción Política: Las Organizaciones de Pobladores en Santiago*, Ediciones ILET, Santiago 1987

Cardoso, Fernando Henrique, 'Associated-dependent Development and Democratic Theory', in Stepan, Alfred, ed., *Democratizing Brazil: Problems of Transition and Consolidation*, Oxford University Press, New York, 1989

Carroll, Thomas, *Intermediary NGOs: The Supporting Link in Grassroots Development*, Kumarian Press, West Hartford, Connecticut, 1992

Chateau, Jorge et al., *Espacio y Poder: Los Pobladores*, FLACSO, Santiago 1987

CIERA, *Sistema Alimentario*, vol. 2 of *La Reforma Agraria en Nicaragua 1979-1989*, CIERA, Managua, 1989

CLACSO, 'Movimientos Sociales y Participacion Popular', *David y Goliath – Boletin CLACSO*, vol. xiv, no. 46, 1984

Clark, John, *Democratizing Development*, Earthscan Publications, London, 1991, p. 19

Cohen, Selina, ed., *Debaters' Comments on 'Inquiry into Participation: A Research Approach'*, UNRISD, Geneva, October 1980

Cornia, G.A., Jolly, R. and Stewart, F., eds., *Adjustment with a Human Face*, 2 vols., Clarendon Press, Oxford, 1987 and 1988

Das, Arvind N., *Research, Participation and Action: Some Methodological and Practical Issues*, unpublished manuscript, UNRISD, 1985

Dasgupta, S., *Understanding Social Reality*, unpublished manuscript, UNRISD, Geneva, 1983

De Soto, Hernando, *The Other Path: The Invisible Revolution in the Third World*, Harper & Row, New York, 1989

Diegues, Antonio Carlos, *The Social Dynamics of Deforestation in the Brazilian Amazon: An Overview*, UNRISD Discussion Paper No. 36, Geneva, July 1992

Eckstein, Susan, *The Poverty of Revolution: The State and the Urban Poor in Mexico*, Princeton University Press, Princeton, N.J. First published 1977; republished with an Epilogue, 1988

Escobar, Arturo and Alvarez, Sonia E., eds., *The Making of Social Movements in Latin America: Identity, Strategy and Democracy*, Westview Press, Boulder, Colorado, 1992

Escobar, Cristina, *Trayectoria de la ANUC (1966-1982)*, UNRISD, unpublished manuscript

Esman, Milton J. and Uphoff, Norman T., *Local Organization and Rural Development: The State of the Art*, Cornell University Press, Ithaca, N.Y., 1982

Esteva, Gustavo, *El Proyecto Político de los Márgenes*, paper presented at the XVI Congreso Interamericano de Planificación, 22-26 August, 1988, San Juan, Puerto Rico

Fadda, Giulietta C., *Participación: Discurso, Política, y Praxis Urbana. Caracas (1973/1983)*, CENDES/Universidad Central de Venezuela, Caracas, December 1987

Fara, Luis, 'Luchas Reivindicativas Urbanas en su Contexto Autoritario. Los Asentamientos de San Francisco Solano', in Jelin, Elizabeth, ed., *Los Nuevos Movimientos Sociales*, vol. 2, Centro Editor de América Latina, Buenos Aires, 1985

Franco, Carlos, ed., *El Peru de Velasco*, 3 vols., CEDEP, Lima, 1983

Friedmann, John, 'Collective Self-Empowerment and Social Change', *IFDA Dossier 69*, January/February 1989

Friedmann, John, and Haripriya, Rangan, eds., *In Defense of Livelihood:*

Comparative Studies in Environmental Action, Kumarian Press, West Hartford, Connecticut, 1993

García Delgado, D.R. and Silva, Juan, 'El Movimiento Vecinal y la Democracia: Participación y Control en el Gran Buenos Aires' in Jelin, Elizabeth, ed., *Los Nuevos Movimientos Sociales*, vol 2, Centro Editor de América Latina, Buenos Aires, 1985

Ghai, Dharam and Vivian, Jessica M., eds., *Grassroots Environmental Action: People's Participation in Sustainable Development*, Routledge, London, 1992

Ghai, Dharam, ed., *The IMF and the South: The Social Impact of Crisis and Adjustment*, Zed Books, London, 1991.

Ghai, Dharam, *Participatory Development: Some Perspectives from Grassroots Experiences*, UNRISD Discussion Paper No. 5, Geneva, 1988

González Bombal, M. Ines, 'Protestan los Barrios (El Murmullo Suburbano de la Política)', in Jelin, Elizabeth, ed., *Los Nuevos Movimientos Sociales*, vol. 2, Centro Editor de América Latina, Buenos Aires, 1985

Gordon Drabek, Anne, 'Development Alternatives: The Challenge for NGOs – An Overview of the Issues', *World Development*, vol. 15, 1987 (special issue on NGOs)

Griffin, Keith, *An Assessment of UNRISD's Research Programmes on Food Systems and Society and Participation*, Oxford, 1987

Guerguil, Martine, 'Some Thoughts on the Definition of the Informal Sector', *CEPAL Review*, no. 35, August 1988

Gunder Frank, André and Fuentes, Marta, 'Nine Theses on Social Movements', *IFDA Dossier*, no. 63, January/February 1988

Hancock, Graham, *Lords of Poverty*, Macmillan, London, 1989

Hardy, Clarissa, *Organizarse para Vivir: Pobreza Urbana y Organización Popular*, Programa de Economia del Trabajo, Santiago 1987

Hewitt de Alcántara, Cynthia, Introduction to *Reestructuración Económica y Subsistencia Rural: El Maíz y la Crisis de los Ochenta*, El Colegio de México, Mexico City, 1992

Hewitt de Alcántara, Cynthia, ed., *Real Markets: Social and Political Issues of Food Policy Reform*, Frank Cass, London, 1992

Hirsch, Philip, *Development Dilemmas in Rural Thailand*, Oxford University Press, Singapore, 1990, pp. 210 and 218

Hirschman, Albert O., *Getting Ahead Collectively: Grassroots Experiences in Latin America*, Pergamon Press, New York, 1984

Hollnsteiner Racelis, Mary, 'Prologue' in Turton, Andrew, *Production, Power and Participation in Rural Thailand*, UNRISD, Geneva, 1987

Hong, Kwan Kai, ed., *Jeux et Enjeux de l'Auto-Promotion*, Presse Universitaire de France, Paris, 1991

Izquierdo Maldonado, Gabriel, *Peasant Popular Participation: Rise and Fall of the Peasant Movement in Manati*, UNRISD, unpublished manuscript

Jelin, Elizabeth, ed., *Los Nuevos Movimientos Sociales*, 2 vols., Centro Editor de América Latina, Buenos Aires, 1985

Jelin, Elizabeth, ed., *Women and Social Change in Latin America*, UNRISD and Zed Books, Geneva and London, 1990

Korten, David C., 'The Third Generation NGO Strategies: A Key to People-

Centred Development', *World Development*, vol. 15, 1987 (special issue on NGOs)

Korten, Frances F. and Siy, Robert Y. Jr., *Transforming a Bureaucracy: The Experience of the Philippine National Irrigation Administration*, Kumarian Press, West Hartford, Connecticut, 1989

Kowarick, Lúcio, *As Lutas Sociais e a Cidade: São Paulo, Passado e Presente*, Paz e Terra, São Paulo, 1988

Landell-Mills, Pierre and Serageldin, Ismail, *Governance and the External Factor*, The World Bank Annual Conference on Development Economics 1991, Washington

Lehmann, David, *Democracy and Development in Latin America*, Polity Press, Cambridge, 1990

Marchetti, Peter, ed., *Cooperativas y Participación Popular en Nicaragua*, unpublished manuscript, Geneva, UNRISD, 1985

Marchetti, Peter, *Guerra, Participación Popular y Transición al Socialismo*, unpublished draft manuscript, UNRISD

Moghadam, Valentine M., 'Development and Women's Exploitation', in Pieterse, Jan Nedreveen, ed., op. cit., pp. 215-55

Moguel, Julio and Velázquez, Enrique, *Organización Social y Lucha Ecológica en una Región del Norte de México*, UNRISD Discussion Paper No. 20, Geneva, April 1991

Molano, Alfredo, *Relatos de la Violencia*, UNRISD, unpublished manuscript

Nandy, Ashis, *Note on a Study of Ethnic Violence*, mimeo, Delhi, February 1990

Oakely, Peter, et al., *Projects with People: The Practice of Participation in Rural Development*, ILO, Geneva, 1991

Omvedt, Gail, *Women in Popular Movements: India and Thailand during the Decade of Women*, UNRISD, Geneva, 1986

Padron, Mario, *Development Cooperation and the Popular Movement: The Non-Governmental Development Organizations*, Westview Press, Boulder, Colorado, 1988

Palomino, Hector, 'El Movimiento de Democratización Síndical', in Jelin, Elizabeth, ed., *Los Nuevos Movimientos Sociales*, vol. 2, Centro Editor de América Latina, Buenos Aires, 1985

Parodi, Jorge, 'La Desmovilización del Sindicalismo Industrial Peruano en el Segundo Belaundismo', in Eduardo Ballón, ed., op. cit. 1986

Parra Escobar, Ernesto, 'ANUC: A History of Peasant Participation', postscript to Rivera Cusicanqui, Silvia, op. cit.

Pearse, Andrew, *The Latin American Peasant*, Frank Cass, London, 1975

Pearse, Andrew, *Seeds of Plenty, Seeds of Want: Social and Economic Implications of the Green Revolution*, UNRISD/Oxford University Press, Geneva and Oxford, 1980

Pearse, Andrew and Stiefel, Matthias, 'Launching the Debate' in *Dialogue about Participation 1*, UNRISD, Geneva, June 1981

Pearse, Andrew and Stiefel, Matthias, *An Inquiry into Participation: A Research Approach*, UNRISD, Geneva, 1979

Petras, James and Morley, Morris, *US Hegemony under Siege: Class, Politics and Development in Latin America*, Verso, London and New York, 1990

References

247

PIDT, *Understanding Social Reality*, unpublished manuscript, PIDT/UNRISD, New Dehli, 1984

Pieterse, Jan Nederveen, *Emancipations, Modern and Postmodern*, special issue of *Development and Change*, vol. 23, no. 3, July 1992, Sage Publications on behalf of the Institute of Social Studies, The Hague

Popov, Gavriil, 'Dangers of Democracy', *New York Review of Books,* 16 August 1990

Quamina, Odida, *Food Systems and Popular Participation in Grenada*, draft final report submitted to UNRISD, February 1981

Quamina, Odida, *Mineworkers of Guyana. The Making of a Working Class,* Zed Books, London, 1987

Quijano, Anibal, 'New Light on the Concepts of "Private" and "Public" ', *CEPAL Review*, no. 35, August 1988

Quijano, Anibal, *Estado y Sociedad en América Latina (Notas de Investigación)*, draft manuscript, 1988,

Rahman, Anisur, ed., *Grass-Roots Participation and Self-Reliance*, Oxford and IBH Publishing Co., New Delhi, 1984

Rahman, Anisur, *Glimpses of the Other Africa*, WEP Working Paper, ILO, Geneva, 1988

Rahman, Anisur, *Some Dimensions of People's Participation in the Bhoomi Sena Movement*, UNRISD, Geneva, 1981

Rau, Bill, *From Feast to Famine*, Zed Books, London, 1991

Rello, Fernando, *Bourgeoisie, Peasants and the State in Mexico: The Agrarian Conflict of 1976*, Geneva, UNRISD, 1986

Rello, Fernando, *State and Peasantry in Mexico: A Case Study of Rural Credit in La Laguna*, UNRISD, Geneva, 1987

Rivera Cusicanqui, Silvia, *Collective Memory and Popular Movements*, UNRISD, unpublished draft manuscript, 1984

Rivera Cusicanqui, Silvia, *The Politics and Ideology of the Colombian Peasant Movement: The Case of ANUC (National Association of Peasant Small-holders)*, Geneva, UNRISD, 1987

Rivera Cusicanqui, Silvia, *'Oppressed but not Defeated': Peasant Struggles among the Aymara and Qhechwa in Bolivia, 1900-1980*, UNRISD, Geneva, 1987

Rodríguez, Alfredo, Riofrio, Gustavo and Walsh, Eileen, *De Invasores a Invadidos*, DESCO, Lima, 1973

Scott, Alan, *Ideology and the New Social Movements*, Unwin Hyman, London, 1990

Scott, James C. and Kerkvliet, Benedict J. Tria, eds., 'Everyday Forms of Peasant Resistance in South-East Asia', *Journal of Peasant Studies*, vol. 13, no. 2, January 1986

Sethi, Harsh and Kothari, Smitu, eds., *The Non-Party Political Process in India: Uncertain Alternatives*, unpublished manuscript, UNRISD, Geneva, 1985

Society for Participatory Research in Asia, *'The Seduction of NGOs?'*, Newsletter, no. 37, January 1992

South Commission, *The Challenge to the South: The Report of the South Commission*, Oxford University Press, New York, 1990

Spence, Jonathan D., *The Search for Modern China*, W. Norton & Company, New York, 1990, p. 736

Stiefel, Matthias and Wertheim, Willem F., *Production, Equality and Participation in Rural China*, Zed Books and UNRISD, London and Geneva, 1983

Stiefel, Matthias and Racelis, Mary, *The Role and Responsibilities of Government and Development and Donor Agencies*, UN Economic Commission for Africa, 1990, paper prepared for the International Conference on Popular Participation in the Recovery and Development Process in Africa

Stiefel, Matthias, *Democratization, Participation and the Search for a New Polity, A Discussion Paper*, ILO, Geneva, November 1991

Stiefel, Matthias, *Sustainable Development and People's Participation: Some Reflections*, paper prepared for the United Nations Conference on Environment and Development (UNCED), Geneva, 1991

Sunshine, Catherine A., 'Grenada', in *The Caribbean Survival: Struggle and Sovereignty*, Ecumenical Programme for Interamerican Communication and Action, Washington, D.C., 1985

Touraine, Alain, *Actores Sociales y Sistemas Políticos en América Latina*, PREALC, Santiago, 1987

Turton, Andrew, *Production, Power and Participation in Rural Thailand*, Geneva, UNRISD, 1987

UN Economic Commission for Africa (ECA), *Alternative Framework to Structural Adjustment Programme for Socio-Economic Recovery and Transformation*, UNECA, Addis Ababa, 1989

UN Economic Commission for Africa (ECA), *African Charter for Popular Participation in Development* (E/ECA/CM.16/11), 1990

UN Economic Commission for Latin America and the Caribbean (ECLAC), *Social Equity and Changing Production Patterns: An Integrated Approach*, CEPAL, Santiago, 1992

UN Economic Commission for Latin America and the Caribbean (ECLAC), *Preliminary Overview of the Economy of Latin America and the Caribbean 1990*, CEPAL, Santiago, December 1990

UN Economic Commission for Latin America and the Caribbean (ECLAC), *Panorama Económico de América Latina 1991*, CEPAL, Santiago, September 1991

UN Economic Commission for Latin America and the Caribbean (ECLAC), *El Desarrollo Sostenible: Transformación Productiva, Equidad y Medio Ambiente*, CEPAL, Santiago, 1991

UNDP, *Human Development Report 1990*, Oxford University Press, New York and Oxford, 1990

UNDP, *Human Development Report 1991*, Oxford University Press, New York and Oxford, 1991

UNRISD, *Rural Co-operatives as Agents of Change: A Research Project and a Debate*, UNRISD, Geneva, 1975

UNRISD, *The Quest for a Unified Approach to Development*, UNRISD, Geneva, 1980

UNRISD Participation Programme, *A Glance at the Past and Directions for the Future*, mimeo, UNRISD, Geneva, July 1980

UNRISD Participation Programme, *Dialogue about Participation*, UNRISD, Geneva, 4 issues published in 1981, 1982 and 1983

Utting, Peter, *The Peasant Question and Development Policy in Nicaragua*, UNRISD Discussion Paper No. 2, Geneva, 1988

Utting, Peter, *The Social Origins and Impact of Deforestation in Central America*, UNRISD Discussion Paper No. 24, Geneva, May 1991

Utting, Peter, *Economic Reform and Third World Socialism: A Political Economy of Food Policy in Post-Revolutionary Societies*, UNRISD and Macmillan, London, 1992

Valladares, Licia, *A Luta pela Terra no Brazil Urbano: Reflexões em Torno de Alguns Casos*, UNRISD, unpublished manuscript

Vera Ferrer, Oscar H., *La Política Económica y el Sector Informal en el Contexto de la Crisis Latinoamericana: La Experiencia Mexicana*, paper presented at XVI Congreso Interamericano de Planificación, San Juan, Puerto Rico, 22-25 August 1988

Vilas, Carlos N., 'What Went Wrong', in *Nicaragua: Haunted by the Past, NACLA Report on the Americas*, vol. XXIV, no. 1, June 1990

White, Sarah C., *Evaluating the Impact of NGOs in Rural Poverty Alleviation, Bangladesh Country Study*, ODI, London, 1991

Wolfe, Marshall, 'Social Structures and Democracy in the 1990s', *CEPAL Review*, no. 40, April 1990

Wolfe, Marshall, *Elusive Development*, Geneva, UNRISD and ECLA, 1981

Wolfe, Marshall, 'Participation: the View from Above', *Cepal Review*, no. 23, August 1984

World Bank, *Involving Nongovernmental Organizations in Bank-Supported Activities*, World Bank, Operational Directive 14.70., August 1989

World Bank, *Managing Development: The Governance Dimension, A Discussion Paper*, World Bank, Washington, D.C., 29 August 1991

World Bank, *Poverty: World Development Report 1990*, Oxford University Press, New York, 1990

World Bank, *The Challenge of Development: World Development Report 1991*, Oxford University Press, Oxford, 1991

World Bank, *Rural Development: World Bank Experience 1965-86*, World Bank, Washington, D.C., 1988, p. 57

Zamosc, León, *The Agrarian Question and the Peasant Movement in Colombia: Struggles of the National Peasant Association, 1967-81*, UNRISD and Cambridge University Press, Geneva and Cambridge, 1986

Annex 1

UNRISD's Popular Participation Programme: main case studies and sub-debates

(carried out between 1979 and 1984)

Case studies

Country	Topic of research	Research Co-ordinators
Bolivia	Peasant Movements and Ethnicity (general and historical)	F. Calderon & J. Dandler, CERES, La Paz
Bolivia	Peasant Movements and Ethnicity (Aymara and Qhechwa struggles 1900-1980)	S. Rivera Cusicanqui
Brazil	Urban Expoliation and Social Struggles in São Paulo	L. Kowarick, CEDEC, São Paulo
Chile	Collective Bargaining as an Instrument of Participation under Authoritarian Conditions	M. Barrera, CES, Santiago
Colombia	Politics and Ideology in the Colombian Peasant Movement: The case of ANUC	A. Angulo, CINEP, Bogota
Guyana	Trade Unionism and Workers' Participation in the Bauxite Mining Enterprise	O. Quamina
India	The Non-Party Political Formations	H. Sethi, ICSSR, New Delhi
India	Comparative Study of Nine Grassroots Movements	S. Dasgupta, PIDT, New Delhi

Country	Topic of research	Research Co-ordinators
Mexico	The Peasant Movement and the State: El Banco Rural in La Laguna	F. Rello, UNAM, Mexico
Nicaragua	Institutionalization of Popular Participation Agriculture	P. Marchetti, CIERA, Managua
Peru	Institutionalization of Popular Participation: the SINAMOS Experience	C. Franco, CEDEC, Lima
Peru	Popular Movements in Peru 1976-1981	H. Pease and E. Ballon, DESCO, Lima
Thailand	Popular Participation in Rural Thailand	A. Turton, SOAS, London, W. Wonghanchao, CUSRI, Bangkok

Global sub-debates

Issue	Co-ordinator
Participation: the View from Above	M. Wolfe
The Urgency Factor and Democracy	W. F. Wertheim
Clientelism, Patronage and Popular Participation	B. Jobert

Regional sub-debates in Latin America

Issue	*Co-ordinator*
Conceptual and Methodological Issues concerning Peasant Movements and Ethnicity in the Andean Region	F. Calderon and J. Dandler, CERES, La Paz
History and Consciousness in Third World Popular Movements	S. Rivera Cusicanqui
The State and the Peasantry	A. Angulo, CINEP, Bogota
Women's Participation in Social Movements	E. Jelin, CEDES, Buenos Aires
Participation and Urban Social Movements	L. Kowarick, CEDEC, São Paulo
The Union as an Instrument of Defence and Transformation in Situations of Political Authoritarianism and/or Extended Economic Crisis	M. Barrera, CES, Santiago
Limitations and Potential of Popular Movements: their Impact on the Political Process	H. Pease and E. Ballon DESCO, Lima
Institutional Control of Popular Participation: the Mexican Example	F. Rello, UNAM, Mexico
Transition and the Institutionalization of Popular Participation	P. Marchetti, CIERA, Managua

Annex 2

UNRISD's Popular Participation Programme: organization and core groups

Central co-ordination

The programme was co-directed by Andrew Pearse and Matthias Stiefel from its start in 1979 until December 1980. After Andrew Pearse's death and until its conclusion in the summer of 1986 it was directed by Matthias Stiefel, assisted by a newly formed central core group.

The following people also assisted in the central co-ordination and direction of the programme:

• Gonzalo Falabella, as regional co-ordinator for Latin America, from January 1981 to October 1982. He was responsible for the programme's sub-office at the University of London.
• Phillipe Egger, from January 1981 to June 1982, who assisted Matthias Stiefel in the central co-ordination of the programme in Geneva.
• Selina Cohen, from December 1979 to August 1982, who was responsible for English publications. After Andrew Pearse's death she was responsible for the programme's sub-office in Oxford.
• Hernan Saez, from April 1981 to August 1982, who assisted in the co-ordination of the Latin American studies and was responsible for Spanish publications.

Central core group

The programme's central core group was formed in March 1981. Besides the programme's regular staff, mentioned above, the following persons were members of the group, for the whole period or for part of it:

Solon Barraclough	Henry Pease
Jan Breman	Jacobo Schatan
Arvind Das	Harsh Sethi
Carlos Fortin	Andrew Turton
Enrique Oteiza	Marshall Wolfe

Regional core group in Latin America

The regional core group in Latin America was composed of the research and sub-debate co-ordinators:

Alejandro Angulo
Manuel Barrera
Fernando Calderon
Silvia Rivera Cusicanqui
Jorge Dandler
Elizabeth Jelin

Lucio Kowarick
Peter Marchetti
Henry Pease
Odida Quamina
Fernando Rello

Annex 3

UNRISD's Popular Participation Programme: publications, research reports and other papers

The programme's many activities generated a large number of research reports, issue papers and other documents. The following list of published and unpublished documents does not list the numerous papers and studies that were contributed to the various Latin American sub-debates or to the UNRISD/CESTEEM Seminar on Social Movements in Latin America that was held in Mexico in August 1982.

Published reports and papers

Barrera, Manuel, *Worker's Participation in Company Management in Chile: A Historical Experience*, UNRISD, Geneva, 1981 (also published in Spanish)

Barrera, Manuel, Henríquez, Helia and Selamé, Teresita, *Trade Unions and the State in Present Day Chile: Collective Bargaining as an Instrument of Popular Participation*. UNRISD and Centro de Estudios Sociales, Geneva and Santiago, 1986 (also published in French and Spanish)

Barrera, Manuel and Falabella, Gonzalo, eds., *Sindicatos bajo Regímenes Militares: Argentina, Brazil, Chile*. UNRISD and CES, Geneva and Santiago, 1990

Calderon, Fernando and Dandler, Jorge, eds., *Bolivia: la Fuerza Histórica del Campesinado*, UNRISD and CERES, Geneva and La Paz, 2nd revised edition 1986

Cohen, Selina, ed., *Debaters' Comments on 'Inquiry into Participation: A Research Approach'*, UNRISD, Geneva, October 1980

Franco, Carlos, ed., *El Peru de Velasco*, 3 vols., CEDEP, Lima, 1983

Jelin, Elizabeth, ed., *Women and Social Change in Latin America*, UNRISD and Zed Books, Geneva and London, 1990 (also published in Spanish as *Ciudadanía e Identitad*, UNRISD)

Kowarick, Lúcio, *As Lutas Sociais e a Cidade*, Paz e Terra, São Paulo and Geneva, 1988 (published in English under the title *Social Struggles and the City: The Case of São Paulo*, Monthly Review Press, New York, 1993)

Omvedt, Gail, *Women in Popular Movements: India and Thailand during the Decade of Women*, UNRISD, Geneva, 1986

Quamina, Odida, *The Social Organization of Plantation Mackenzie: An Account of Life in the Guyana Mining Enterprises*, UNRISD, Geneva, 1981 (also published in Spanish)

Quamina, Odida, *Mineworkers of Guyana: The Making of a Working Class*, Zed Books, London, 1987

Rahman, Anisur, *Some Dimensions of People's Participation in the Bhoomi Sena Movement*, UNRISD, Geneva, 1981 (also published in Spanish)

Rello, Fernando, *Bourgeoisie, Peasants and the State in Mexico: The Agrarian Conflict of 1976*, UNRISD, Geneva, 1986 (also published in Spanish)

Rello, Fernando, *State and Peasantry in Mexico: A Case Study of Rural Credit in La Laguna*, UNRISD, Geneva, 1987 (also published in Spanish)

Rivera Cusicanqui, Silvia, *The Politics and Ideology of the Colombian Peasant Movement*, UNRISD, Geneva, 1987 (also published in Spanish)

Rivera Cusicanqui, Silvia, *'Oppressed but not Defeated': Peasant Struggles among the Aymara and Qhechwa in Bolivia, 1900-1980*, UNRISD, Geneva, 1987 (also published in Spanish)

Stiefel, Matthias and Wertheim, Willem F., *Production, Equality and Participation in Rural China*, Zed Books and UNRISD, London and Geneva, 1983

Turton, Andrew, *Production, Power and Participation in Rural Thailand*, Geneva, UNRISD, 1987

UNRISD Participation Programme, *Dialogue about Participation*, UNRISD, Geneva, 4 issues published in 1981, 1982 and 1983 respectively (also published in Spanish)

Wolfe, Marshall, 'Participation: the View from Above', *Cepal Review*, no. 23, August 1984

Zamosc, León, *The Agrarian Question and the Peasant Movement in Colombia: Struggles of the National Peasant Association, 1967-81*, UNRISD and Cambridge University Press, Geneva and Cambridge, 1986 (also published in Spanish)

Mimeographed and unpublished reports

Ballón, E. and Tovar, T., *The Development of Popular Movements in Peru, 1968-1982*, unpublished manuscript, 1985

Biro, Andras, *Apprenticeship in Participation: An Experience of Dialogical Research in a Mexican Village*, unpublished manuscript, 1981

Das, Arvind N., *Research, Participation and Action: Some Methodological and Practical Issues*, unpublished manuscript, 1985

Dasgupta, S., *Understanding Social Reality*, unpublished manuscript, 1983

Escobar, Cristina, *Trayectoria de la ANUC (1966-1982)*, unpublished manuscript

Fortin, Carlos and Stiefel, Matthias, *Of People, Power and Participation*, mimeo, UNRISD, Geneva, June 1985

Henfrey, Colin, *Cante Amigo: Cultural Participation and the Struggle for Democracy in Chile*, unpublished manuscript, 1985

Izquierdo Maldonado, Gabriel, *Peasant Popular Participation: Rise and Fall of the Peasant Movement in Manati*, unpublished manuscript

Jobert, Bruno, *Clientelism, Patronage and Popular Participation*, mimeo, UNRISD, Geneva, 1983

Marchetti, Peter, ed., *Cooperativas y Participación Popular en Nicaragua*, unpublished manuscript, 1985

Marchetti, Peter, *Guerra, Participación Popular y Transición al Socialismo*, draft manuscript

Molano, Alfredo, *Relatos de la Violencia*, unpublished manuscript, 1984

Pearse, Andrew and Stiefel, Matthias, *An Inquiry into Participation: A Research Approach*, mimeo, UNRISD, Geneva, 1979

PIDT, *Understanding Social Reality*, unpublished manuscript, 1984

Quamina, Odida, *Food Systems and Popular Participation in Grenada*, unpublished report, February 1981

Rivera Cusicanqui, Silvia, *Collective Memory and Popular Movements*, draft manuscript, 1984

Santana, Roberto, *Los Suhars del Ecuador: Otro Desarollo y Otra Participación?*, draft manuscript, 1980

Sethi, Harsh and Kothari, Smitu, eds., *The Non-Party Political Process in India: Uncertain Alternatives*, unpublished manuscript, 1985

Stiefel, Matthias and Wolfe, Marshall, *The Quest for Participation: Social Movements, the State and People's Participation in Latin America and Some Countries of Asia*, mimeo, UNRISD, Geneva, June 1984

Valladares, Licia, *A Luta pela Terra no Brazil Urbano: Reflexões em Torno de Alguns Casos*, unpublished manuscript

Wertheim, Willem F., *The Urgency Factor and Democracy, Participation and Type of Government in the Third World*, mimeo, UNRISD, Geneva, 1980

Annex 4

Recent UNRISD Research and Publications
in the Field of Participation

While no separate research programme on participation has existed at UNRISD since the end of its Participation Programme in 1986, most UNRISD work has continued to investigate many of the key questions that have been discussed in this volume. Such is the case, for example, in the research presently carried out on environment and sustainable development, on crisis and adjustment, on present changes in Eastern Europe, on ethnic conflict, and on political violence and social movements. Participation is also an important theme in the preparatory work for the 1995 World Summit for Social Development that UNRISD is at present carrying out. Some of the recent UNRISD publications relevant to the issues discussed in this volume are:

Bangura, Y., Gibbon, P. and Ofstad, A., *Authoritarianism, Democracy and Adjustment: The Politics of Economic Reform in Africa*, UNRISD, Scandinavian Institute of African Studies and Christian Michelsen Institute, Uppsala, 1992

Barraclough, Solon, *An End to Hunger? The Social Origins of Food Strategies*, UNRISD and Zed Books, London, 1991

Barraclough, Solon and Ghimire, Krishna, *Forest and Livelihoods: The Social Dynamics of Deforestation in Developing Countries*, UNRISD, forthcoming 1993

Colchester, Marcus, *Sustaining the Forests: The Community-Based Approach in South and South-East Asia*, UNRISD Discussion Paper, Geneva, May 1992

Friedmann, John and Haripriya, Rangan, eds., *In Defense of Livelihood: Comparative Studies in Environmental Action*, Kumarian Press, West Hartford, Connecticut, 1993

Ghai, Dharam and Vivian, Jessica M., eds., *Grassroots Environmental Action: People's Participation in Sustainable Development*, Routledge, London, 1992

Ghai, Dharam, ed., *The IMF and the South: The Social Impact of Crisis and Adjustment*, Zed Books, London, 1991

Hewitt de Alcántara, Cynthia, ed., *Real Markets: Social and Political Issues of Food Policy Reform*, Frank Cass, London, 1992

Kurien, John, *Ruining the Commons and Responses of the Commoners: Coastal Overfishing and Fishermen's Actions in Kerala State, India*, UNRISD Discussion Paper, May 1991

Premdas, Ralph R., *Ethnic Conflict and Development: The Case of Guayana*, UNRISD Discussion Paper, January 1992

Stahl, Michael, *Constraints to Environmental Rehabilitation through People's Participation in the Northern Ethiopian Highlands*, UNRISD Discussion Paper, July 1990

Utting, Peter, *Economic Reform and Third-World Socialism: A Political Economy of Food Policy in Post-Revolutionary Societies*, UNRISD and Macmillan, 1992

Index